Spiritual Renewal in Japan

Christian Heritage Rediscovered

The Series, as the name suggests, is meant to focus on Christian Faith & Living vis-à-vis topics like Literature & Poetry, Indigenous Philosophizing, Ethical response towards Agriculture, Health & Healing, Science & Technology, Ecofeminist Theology, Sociological approach towards Human Rights, Law & Politics, Arts, History of Ideas, Ancient Civilizations, Cultural Contiguity, Religious Cosmologies & Mysticism, Footsteps of famous Theologians, World Peace & Harmony, Global Capitalism, Network Marketing, Cybertheology, Population & Demographics, Epigraphic Studies, Contextualized Education, and many others. We welcome a Mss. on any topic/s mentioned, whether they are original works, scholarly monographs, collections of conference papers, revised dissertations, or translations of historical documents. Through the Series we, the Publishers, are striving to put forward published works that may help Institutions, Academic Bodies, Researchers, Scholars and the World at large in furthering their respective knowledge and understanding on the concerned subject. We welcome your comments on our efforts and further suggestions on how we can foster the upcoming thoughtful theologically grounded books.

Christian Heritage Rediscovered - 17

Spiritual Renewal in Japan

Journey of the Catholic Charismatic Renewal Movement

Reginald Alva SVD

CWI

Christian World Imprints™

First Published in 2015 by

Christian World Imprints(TM)
Christian Publishing & Books from India
H-12 Bali Nagar, **New Delhi-110015**
info@christianworldimprints.com
www.ChristianWorldImprints.com
Phone: +91 11 25465925 Fax: +91 11 25173055

ISBN-13: 978-93-5148-051-8 ISBN-10: 93-5148-051-8

Cataloging in Publication Data--DK
Courtesy: D.K. Agencies (P) Ltd. <docinfo@dkagencies.com>

Alva, Reginald, author.
Spiritual renewal in Japan : journey of the Catholic Charismatic Renewal Movement / Reginald Alva SVD.
pages cm. -- (Christian heritage rediscovered ; 17)
Includes bibliographical references (pages) and index.
ISBN 9789351480518
ISBN 9351480518

1. Pentecostalism--Japan--Catholic Church--History. I. Title. II. Series: Christian heritage rediscovered ; 17.

DDC 289.940952 23

Printed at Replika Press Pvt. Ltd.

The Book

This is the first book which examines in depth the history and growth of the Catholic Charismatic Renewal Movement (CCRM) in Japan. The Charismatic Renewal Movement has registered a great success in Japan. It has touched the lives of many Japanese. It has helped them to have a freshness in their spiritual lives. This book studies actual cases of individuals who have experienced the fruits of renewal in their lives. The CCRM has the potential of turning the flame of the Holy Spirit into a mighty fire.

Equipped with detailed Bibliography and supplementing Appendices this scholarly work also provides a critical analysis of the CCRM for its self-introspection and growth. The study concludes that though the CCRM has adapted itself to the situation of Japan, basic features of the Charismatic spirituality in it being intact. The book is a must have for those who are into International Studies, Religious Leaders, Historians, Christian Laity, Church Clergies, Researchers and all those who are somehow connected to the CCRM.

The Author

Reginald Alva is a Catholic Priest belonging to the Society of the Divine Word (SVD). He is presently teaching at Nanzan University, Japan. He is also involved in pastoral and renewal work in the Catholic Church of Japan. He holds degrees in English Literature, Social Work, Political Science, Philosophy and Theology. He has a licentiate in Biblical Theology and he took his doctorate in Theology (Spirituality) from Pontificia Università San Tommaso D'Aquino, Angelicum, Rome. He has also authored a book titled *"The Spirituality of the Catholic Charismatic Renewal Movement"*.

Acknowledgments

I thank God for His grace and support to complete this work. This work includes parts of my doctoral thesis *The Theological Basis of the Catholic Charismatic Renewal Movement and its Role in the Renewal of the Catholic Church of Japan*, defended at Pontifical University of St. Thomas Aquinas (Angelicum), Rome in 2010. I thank Prof. Luke Buckles for his guidance in writing my doctoral thesis. Also, I am thankful to the university for allowing me to publish parts of my thesis.

The Catholic Charismatic Renewal Services Office of Japan supplied me the data and materials on their activities. This material helped in my research on the CCRM in Japan. I appreciate their generosity.

I thank my parents, Celina and Jockim Alva for forming my faith life. It is their prayers and encouragement, which strengthened me to undertake this task for the greater glory of God. I also thank my brother and sisters for their moral and spiritual support. I am also grateful to all those who have helped me in the completion of this work.

Preface

There have been various movements in the life of the Church. The Catholic Charismatic Renewal Movement is one of such movements. It focuses on the spiritual renewal of the Church. In 1967, it began in the USA. However, it soon spread all around the world. It reached Japan in 1972.

Generally, the Charismatic prayers meetings have distinctive features like singing, dancing, clapping and loud praises. However, the Japanese are quite by nature. Therefore, the Catholic Charismatic Renewal Movement has adapted to the Japanese culture. It gives more time for silence during the prayer meetings. Thus, the Charismatic Renewal Movement in Japan differs from the Charismatic Renewal Movement in other nations.

The Catholic Church is minority in Japan. Moreover, it also faces the challenges posed by secularization. Christian values have little relevance in the Japanese society. Thus, the Church has a difficult task of continuing its mission in Japan. The Charismatic Renewal Movement is helping the Church by seeking renewal of faith. It emphasizes on the role of the Holy Spirit in faith formation. People associated with the Charismatic Renewal Movement have experienced renewal of their spiritual lives. Their lives show the fruits of the renewal. Their testimonies attract others. Charismatics are active members of their parishes. They are reaching out to all those who are seeking spiritual help. They also engage in ecumenism, interreligious dialogue and social action. Thus, the Charismatic Renewal Movement is both the chance and the hope of the Catholic Church in Japan.

Abbreviations

AA	*Apostolicam Actuositatem*
AAS	*Acta Apostolicae Sedis*
AG	*Ad Gentes*
AJPS	Asian Journal of Pentecostal Studies
CBCJ	Catholic Bishops' Conference of Japan
CCC	Catechism of the Catholic Church
CCCAP	Catholic Charismatic Council for Asia-Pacific
CCRJ	Catholic Charismatic Renewal Japan
CCRM	Catholic Charismatic Renewal Movement
CE	Common Era
DV	*Dei Verbum*
GS	*Gaudium et Spes*
HSRO	Holy Spirit Renewal Office of Japan
ICCRO	International Catholic Charismatic Renewal Office
ICCRS	International Catholic Charismatic Renewal Services
ISAO	International Sub-Committee for Asia-Oceania
JAG	Japan Assemblies of God
JCY	Japan Christian Yearbook
LG	*Lumen Gentium*
MEP	*Missions Etrangères de Paris*
NICE	National Incentive Convention for Evangelization

NA	*Nostra Aetate*
NTS	New Testament Studies
PMU	Pentecostal Missionary Union
PO	*Presbyterorum Ordinis*
RM	*Redemptoris Mater*
SC	*Sacrosanctum Concilium*
TDNT	Theological Dictionary of the New Testament
UR	*Unitatis Redintegratio*
USCCB	United States Conference of Catholic Bishops

Old Testament

Am	Amos
Bar	Baruch
1 Chr	1 Chronicles
2 Chr	2 Chronicles
Dn	Daniel
Dt	Deuteronomy
Eccl	Ecclesiastes
Est	Esther
Ex	Exodus
Ez	Ezekiel
Ezr	Ezra
Gn	Genesis
Hb	Habakkuk
Hg	Haggai
Hos	Hosea
Is	Isaiah
Jer	Jeremiah
Jb	Job
Jl	Joel
Jon	Jonah
Jo	Joshua
Jgs	Judges

Jdt	Judith
1 Kgs	1 Kings
2 Kgs	2 Kings
Lam	Lamentations
Lv	Leviticus
1 Mc	1 Maccabees
2 Mc	2 Maccabees
Mal	Malachi
Mi	Micah
Na	Nahum
Neh	Nehemiah
Nm	Numbers
Ob	Obadiah
Prv	Proverbs
Ps	Psalms
Ru	Ruth
1 Sm	1 Samuel
2 Sm	2 Samuel
Sg	Song of Solomon
Sir	Ecclesiasticus (Sirach)
Tb	Tobit
Ws	Wisdom of Solomon
Zec	Zechariah
Zep	Zephaniah

New Testament

Acts	Acts of the Apostles
Col	Colossians
1 Cor	1 Corinthians
2 Cor	2 Corinthians
Eph	Ephesians
Gal	Galatians
Heb	Hebrews

Jas	James
Jn	John
1 Jn	1 John (Epistle)
2 Jn	2 John (Epistle)
3 Jn	3 John (Epistle)
Jude	Jude
Lk	Luke
Mt	Matthew
1 Pt	I Peter
2 Pt	2 Peter
Phil	Philippians
Phlm	Philemon
Rv	Revelation (Apocalypse)
Rom	Romans
1 Thes	1 Thessalonians
2 Thes	2 Thessalonians
1 Tm	1 Timothy
2 Tm	2 Timothy
Ti	Titus

Introduction

The Charismatic Renewal Movement started in the Catholic Church in 1967. Through its efforts, many Catholics have rediscovered the value of their faith. This spiritual experience has changed their life radically.

In this book, we shall study about the Catholic Charismatic Renewal Movement (CCRM) in Japan. Japan is a fascinating nation. One can find many contrasts in Japan. It is modern yet very traditional. People in general are disinterested in matters about religion or faith. Nevertheless, surprisingly many religions co-exist in Japan. In addition, there are cults. Even though, people do not have interest in religious matters, they go to cults to seek favors.

Christianity is a minority religion. The government statistics of 2014 shows that Christians form 1% of the population.[1] The 2014 statistics of the Catholic Bishops' Conference of Japan shows that there are around 444,441 Catholics, about 0.35% of the Japanese

1 Ministry of Education, Culture, Sport, Science and Technology, Japan, "*Zenkoku Jinja Kyokai Nado Shukyo Dantai, Kyoshi, Shinjasu*" [National Statistics of Shrines, Churches etc, Religious Organizations, Adherents]. http://www.e-stat.go.jp/SG1/estat/List.do?bid=000001052797&cycode=0 However, David Barrett puts the figure at 3% in *World Christian Encyclopedia*. David Barrett, George Kurian and Todd Johnson. *World Christian Encyclopedia: A Comparative Survey of Churches and Religions in the Modern World*, 2nd ed. Vol.1 (New York: Oxford University, 2001), 412.

population. Besides being minority, the Catholic Church also faces challenges from rapid secularization and degradation of moral values in the society. The Catholic Church in Japan seeks the power of the Holy Spirit to continue her mission in these difficult times. The CCRM, which reached Japan in 1972, has worked for the renewal of the Church. Even though, religion has hardly any relevance in Japan, the CCRM continues with its activities.

The Charismatic prayer meetings are usually lively with clapping, singing and dancing. However, the CCRM has adapted itself to the situation in Japan. Even though, it retains the characteristic features of the Charismatic spirituality, it has made certain changes to integrate itself with the Japanese society.

In this book, we shall trace the history of the CCRM in Japan. Further, we shall examine its various activities. We shall also examine its role in the renewal of the Catholic Church in Japan. We shall study actual cases of people who have renewed their spiritual life, because of the efforts of the CCRM. Finally, we shall also critically analyze the CCRM for its self-introspection and growth.

Contents

Chapter 1

The Beginning of the Charismatic Renewal Movement in the Catholic Church

Pope John XXIII promulgated the Second Vatican Council to renew the Church. He prayed, "Divine Spirit... renew your wonders in our time, as though for a new Pentecost."[1] The documents of the Council emphasized on the renewal of the Church in the light of the needs of the changing times.[2] The documents also placed importance on the role of the Holy Spirit in the life of the Church. It urged the faithful to use the charisms of the Holy Spirit for common good.[3] It stressed on interior renewal and conversion.[4] The Second Vatican Council was revolutionary in redefining the Church, as the people of God.[5] Thus, it highlighted the importance of laity.

The teachings of the Second Vatican Council influenced the beginning of the Pentecostal-Charismatic Movement in the Catholic

1 "Prayer to the Holy Spirit for the Success of the Ecumenical Council," *AAS* 51 (1959): 832.

2 See John Paul II, "Encyclical *Redemptoris Missio*," *AAS* 83.1 (1991): 249.

3 See Conciliar Document *Lumen Gentium*, No. 4, 12.

4 See Conciliar Document *Ad Gentes*, No. 35.

5 See Conciliar Document *Lumen Gentium*, No. 11-14.

Church. In the fall of 1966 several Catholic lay people of the faculty of the Duquesne University, a Catholic University in Pittsburg run by the Congregation of the Holy Spirit (a Catholic Religious Order founded in France in 1703) gathered to pray on a weekend. They were sincere Catholics who were longing for a more tangible experience of their faith. As a preparation for this prayer weekend, they prayed that the Holy Spirit would renew the graces of their baptism and confirmation. They prayed the sequence for the liturgy of Pentecost Sunday, "Come Holy Spirit." As they prayed for a deeper experience of the Holy Spirit in their lives, they also started studying the New Testament, particularly the sections that dealt with the life of the primitive church found in the Acts of the Apostles. In August 1966 two of their friends, Steve Clark and Ralph Martin of the National Cursillo Convention (a Christian movement promoting Gospel values) were staff members of Saint John's Student Parish in East Lansing, Michigan. They suggested them to read a book, *The Cross and the Switchblade* (1963, written and edited by John Sherril) about the Protestant preacher David Wilkerson's experience with the juvenile drug addicts of New York and the dramatic conversion of these juveniles by the mighty power of the Holy Spirit working in them. Ralph Keifer one of the faculty members of Duquesne University read the book by John Sherrill, *They Speak with Other Tongues* (1964). This book was about Pentecostalism. It impressed Keifer very much.[6]

Ralph Keifer and his colleague, Patrick Bourgeois were very eager to have this personal experience of the Holy Spirit in their lives, but did not know how to approach someone who could pray for the outpouring of the Holy Spirit on them. The only thing, which came to them, was to go to a Pentecostal church. Having this thought in mind they approached William Lewis, an Episcopal pastor who introduced them to Betty Schomaker, an Episcopalian lady, a member of the Pentecostal prayer group. Betty Schomaker invited Ralph Keifer and his colleagues to a prayer meeting at the home of Miss Florence Dodge on January 13, 1967. They attended this meeting and asked those gathered there to pray over them for

6 Kevin Ranaghan and Dorothy Ranaghan, *Catholic Pentecostals* (New York: Paulist Press, 1969), 9-11.

the baptism in the Holy Spirit. Ralph Keifer and Patrick Bourgeois who had received the baptism in the Holy Spirit had a new awareness of the love of God. They had a greater desire for prayers, especially praise and thanksgiving. They found a new joy in reading the Bible. They grew in their faith. In the following week, Ralph Keifer laid hands on two others, and they too, received the baptism in the Holy Spirit. Those who received the baptism in the Holy Spirit found that this experience opened them to have a deeper love for the sacraments. They did not consider baptism in the Holy Spirit as a sacrament replacing the sacrament of baptism or confirmation, but as revival of the graces received during baptism and confirmation. They did not consider the laying of hands as a magical act of giving the Holy Spirit, but a gesture of love and concern for the other.[7]

In mid-February of 1967, a small groups of students together with the faculty members of Duquesne University who had the experience of the baptism in the Spirit decided to have a weekend of intense prayer. They meditated on the first four chapters of the Acts of the Apostles. The faculty members recommended these students to read David Wilkerson's, *The Cross and the Switchblade*. Majority of the students read this book before attending the weekend prayer meeting. It was during this prayer meeting the students had the experience of the baptism in the Holy Spirit.[8] This weekend prayer is the beginning of the Pentecostal-Charismatic Movement in the Catholic Church.[9]

---

7 Kevin Ranaghan and Dorothy Ranaghan, *Catholic Pentecostals* (New York: Paulist Press, 1969), 15-20.

8 Ibid., 20-23.

9 Classical Pentecostalism refers to independent churches that grew out of the earlier Azusa Street Revival. Charismatic or Neo-Pentecostal Movements are Pentecostal type prayer meetings organized within mainline churches. In the late 1960s and early 1970s, Christians from mainline Protestant churches especially in U.S.A, accepted partly the doctrines of the Pentecostal movement like the baptism in the Holy Spirit and the manifestations of the Holy Spirit. They continued to be members of their respective churches and carried out Pentecostal type prayer meetings in their own churches. Mainline Churches refer to these prayer meetings as Charismatic prayer meetings. See Edward O'Connor, *The Pentecostal Movement in the Catholic Church* (Notre Dame: Ave Maria Press, 1979), 28-29.

The news about these events at Duquesne University spread quickly to other Catholic university campuses. Some people welcomed these events as a genuine sign of the revival of the gifts and charisms of the early church in the modern times, but there were also others, who were skeptical about these happenings. They considered it more of Protestant Pentecostalism. However, two major publications, *The National Catholic Reporter* and *Our Sunday Visitor* took note of the new Charismatics in April 1967, when about 100 students and a number of faculty members from several universities had gathered at the Notre Dame campus for a weekend of prayer. Many students all over the USA read this news report. After reading the spiritual experience of the students, they too decided to join this type of prayer meeting. Thus, there was an overall increase in the charismatic prayer meetings all over in the USA.[10]

Soon the CCRM spread to different parts in the USA and the world. The Second Vatican Council promoted the growth of the movement. Moreover, the Belgian Cardinal, Léon Joseph Suenens, a prominent member of the Second Vatican Council supported the CCRM.[11] The cardinal hosted a series of conferences at Malines that published documents on the CCRM. He published a series of six books known as the Malines Documents. They are as follows: *Charismatic Renewal,* with Kilian McDonnell as lead consultant, *Ecumenism and Charismatic Renewal* (1978), *Charismatic Renewal and Social Action* (1979) with Dom Helder Camara of Brazil as the co-author, *Renewal and the Powers of Darkness* (1982), with a Foreword by Cardinal Joseph Ratzinger (Emeritus Pope Benedict XVI). The final two Malines Documents, *Le Culte du Moi et Foi Chretienne* (1985) and *Resting in the Spirit* (1986) dealt with the controversial issues of the CCRM and Pentecostal Movements. The Malines Documents served as a precious guide to the CCRM, to root itself in the tradition of the Catholic Church and to be a dynamic force within the church.

---

10 Paul Thigpen, "Catholic Charismatic Movement," in *The New International Dictionary of Pentecostal and Charismatic Movements*, eds. Stanley Burgess and Eduard Van Der Maas (Grand Rapids: Zondervan, 2003), 460-467.

11 See Ibid.

As the CCRM was growing rapidly in the 1970s, Cardinal Suenens set up an office in Brussels for the CCRM. In 1981, he moved this office to Via Ferruccio in Rome and named it as the International Catholic Charismatic Renewal Office (ICCRO) to work in coordination with other dicasteries of the Holy See and to be in close relationship with the Holy See. In 1985, the Holy See shifted ICCRO to Vatican City. In 1993, the leaders renamed ICCRO as International Catholic Charismatic Renewal Services (ICCRS). They shifted its office to Piazza San Calisto, Rome.[12]

1.1 The Characteristic Features of the Catholic Charismatic Renewal Movement

Along with the teaching of the Second Vatican Council, Pentecostalism also influenced the CCRM. Like Pentecostalism, the CCRM stresses on the spiritual renewal in the Holy Spirit. It recognizes the importance of the phenomena of the baptism in the Holy Spirit for living an authentic Christian life. It also emphasizes on the use of the charisms for the good of the community. Repentance, holiness and deepening of spiritual life are some of the common features of both, the CCRM and Pentecostalism. However, the CCRM differs from Pentecostalism. The CCRM is a movement within the Catholic Church, unlike the Pentecostal Independent Churches. It considers itself as a grace within the Church and for the Church.

The CCRM considers the experience of the baptism of the Holy Spirit as a grace. However, it does not consider baptism of the Holy Spirit as a sacrament but a release of the power of the sacraments of initiation.[13] It also does not consider the gift of tongues as indispensable sign of baptism in the Holy Spirit. Pentecostals relate baptism in the Holy Spirit with gift of tongues. They consider it as indispensable sign of the experience of the baptism in the Holy Spirit. The CCRM draws its spirituality from the richness of

---

12 David Barrett and Todd Johnson, *Then Peter Stood Up*, (Rome: ICCRS, 2000), 117.

13 See Paul Thigpen, "Catholic Charismatic Movement," in *The New International Dictionary of Pentecostal and Charismatic Movements*, 465. See also Walter Hollenweger, *Pentecostalism: Origins and Developments Worldwide* (Peabody: Hendrickson Publishers, 1997), 156-159.

the tradition of the Church. Thus, the CCRM has integrated the devotions of the Catholic Church in its spirituality. The CCRM does not consider the phenomenon of baptism in the Holy Spirit as new. This is because the Church history shows that some individuals and movements had the experience of the baptism in the Holy Spirit. They too used the charisms of the Holy Spirit like the Pentecostals of our times.[14] Thus, the CCRM spirituality draws strength from the teachings of the Church for spiritual growth. It is at the service of the Church.

1.2 The Growth of the Catholic Charismatic Renewal Movement

In 1967, the CCRM organized its first conference. Only a few people attended it. However, the following year, in 1968, there were around 150 participants. In 1969, the number grew to 450 people. In 1970, more than 1300 people attended the annual conferences of the CCRM. After the 70s, the movement started spreading to other countries. At the 1971 gathering, representatives from 11 countries attended the annual conference and the total number of people who were present was more than 5000. By 1977, at the regional conference in Atlantic City alone the attendants numbered more than 30,000.[15]

In the 1980s, the number of people attending the CCRM conferences declined in the USA. By 1982 Stephen Clark, one of the pioneers of the CCRM in the USA acknowledged that the CCRM had peaked.[16] Theologian Edward O'Connor noted the following about the disinterest in the CCRM.

> It is relatively easy for a person, while still buoyed up by the first Pentecostal grace, and supported by the community around him, to believe in the work of the spirit.

---

14 See Kilian McDonnell and George T. Montague, Christian Initiation and Baptism in the Holy Spirit: Evidence from the First Eight Centuries (Collegeville: The Liturgical Press, 1991).

15 Paul Thigpen, "Catholic Charismatic Movement," in The New International Dictionary of Pentecostal and Charismatic Movements, 460-467.

16 Steve Clark, "Are We Charismatic?" *New Covenant* 12, No. 7, (February 1983): 24.

> But after some weeks, when the early effects of the baptism subside, he is frequently assailed by grievous doubts about the reality of his experience. If in addition, he finds himself isolated, or surrounded by skeptics, it is very difficult to maintain his enthusiasm.[17]

Those involved actively with the CCRM were praying for its growth. They were seeking new ways to spread their message. In 1986, in response to Pope John Paul II's stress on the "New Evangelization," the CCRM started organizing programs with the aim of evangelization. Through the 1990s, the CCRM programs trained many people for the task of evangelization. Most of the people who attended these programs and courses were lay people with full time jobs.[18]

In the international context, especially in the developing countries the CCRM also took active interest in social justice activities. In the late 1990s, the number of Charismatics swelled to 72 million, worldwide. The numbers may have declined in the U.S.A but there was a great increase in South America, Europe and Asia. Nations like Korea, Pakistan, Malaysia, and even Papua New Guinea had a significant number of people involved with the CCRM.[19]

From a humble beginning at Duquesne University, the CCRM surged ahead in spite of all difficulties and uncertainties and by 2000 spread to 235 countries. The CCRM, which began in 1970s with a modest figure of 2000 people rapidly grew to 40 million by 1980s and by 2000, it further grew to 119 million. The 30 year growth rate is 14.6%. There were 1,057,447,000 baptized Catholics as of the data of 2000.[20] This means that 11.3% of the globe's Catholic population is involved with the CCRM.

Thus, the CCRM had a phenomenal growth worldwide. In the next chapter, we shall examine the spread of the CCRM to Japan.

---

17 O'Connor, The Pentecostal Movement in the Catholic Church, 87-88.

18 Ibid.

19 David Barrett and Todd Johnson, *Then Peter Stood Up*, 117.

20 Ibid.

Chapter 2

The Beginning of the Catholic Charismatic Renewal Movement in Japan

The CCRM started in 1972 in Japan. However, Christianity is much older in Japan. We shall trace the history of the Catholic Church in Japan in order to understand the place of Christianity in the Japanese society. The history of Christianity is remarkable because in spite of difficulties and persecutions, it continued to survive.

2.1 A Brief History of Catholic Church in Japan

2.1.1 Arrival of St. Francis Xavier and the Beginning of the Catholic Church in Japan

Japan and Portugal started trade relationship in 1543. This trade relation helped the Catholic Church to spread in Japan. It was on August 15, 1549 the solemnity of the Assumption of our Lady in heaven, the great missionary St. Francis Xavier landed in Kagoshima along with fellow Jesuits, Cosme de Torres, John Fernandez and three Japanese converts. Xavier had baptized these three Japanese in Malacca in 1547. During these times, neither the Emperor of Japan nor the Ashikaga *shogunate* (ruling powers) wielded an absolute authority over the country. In such a situation, Xavier had no other way, but to rely on the local warlords for carrying out his mission work. Xavier approached Takahisa Shimazu feudal lord of Satsuma, Kagoshima and sought his permission to begin the missionary work. As the local warlords were keen on establishing trade ties with the West, they willing granted the permission. However, initially the *daimyo* (feudal lord) of Yamaguchi refused to give audience to Xavier because of his poor dress. However, later when Xavier presented him good clothes and gifts he readily offered him a temple to live in and the permission to preach in his territory. Otomo Yoshishige, the most influential *daimyo* of Kyushu assured Xavier, protection to the missionaries. With this assurance, Xavier departed from Japan in 1551 leaving the Church to the care of Torres. The teachings of Xavier had a great influence on Yoshishige. He had a great admiration and respect for Xavier. He received Baptism and his Christian name was Francisco. Xavier's missionary work yielded a great fruit. When he left Japan, there were about 2000 Catholics in Kagoshima, Hirado, Yamaguchi and Funai. After Xavier left for India, Torres took over the charge of directing the mission work in Japan.[21]

2.1.2 Mission of Torres and Cabral

Torres became Xavier's successor in Japan. He moved from Yamaguchi to Bungo and established there a center for the Japanese Christian Church. Lack of priests and imprudent methods of evangelization hampered the progress of missionary work. However, Luis d'Almeida, a physician by profession started a clinic in Funai in 1557 and it was very successful. His work resulted in the founding of new mission areas in Omura, Shimabara, Goto Islands, Amakusa Islands and Nagasaki. In southern Japan, many of the converts were belonging to the lower strata of the society but in central Japan, many noblemen became Christians. Kyoto, Sakai and Iimori became the first Christian centers in central Japan. Torres died in 1570 and his successor was Francisco Cabral. When Torres died after spending 18 years in propagation of faith, there were around 30,000 Christians in Japan but the unofficial record claims that there were more than

21 Arcadio Schwade, 'Japan,' in *New Catholic Encyclopaedia*. Vol. 7, (New York: McGraw-Hill Book Company, 1967), 828.

100,000 Christians.[22] Torres always insisted his fellow missionary companions to carry out prudently the mission work. He suggested them to adapt to the culture and language of the people where they were working.[23]

Under the reign of Oda Nobunaga, the Christians enjoyed protection and encouragement. Nobunaga was generous in granting the Jesuits a property near his castle in Azuchi to build their house. Organtino, a Jesuit priest constructed a seminary and a Church on the gifted land.

After the death of Torres, Francisco Cabral became the superior of the Jesuit Japan missions. Cabral was opposed to the policies of Torres of adaptation to the culture of the people and discouraged missionaries from learning Japanese. He also banned the use of wearing silk after the fashion of Buddhist monks.[24] This hostile behavior of Cabral brought a deep dissension within the Jesuit missionaries, who were in favor of adaptation to local culture and language.

2.1.3 The Visitation of Alessandro Valignano

Alessandro Valignano came to Japan in 1579 as the first official visitator general. He began visiting the missionaries and the Christians, which numbered around 150,000 at that time. He got an impression that the missionaries had not given enough catechesis to converts especially some warlords. He felt that they had embraced Christianity to get favors from the Western missionaries and that they forced their soldiers to embrace Christianity to please the missionaries. As a result, there were mass conversions but on the other hand, there were also mass desertions because of inadequate follow up in Christian education. Valignano attempted to visit as many Christian centers and missionaries. He tired to reorganize the mission strategy in the light of his visitation. One of the defects he found with the mission strategy was that of the inadequate knowledge of the Japanese

22 Arcadio Schwade, 'Japan,' in *New Catholic Encyclopaedia*. Vol. 7, (New York: McGraw-Hill Book Company, 1967), 828.

23 George Mueller, *The Catechetical Problem in Japan: 1549-1965* (Tokyo: Oriens Institute for Religious Research, 1967), 13.

24 Ibid., 15.

language by the missionaries. He promoted the study of Japanese language, culture and history. In order to solve the problem of the lack of missionaries, he decided to start a novitiate and a theologate to train seminarians in Japan. He also constructed two seminaries for young Japanese boys who wished to join the priesthood or become catechists. Cabral, the then superior was bitterly opposed to adaptation to local culture and language. He disagreed with Valignano over his open policies. Valignano removed him from his post and sent him to Macao. He replaced him with Gaspar Coelho, who became the first Jesuit vice provincial of Japan.[25]

After the conclusion of the General Visitation to Japan in 1582, Valignano decided to send a delegation of young Catholic Japanese boys to Europe as envoys from the Christian *daimios* of Bungo, Arima and Omura to the Pope and then to the King of Spain. There was a two-fold purpose in sending this delegation. Firstly, Valignano wanted the Western world to see the fruits of the Jesuit missionaries in Japan. He thought that this could arouse interest for mission work in Japan among Europeans. He expected some of them to volunteer to go to Japan as missionaries or give donations for mission work in Japan. The second purpose was to give the young Japanese boys an exposure to the Western world especially to the European culture. The envoys left Japan on February 20, 1582 with Valignano and Diogo Mesquita, going all the way to India and from there to Rome. They returned to Japan in 1590. Mansho Ito, Miguel Chijiwa, Martino Hara and Julian Nakaura were the envoys selected to travel to Europe. They arrived in Portugal in 1584 and met the Spanish King, who ruled over Portugal during that time. Later they visited Pope Gregorio XIII on March 23, 1585. The Pope welcomed them in Rome and gave them the title of honorary citizens of Rome. After the Papal audience, many people invited them to share their experiences of mission. Their presence, especially in Japanese traditional dress, *kimono* created a lot of enthusiasm among the Europeans. In 1586, the delegation left to return to Japan, but due to restrictions in Japan, they stayed back in Macao for two years and reached back to Japan only in 1590.[26]

25 Schwade, 'Japan,' in *New Catholic Encyclopaedia*, 828.

26 Ibid.

2.1.4 The First Persecution of Christians and Prohibition on Practicing Christianity

After Nobunaga's assassination in 1582, his general Toyotomi Hideyoshi succeeded him as the ruler. Initially like Nobunaga, Hideyoshi too was very generous and sympathetic towards the Christians. He helped the Christians in their struggle against the anti-Christian ruler Shimazu, by sending an army of 200,000 soldiers. He had many generals who were Christians and he granted them permission to construct new Churches and start new mission centers. However, at the instigation of the Seyakuin Senso, a Buddhist priest who was having grudge against Takayama Ukon, a Christian general, Hideyoshi became enemy of Christians. He sent Ukon into exile and published a decree on July 15, 1587 banning the practice of Christianity and ordering all the missionaries to leave Japan within 20 days of issuing the decree.[27] Nevertheless, the actual reason (besides the instigation of the Buddhist priest) behind Hideyoshi's hatred towards Christians is not clear. Moreover, his decision to ban missionaries and Christianity remains unclear. Historians suggest that one of the most likely reasons could be the refusal of a Jesuit missionary, Coelho to deliver him a well-armed Portuguese ship. After Hideyoshi issued a decree banning Christianity, most of the missionaries gathered in the port of Hirado while a few defied the order and went into hiding. However, the authorities could not enforce Hideyoshi's decree because there were no ships departing from Japan for overseas for the next 20 days. Thus, most of the missionaries could remain in Japan, under the protection of the Christian lords of Southern Japan, Kyushu.[28] However, Hideyoshi's soldiers destroyed many Churches and Christian properties. The Church, which administered the port of Nagasaki, lost its right of administration. Besides the port of Nagasaki, the Church also lost the ownership of the port at Mogi and the Church properties in Urakami. Hideyoshi imposed oppressive fines on the Christians in Nagasaki. Later Hideyoshi agreed to relax the ban against the missionaries and allowed them to stay in Japan

27 Richard Drummond, *A History of Christianity in Japan* (Grand Rapids: William B. Eerdmans, 1971), 79-81.

28 Ibid., 830.

until the next year. However, he told them that this relaxation was temporary and they need to settle around the port of Hirado and get ready for their departure.[29]

Hideyoshi vacated all the Church properties in central Japan (Shikoku). He forced most of the missionaries to leave Kyushu and go to Hirado. However, some missionaries decided to defy the order of Hideyoshi and secretly continued to live in Japan under the protection of local Christian feudal lords. Hideyoshi tried to enforce the ban on professing Christianity and ordered all the missionaries to leave Japan. In February 1588, before sailing for Macao, the captain of the ship Domingos Monteiro sent a message to Hideyoshi that it was not possible to accommodate all the missionaries on the boat and some will have to remain back and travel on another vessel the next year. Hideyoshi was not happy with this and gave orders to destroy all the Jesuit houses in Miyako, Osaka, Gifu, Akashi and Sakai.

A Portuguese vessel called Nao landed in Japan on August 17, 1588. The captain Jeronymo Pereira assured Hideyoshi that he could accommodate all the missionaries on his vessel. In spite of this assurance, Hideyoshi knew that some missionaries would not leave Japan and continue to remain in hiding.

Surprisingly Hideyoshi sometimes acted favorably towards the Christians and sometimes was too harsh. Historians find it difficult to comprehend, as to why Hideyoshi kept on changing his mind about Christians. Some historians reason out that he persecuted Christians because he feared that the missionaries with the help of their native kings (European empires) would invade Japan. On the other hand, with the intention to improve the trade relations between the Western worlds, he tried to have good relations with Christians. Even though he asked the missionaries to leave Japan, he did not enforce his edicts with full vigor.

In spite of the persecutions, the Church survived in Japan. However, there was a significant decline in number of Baptisms and conversions.[30] In 1588, Pope Sixtus V created the Diocese of

---

29 Richard Drummond, *A History of Christianity in Japan* (Grand Rapids: William B. Eerdmans, 1971), 837.

30 Joseph Jennes, A History of the Catholic Church in Japan, from Its Beginnings to the Early Meiji Era (1549-1873) (Tokyo: Oriens Institute for Religious Research, 1973), 62-85.

Funai (Oita), the first see in Japan. Pope Sixtus V was unaware of the persecutions started against the Christians in Japan. About the same time the Jesuit, Valignano who had earlier come to Japan as Visitator General, revisited Japan from 1590-1592. The four Japanese delegates who went to Europe as envoys accompanied him. However, this time he came to Japan in his capacity as the ambassador of the Portuguese viceroy of India. Hideyoshi welcomed him and gave him an audience.[31] Valignano presented Hideyoshi gifts including an Arabian stallion and a printing press with the movable metal type, which was not available in Japan.[32] Valignano's diplomacy yielded some fruits. He could not persuade Hideyoshi to abrogate his edict banning missionaries but he was successful in getting stay permit for 10 Jesuits to reside in Japan. This permission implied that Hideyoshi had allowed the missionaries to stay in Japan. Nevertheless, he did not abrogate his edict banning Christianity and missionaries.[33] Even though, Hideyoshi welcomed Valignano, he continued to persecute Christians and missionaries.

In August 1592, Hideyoshi's minister destroyed the Church in Nagasaki. The real reason to destroy the Church building was to use the Church property for his personal motives. During the Korean War (1592-1598), Hideyoshi often traveled to Kyushu to overlook the military operations against Korea and this resulted in indirect control of missionaries in Kyushu. However, Hideyoshi relied heavily on the famous Christian general Konishi Yukinaga and his eighteen thousand Christian soldiers from Kyushu, who invaded the Korean capital.[34] Hideyoshi was in favor of taking help from Christian feudal lords like Kuroda of Fukuoka, Asano of Wakayama and Hosokawa Tadoki of Tango and Buzen. In the meantime, in Central Japan noblemen and noblewomen came into the Christian fold. The grandson of Oda Nobunaga was one of them.

31 Samuel Hugh Moffett, *A History of Christianity in Asia,* Vol. 2, (New York: Orbis Books, 2005), 81.

32 Ibid.

33 Jospeh Schütte, 'Japan, Martyrs of,' in *New Catholic Encyclopaedia*, Vol. 7, (New York: McGraw-Hill Book Company, 1967), 838.

34 James Mudroch and Isoh Yamagata, *A History of Japan during the Century of Early Foreign Intercourse (1542-1651)*, Vol. 2, (Kobe: The Chronicle, 1903), 317-324.

Among the various factors, which favored Christianity, was the social welfare schemes of the Church. The Church built hospitals for the sick, houses to take care of the poor and schools to educate. These social welfare works were very successful in creating a positive impact on the Japanese people. The printing press brought by Valignano also had a very positive effect. He used it to print books not only on Christianity but also on the language and culture of Japan that included the first trilingual Japanese-Latin-Portuguese dictionary. In addition, he published a book on Japanese-Latin grammar to help the Japanese seminarians. Besides these, he also published an anthology of Chinese and Japanese prose and poetry. However, one may be surprised to know that in spite of all these publications there was not one single publication of the full Bible in Japanese. Manuscripts of certain texts existed with Japanese translations but there was no one complete work.[35]

In spite of the various difficulties, the missionaries continued with their work of evangelization. In 1593, Franciscan Missionaries got permission to enter Japan. They came from Spain and Philippines. Initially Hideyoshi welcomed them. He wanted to use their influence to negate the strength of the Portuguese and the Jesuits. Even though, he had issued an edict ordering all the missionaries to leave Japan, he himself granted favors to the new missionaries by gifting them land to construct new Churches and monasteries in the capital. Besides building Churches, the Franciscans also built a hospital in Osaka. They were preparing to construct another hospital in Nagasaki. The missionary work of the Franciscans differed from that of the Jesuits. The Franciscans were more involved in humanitarian works rather than evangelizing the noblemen. The Jesuits on the other hand worked for the evangelization of the higher-class people. They believed that if the upper class people convert then within no time all the people who serve them, would also follow their masters and become Christians.[36]

35 Johannes Laures, Kirishitan Bunko: A Manual of Books and Documents on the Early Christian Missions in Japan, 3rd ed. (Tokyo: Sophia University, 1957), 1-26. See also Jennes, A History of the Catholic Church in Japan, 78-82, 121-124.

36 Moffett, A History of Christianity in Asia, Vol. 2, 84. See also Jennes, A History of the Catholic Church in Japan, 69ff.

The differences among the Jesuits and Franciscans damaged the missionary work in Japan. The rift among the missionaries resulted in more persecutions on Christians in Japan. After the appointment of the first resident bishop in Japan, Martinez, people expected that he would build bridges between the Jesuits and the Franciscans. However, unfortunately, the bishop was not interested in unifying the missionaries but only in becoming famous and amassing ecclesiastical power. He himself had serious differences with Valignano, the head of the Jesuit's Asian missions in Japan. He had differences not only with the religious but also with the Japanese government. He was insensitive to the local customs and did not find favor among the people. The Japanese government forced him to leave Japan within a year. The Pope replaced him with Monsignor Luis de Cerqueira, a Jesuit who remained in Japan for fifteen years (1598-1614). He was much more sober person than Martinez. However, he too had little success in unifying the two major religious orders.[37] Mudroch sums up the differences between the two religious orders as "Between the Jesuits and Franciscans in Japan it was all but war to the knife."[38]

The constant infighting of the missionaries and the differences between the Portuguese and the Spanish was creating great damage to the Church in Japan. This resulted in Hideyoshi becoming more suspicious of the missionaries and their plans. The infighting clearly gave an impression that the main intention of the missionaries was to capture power in Japan. In the meantime, the Buddhist priests were constantly warning Hideyoshi of the danger of invasion by Western forces. Hideyoshi's fear grew with the landing of the ship *San Felipe*. This Spanish ship from Manila landed in Japan in 1596. It was loaded with guns, ammunitions and seven missionaries. Some historians claim that the captain of the ship made some indiscreet and imprudent remarks, saying that Spaniards send the missionaries first and then the soldiers follow them. His remarks suggested that the Spaniards would capture Japan, just as they had captured the

37 Jennes, *A History of the Catholic Church in Japan,* 75-76. See also Frank Cary, *History of Christianity in Japan,* Vol. 1, (Tokyo: Kyo Bun Kan, 1960), 122-123.

38 Mudroch and Isoh Yamagata, A History of Japan during the Century of Early Foreign Intercourse (1542-1651), Vol. 2, 490.

countries of Latin America and the Philippines. However, some historians dispute this claim. Some historians believe that this story about the captain, which led to the execution of 26 Christians, is untrue. Nevertheless, whatever the truth is, the fact remains that Hideyoshi became very suspicious of Christian missionaries with the landing of the ship *San Felipe*.[39]

Hideyoshi ordered the execution of 26 Christians. This list includes six Franciscans, three Japanese Jesuits, fifteen Japanese Christians from the Franciscan hospital in Kyoto and two others. The court prosecuted them in Kyoto and then sent them to Nagasaki for public crucifixion. The authorities killed them on the hill of Nishizaka, Nagasaki on February 5, 1597 and left their bodies in the open for nine months to give the stern message to all Christians that if anyone dared to go against Japanese interests, they would also meet the same fate as them.[40] Hideyoshi ordered the closure of Jesuit colleges and seminaries. He wanted to deport all the Jesuits from Japan. By February 17, 1597, he destroyed more than 130 Churches and Church properties.[41] The first great persecutions against the Christians ended with the death of Hideyoshi in September 1598. Christian missionaries came out of hiding, the war with Korea ended and the Christian feudal lords and generals returned, and there was temporary peace and progress in the mission work.[42]

2.1.5 Christendom Under Tokugawa Ieyasu

Tokugawa Ieyasu was the successor of Toyotomi Hideyoshi. Due to the tremendous pressure of the Catholic feudal lords of Arima and Omura, Ieyasu decided to be tolerant towards Christian missionaries and allowed them to practice freely Christianity. He also permitted the Franciscan missionaries to return to Japan. Thus, there was a tremendous increase in the number of Christians from 1601-1612. The increasing strength and influence of the Catholic *daimyos* was

39 Charles Boxer, *The Christian Century in Japan, 1549-1650* (London: Cambridge University Press, 1951), 166-170. See also George Bailey Samson, *A History of Japan*, Vol. 2, (Stanford: Stanford University Press, 1963), 374.

40 See Schütte, 'Japan, Martyrs of,' in *New Catholic Encyclopaedia*, Vol. 7, 838.

41 Ibid.

42 Ibid. See also Moffett, *A History of Christianity in Asia*, Vol. 2, 85.

making Ieyasu insecure and jealous. Ieyasu considered the growing strength of the *daimyos* as a threat to his plan to unify Japan as one nation. In the meantime, to make the matters worse, in the civil war, which broke out in 1600 between Ieyasu and the heirs of Hideyoshi, the Christian commander Konishi decided to support the cause of the heirs of Hideyoshi and fought against Ieyasu. Ieyasu won the war and executed Konishi for his anti-government activities. This also resulted in the beginning of the second phase of persecutions against the Christians in Japan. Ieyasu handed over the territory governed by Konishi to the Buddhist general Kato under whose reign the number of Christians reduced drastically.[43] On June 13, 1612, he expelled all missionaries from his territory. He ordered his Christian subjects to renounce Christianity. Nevertheless, the Christians were strong in their faith and refused to give up their Christian faith.

2.1.6 The Second Persecution of Christians

In 1612, Ieyasu burnt down a Franciscan Church in Tokyo. In addition, the destruction of Christian properties spread to other parts of Japan. In November 1613, some Buddhists in Miyako accused Christians of worshipping the dead. This incident triggered further persecutions against Christians.[44] Further, the soldeirs arrested the famous *daimyo* of Arima, whose family had long been supporting the Jesuits on charges of bribery. Later they executed him. The son of the *daimyo* renounced his Christian faith and became a bitter opponent of Christians. He killed many Christians and tried to make many Christians renounce their faith but with little success as a large number of Christians resisted his attempts.[45]

The Christians in Japan soon realized that the government was increasingly becoming suspicious of them as anti-nationals who were working against the unification of Japan. Moreover, Ieyasu Tokugawa started to disdain Christianity. He wanted to give more importance to religions like Shinto, Buddhism and Confucianism. He considered Shinto a national pride and reconstructed the imperial shrine at Ise (*Ise Gingu*). In January 1614, Tokugawa Ieyasu issued a

43 Jennes, A History of the Catholic Church in Japan, 88-89, 103.

44 Schütte, 'Japan, Martyrs of' in *New Catholic Encyclopedia*, Vol. 7, 838.

45 Moffett, A History of Christianity in Asia, Vol. 2, 88.

very harsh edict expelling all missionaries from Japan and forbidding the practice of Christianity in Japan. This edict led to the closure of all Churches, the deportation of all missionaries and a complete ban on practicing Christianity by all the Japanese whether in public or private. He accused Christianity of hurting the national pride by going against the traditional and great religions of Japan.[46] This edict almost passed a death sentence on Christianity in Japan. To make the matters worse for Christians he ordered that everyone in Japan must enroll himself or herself as a member of one or the other Buddhist sect.[47]

The edict issued in January 1614 brought the deportation of many Christian missionaries from Japan. Ieyasu wanted to send out all the missionaries at once but he could not do so because of the lack of vessels sailing for overseas from Japan. There was also unrest among the missionaries, as Monsignor Luis Cerqueira had died and there was a dispute regarding his successor among the missionaries. Some Jesuits and diocesan clerics favored the Jesuit provincial Valentin Carvalho as interim apostolic administrator but a group of Franciscans and Dominicans wanted a Dominican priest, Zumàrraga to be the leader. Zumàrraga was a wise person and knew that disunity among missionaries would only add to the problems of the Christians in Japan and so he suggested that all accept Carvalho as the apostolic administrator.[48]

In 1615, there was a domestic political struggle in Japan and Ieyasu was more concerned about holding on to power than actually implementing anti-Christian edicts. The total numbers of martyrs during the lifetime of Ieyasu remained comparatively low. Tokugawa Ieyasu was not favorable towards Christians but he did not order many executions, he tried to make the Christians renounce their faith and come back to the Buddhist fold. However, things turned worse after his death in 1616 and the succession of his son Tokugawa Hidetada as the new ruler.[49]

46 Boxer, The Christian Century in Japan, 1549-1650, 317-318.

47 Jennes, A History of the Catholic Church in Japan, 97ff.

48 Ibid., 119.

49 Mudroch and Isoh Yamagata, A History of Japan during the Century of Early Foreign Intercourse (1542-1651), Vol. 2, 617.

2.1.7 The Horror Under the Rule of Tokugawa Hidetada

Following the policy of his father, Tokugawa Ieyasu, Hidetada published a new edict in 1616 banning all Christian activities. Many of the Christian *daimyos* of Kyushu were not able to resist the pressure and so, renounced their faith and became persecutors of fellow Christians. Hidetada ordered the beheading of entire Christian families who protected the missionaries or gave them shelter. His soldiers burnt many people alive in Nagasaki. They did not spare women and children too. The barbaric acts against Christians grew day by day.[50]

2.1.8 Total Isolation of Christians Under the Rule of Tokugawa Iemitsu

Tokugawa Hidetada appointed his son, Iemitsu as his successor in 1623. The long rule of Iemistu from 1623-1651 meant a total isolation and doom for the Church in Japan. Iemistu tortured the Christians and executed them. The soldiers hunted for Christians and made them to renounce their faith. They asked them to do *fumie* (stamp on the picture of Jesus and Mary) to prove their renunciation of the Christian faith.[51] Tokugawa Iemitsu did not permit new missionaries to enter Japan. The immigration authorities thoroughly checked all foreign vessels entering Japan. If they would find any missionary on the vessel, then they would execute the captain of the ship along with his crew. Iemitsu also forbade the postal correspondence with priests abroad.[52]

The Shimabara uprising (1637-1638) brought the final collapse of the Church in Japan. The agrarian population in Amakusa and Takaku in the Shimabara peninsula, which was entirely Christian, rebelled against Tokugawa due to the deteriorating economic and social situation. Their leader was the 18-year-old son of a Christian samurai named Masuda Shiro. Veteran military leaders helped him to fight against Tokugawa Iemitsu. The government sent a huge army to fight against them and so the rebels had no other choice but

50 See Moffett, *A History of Christianity in Asia,* Vol. 2, 90. See also Schütte, 'Japan, Martyrs of' in *New Catholic Encyclopaedia*, Vol. 7, 839.

51 Ibid.

52 Jennes, A History of the Catholic Church in Japan, 138.

to take refuge in Hara. The government laid complete siege around Hara and cut off all food and water supplies. The rebels could not continue with their fight and fell to their enemy in mid-April 1638. The government suspected that the rebellion was encouraged by foreign powers and so all the ships coming to Japan were subject to strict checking.[53] Meanwhile, anti-Christian activities were increasing. The soldiers were asking Christians to do *fumie.* Their refusal would result in execution and complete confiscation of their property. The government later decided to put the Christians in the hot sulfur springs of Mount Unzen. The Christians were further humiliated by dipping their head in the pits of excrement until they would apostatize or die.[54]

In 1639, Japan broke all trade and diplomatic relations with Portuguese. This marked the closure of Japan to the Western world. Christianity virtually ended in Japan. Harassment and public executions of missionaries and banning the entry of new missionaries all added up to the almost complete annihilation of missionaries in Japan.[55]

The last European missionary to enter Japan was the Sicilian secular priest Giovanni Battista Sidotti. The government arrested him, soon after he landed in Japan in October 1708 and kept him in the prison until his death in December 1715. The Tokugawa *Shoguns* were happy that their mission to eliminate Christians and missionaries was a success. The government tried to wipe out completely Christianity by halting all the missionary activities. The Japanese *Shoguns* succeeded in prohibiting public Christian worship. They killed and humiliated Christians, but they could never kill the Christian spirit of the faithful. The *Shoguns* were happy because they drove out Christianity out of Japan. However, history has proven them wrong as Christianity survived in Japan, in spite of the various persecutions.[56]

---

53 See Schütte, 'Japan, Martyrs of' in *New Catholic Encyclopaedia*, Vol. 7, 840.

54 Ibid. See also Moffett, *A History of Christianity in Asia,* Vol. 2, 91.

55 See Jennes, A History of the Catholic Church in Japan, 146-148.

56 See Moffett, *A History of Christianity in Asia,* Vol. 2, 93-94. See also Schütte, 'Japan, Martyrs of' in *New Catholic Encyclopaedia*, Vol. 7, 840.

2.1.9 The Reappearance of Christianity in Japan in 1859

Christianity faced the worst persecution in the 17th century at the hands of the Japanese government. However, no persecutions could extinguish the flame of the Christ spirit. Christianity survived in spite of all the trials and difficulties. When Xavier left Japan in 1551, there were around 3,000 Christians. However, due to the efforts of the missionaries by 1614, the number of Christians had risen to 300,000. Moreover, in a span of less than 100 years the number of Christians increased dramatically in Japan.[57] These figures clearly show that the missionaries had done a remarkable work of evangelization in Japan. It is not only the numbers but also the fidelity of Japanese Christians, which is very impressive. Even though, there were repeated persecutions, Japanese Christians always kept their faith and remained firm.

From 1639, the Church in Japan did not have any contact with the outside world.[58] After about 2 centuries a Christian, missionary Thoedore Forcade a priest belonging to the Paris Missionary Society (*Missions Etrangères de Paris*) tried to enter Japan in 1844 but in vain. The government did not allow him to enter the mainland. However, the diplomacy of the Navy commander Matthew Perry helped another priest, Louis Thèodore Furet, MEP to enter Japan as an interpreter for a short period in 1855. Japan signed trade and commercial treaties with USA, England, Russia and France from 1858-1859. This opening of Japan to the outside world helped the MEP missionaries to secure permission to remain in Japan and to carry out their religious services for the foreigners who would come to Japan for trade purposes. The earlier edict prohibiting Christianity continued for the Japanese, but the government exempted the foreigners from it.[59]

Bernard Petitjean, a MEP priest discovered that some Christians in Nagasaki continued to keep their Christian faith throughout all

57 Drummond, A History of Christianity in Japan, 57-58.

58 See Klaus Koschorke, Frieder Ludwig and Mariano Delgado, eds. *A History of Christianity in Asia, Africa and Latin America, 1450-1990: A Documentary Sourcebook* (Grand Rapids: William B. Eerdmans Publishing Company, 2007) 31-32.

59 See Schwade, 'Japan' in *New Catholic Encyclopedia*, 832.

the centuries in spite of the absence of the missionaries in Japan. In March 1865, Bernard Petitjean observed that a group of Japanese people had gathered around his new built Church in Nagasaki. A woman came near to him and confessed her faith. He soon discovered that there were many others Christians in Urakami and the Goto Islands of the South Japan. Even though they had registered themselves as Buddhist and were giving Buddhist funerals to their dead, they never gave up their faith. Historians say that the years of persecution, isolation and lack of proper catechism resulted in the dilution of the faith and inclusion of non-Christian religious and superstitious practices in their worship. Therefore, of the 30,000 *Kakure Kirishitan* (hidden Christians), only about 10,000 returned to Roman Catholic Church. The others could not identify their faith with the Roman Catholic faith.[60]

The return of a priest among the *Kakure Kirishitan* infused life and vigor among them and there was lot of excitement in the Christian community. The Japanese government had not lifted the ban against the practice of Christianity by Japanese, so the authorities did not like the Christian activities and started harassing them. In the meantime, Bernard Petitjean became the bishop and tried to mobilize the Christian community, but there was no much growth in Christian population.[61]

On January 3, 1868, a coup d'état threw out the *Shogun* and restored the emperor system in Japan. The new emperor named Meiji was only a youth of 16 years when he inherited the throne. He was heavily dependent on veterans for counsel and planning. He turned out to be one of the most liberal rulers of Japan. Initially, the restoration of imperial rule did not bring any respite to the persecuted Christians. An imperial edict reaffirmed the disdain of the emperor against the sect of the Christians. The emperor was more favorably disposed towards the traditional Japanese religion Shinto. However, interestingly during this time, the government did not even spare

60 See Jennes, A History of the Catholic Church in Japan, 216-217. See also Stephen Turnbull, The Kakure Kirishitan of Japan: A Study of Their [the hidden Christians] Development, Beliefs and Rituals to the Present Day (Surrey: Japan Library, 1998), 55-81.

61 See Jennes, A History of the Catholic Church in Japan, 223-224.

the Buddhists. They placed them under severe restrictions like the Christians. However, the Christians suffered more as the government burnt their homes and got their properties confiscated.[62]

It was only in 1873 that the Japanese government granted tentatively religious freedom because it wanted to re-establish trade relations with United States and Europe. The governments in United States and Europe were keen on the removal of all restrictions on practice of the Christianity in Japan. It was keeping in mind these sentiments and to have trade benefits that the Meiji government wisely removed the public notices of the edict against Christianity, but still the government was more favorable towards the traditional religion Shinto, which it considered as the force of unity and national spirit.[63] Catholics who scattered all over Kyushu due to persecutions started to return to Nagasaki. The government allowed a big number of foreigners to enter Japan. However, some minor restrictions on the travel of missionaries continued, though they were not troubled. The government spared Buddhism too of severe restrictions and considered it as a co-national religion along with Shinto. The government did not consider Christianity as a powerful religion of any national importance. Slowly the government abrogated the anti-Christian edicts and towards the beginning of 1889, the new Meiji constitution granted full religious freedom in Japan.[64]

Even though Japan opened herself to the Western culture in the 19th century, it was merely to gain access to trade and scientific knowledge. Japan's contact with the Western world had hardly any influence on the political, social and religious structures. The traditional religions of Japan, especially Shinto and Buddhism enjoyed a special status as the Japanese government considered them as symbols of national pride. The Japanese society thought that their culture was far superior to others. This ideology helped Japan to work harder in order to surpass all other nations. Even though the

62 See Jennes, A History of the Catholic Church in Japan, 223-224. See also Otis Cary, *History of Christianity in Japan*, Vol. 1, (New York: Fleming H. Revell, 1909), 306-308.

63 Marius Jansen, *The Making of Modern Japan* (Cambridge: Harvard University Press, 2000), 355-356.

64 Jennes, A History of the Catholic Church in Japan, 228-230. See also Moffett, A History of Christianity in Asia, Vol. 2, 507-508.

Japanese government removed all restrictions on Christianity, it could not spread rapidly because of the wide spread presence of the spirit of nationalism, which favored Shinto and Buddhism. The hard work of the Roman Catholic and Protestant missionaries did not yield much fruit. Nationalism, veneration of emperor as god and cultural differences did not favor the growth of Christianity in Japan.[65]

In 1891, Pope Leo XIII established the Japanese hierarchy in the Catholic Church by erecting the Archdiocese of Tokyo as the metropolitan see, with three suffragan bishoprics, Osaka, Nagasaki and Hakodate. The Bishops of Japan and Korea held their first synod at Nagasaki in 1890. However, they held the later synods in Tokyo. In 1924, the Holy See decided to establish a major seminary in Tokyo in order to recruit and train local missionaries. The Holy See erected new dioceses as the population of Catholics grew. The Holy See elevated Nagasaki diocese to the rank of an Archdiocese in 1959 and later raised Osaka diocese to the rank of an Archdiocese in 1969. In the 19th century, the Paris Missionary Society (*Missions Etrangères de Paris*) pioneered the work of evangelization in Japan. Many other religious congregations both of men and of women lined up to begin their missionary and apostolic work in Japan. The mushrooming of new missionary orders, initiated the phase of building educational and social welfare facilities in Japan. The Japanese government had put some restriction on foreign missionaries until 1899. However, it removed all restrictions afterwards. The missionaries were free to do their missionary work.[66]

As Japan opened herself to the outside world, the Congregation for the Propagation of Faith invited many other religious congregations to send their members to Japan. In response to this call, the Marianists began their educational apostolate in Japan in 1888; Trappists in 1896, Dominicans in 1905, and the Society of the Divine Word followed them in 1907. The Franciscans returned in 1906 and the Jesuits in 1908. The bishops of Japan decided to merge the major seminary in Tokyo with Sophia University run by the Jesuits. Later

---

65 Kenneth Scout Latourette, A History of the Expansion of Christianity: The Great Century in Northern Africa and Asia, A. D.1800-A. D. 1914, Vol. 6, (London: Eyre and Spottiswoode Limited, 1944), 371.

66 See Schwade, 'Japan' in *New Catholic Encyclopedia*, 833-834.

in 1948, they decided to open another regional seminary in Nagasaki and gave charge to the Sulpicians, to administer it.[67]

The Jesuits started the Sophia University in 1913 in Tokyo, a task entrusted to them by Pope Pius X. Many other religious congregations started establishing middle and secondary schools for both boys and girls. The Society of the Divine Word also started the Nanzan University in Nagoya in 1946. Along with the University, the Nanzan School Corporation runs primary, middle and secondary schools. Catholic Churches also started kindergartens as part of their apostolate. Besides the educational apostolate, the Catholic Church was also actively involved with the printing press ministry. The Franciscans and the Salesians founded printing centers and publishing houses. These publishing houses published many scholarly periodicals, newsletters and Christian journals. The missionaries realized that the terminology used for Christian terms in the past was not making any sense to the people. This happened because in the past the missionaries did not give much importance to the study of the language and culture of the local people. However, in spite of the efforts of the missionaries to adapt to local culture and language, one can fine that there are still many words used in Catholic liturgy and scriptures, which do not have a suitable and appropriate Japanese translation.

The Japanese society recognizes the social and charitable works done by the Catholic Church. The generosity and the selfless hard labor of the missionaries always gained admiration from the people. A number of religious congregations run hospitals, hospices and homes for the aged people.[68]

Even though the Meiji constitution lifted the restrictions on the practice of religion there was no phenomenal growth of the Catholic Church. This was in spite of the fact that, the Roman Catholic Church found many of her members *Kakure Kirishitan* (Hidden Christians). On the other hand, the Protestant Churches that had hardly any presence in Japan saw more growth than the Catholics. The Russian Orthodox Church too had a growth in her membership. Protestants, mostly from the USA, concentrated on the missions in Japan, and

67 See Schwade, 'Japan' in *New Catholic Encyclopedia*, 833-834.

68 Ibid.

sent a large number of missionaries to evangelize. They distributed copies of the New Testament and literature on Christianity to attract young Japanese to the Christian faith. The sending countries funded the missionaries in Japan and so they were well equipped to carry out their mission work. They worked zealously for the spread of Protestantism in Japan.[69] One of the remarkable achievements of the Protestants was the translation of Bible. Jonathan Goble a Baptist missionary produced a translation of the Gospel of Matthew, even though it was not a good translation. He started to sell copies of this Gospel and many Japanese came forward to buy it.[70] Protestants published the entire New Testament in Japanese in 1879, followed by the Old Testament in 1883. Catholics lagged behind. The first Catholic translation of the New Testament appeared in 1910 and the Old Testament much later in 1959.[71]

Initially in the 1890s, there was a rapid growth of the Protestant churches as compared to the Roman Catholic Church, but by the beginning of the 20th century, there was a significant reduction in the number of converts in all the denominations. One of the reasons for the sudden change is that Christianity lost its charm. Initially the Japanese were greatly excited about the Western religions, but gradually that excitement died out. At the same time, Buddhism and Shinto were gaining popularity. Even though there were no direct threats to Christianity as such in Japan, the mission work did not produce the desired fruit. However, the mission work continued and till this day missionaries toil for the growth of the Church in Japan.[72]

Even though there has been no phenomenal growth of Christianity, it is evident from the statistics published by Barrett in *World Christian Encyclopedia* (2001) that Christianity is growing gradually. In 1979s, only 3.0% of the Japanese population was Christians but my mid 2000 the figure increased to 3.6%. There has been a marginal growth of 0.6% in 30 years. The following table

69 Latourette, A History of the Expansion of Christianity: The Great Century in Northern Africa and Asia, A. D.1800-A. D. 1914, 381-382.

70 See Cary, History of Christianity in Japan, Vol. 2, 84-85, 149.

71 Drummond, A History of Christianity in Japan, 313, 316, 331.

72 Moffett, A History of Christianity in Asia, Vol. 2, 518-519.

Table 2.1: Religious adherents in Japan, 1900-2025[1]

Year	1900		1970		Mid 1990		Mid 1995		Mid 2000		Mid 2025	
Name	Adherents	%	Adherents	%	Adherents	%	Adherents	%	Adherents	%	Adherents	%
Buddhists	35,666,000	79.6	64,605,740	62	68,605,740	56	69,510,900	55.4	69,931,454	55	61,993,500	51.2
New Religionists	2,000,000	4.5	21,3000,000	20	31,600,000	25.6	32,400,000	25.8	32,827,640	25.9	32,500,000	26.8
Non Religious	0	0	9,373,200	9	12,400,000	10	12,700,00	10.1	12,905,945	10.2	14,000,000	11.6
Christians	430,000	1	3,100,000	3	4,375,000	3.5	4,450,000	3.6	4,559,573	3.6	5,000,000	4.1
Independent Christians	10,000	0	460,479	1	1,1510,000	1.2	1,552,452	1.2	1,600,000	1.3	1,800,000	1.5
Marginal Christians	0	0	170,722	0	680,000	0.6	697,561	0.6	720,000	0.6	850,000	0.7
Protestants	75,000	0.2	436,059	0	540,000	0.4	553,598	0.4	570,881	0.5	600,000	0.5
Roman Catholics	55,090	0.1	360,679	0	439,000	0.4	447,482	0.4	460,000	0.4	500,000	0.4
Anglicans	11,000	0	49,100	0	56,000	0.1	62,000	0.1	60,000	0.1	75,000	0.1
Orthodox Christians	26,000	0.1	24,502	0	24,000	0	24,000	0	26,000	0	30,000	0
Evangelicals	73,000	0.2	256,000	0.3	405,000	0.4	445,452	0.4	460,000	0.4	500,000	0.4
Pentecostals/ Charismatics	0	0	3,330,000	0.3	1,235,000	1	1,508,974	1.2	1,760,000	1.4	2,060,000	1.7
Atheists	0	0	1,280,000	1.2	34,000,000	2.8	3,500,000	2.8	3,642,371	2.9	3,470,000	2.9
Shintoists	6,720,000	15	4,173,000	4	2,999,510	2.4	2,750,000	2.2	2,669,167	2.1	2,000,000	1.7
Muslims	0	0	0	0	160,000	0.1	168,000	0.1	178,434	0.1	220,000	0.2
Chinese folk religions	5,000	0	40,000	0	140,000	0.1	145,000	0.1	149,000	0.1	75,000	0.1
Confucianists	0	0	9,800	0	14,400	0	15,000	0	15,579	0	25,000	0
Hindus	4,000	0	5,000	0	21,000	0	23,000	0	24,228	0	40,000	0
Bahais	0	0	0	0	14,400	0	15,000	0	15,579	0	25,000	0
Ethnoreligionists	0	0	1,000	0	9,000	0	9,400	0	9,884	0	15,000	0
Jews	0	0	0	0	2,350	0	1,700	0	1,646	0	1,500	0

1 David Barrett, George Kurian and Todd Johnson. *World Christian Encyclopedia: A Comparative Survey of Churches and Religions in the Modern World*, 2nd ed. Vol. 1, 412.

gives the figures of the different religious adherents in Japan from 1900 and gives projection for the year 2025. It is evident from the statistics that even major religions like Buddhism and Shinto are on the path of decline in Japan.

The table 2.1 enumerates the population of different religious adherents in Japan since 1900. Buddhism is the single largest religion in Japan. 79.6% of the Japanese population practiced it in the 1900s. However, Buddhist population gradually decreased to 62% in the 1970s, 55.5% in the 1990s and reduced further to 55.4% in mid-1995. In mid-2000, 55.2% of the Japanese population was Buddhist and according to Barrett by 2025, it may reduce to 51.2%.

The second major religion in the 1900s was Shinto. It had 15% of the population as its adherent in the 1900s but decreased rapidly to 4% by the 1970s and to 2.4% by mid-1990s. In mid-1995, it was around 2.2% and further reduced to 2.1% in 2000. Barrett projects it to shrink to 1.7% by 2025.

New-Religionists, Non-Religious, Christians and Atheists fill the space emptied by Buddhism and Shinto. The New Religionist were mere 4.5% in the 1900s but rose to 20.4% by the 1970s and 25.6% by the mid-1990s. It grew to 25.9% in mid-2000 and Barrett estimates it to grow further to 26.8% by 2025. The Non-Religious had phenomenal growth from nil in the 1900s to 9.3% in the 1970s and rising to 10% by mid-1990. They grew gradually to 10.1% in mid-1995 and to 10.2% by mid-2000. Barrett expects that non-religious group will grow to 11.66% by the year 2025.

Christianity had a rapid growth initially. Around 1% of the Japanese population was Christian by 1900s and grew to 3% by the 1970s but later had marginal growth to 3.6% in mid-1995 and remaining stagnant till 2000. Barrett estimates it to grow to 4.1% by 2025. Surprisingly the number of atheists is steadily growing in Japan. In the 1900s, there were no atheists but by 1970, 1.2% of the population was atheist, a percentage that rose to 2.8% by the mid-1990s and to 2.8% by mid-1995 and to 2.9% by mid-2000. Japan may have 4.5% atheists by 2025. Japan may have more atheists than Christians by 2025.

The 1946 constitution of Japan guaranteed freedom of practice of religion. However, it is evident from the above figures and statistics that Christianity has not grown significantly. The overall population of Christians, including Catholics has been more or less the same since the 1970s. However, a large influx of Japanese Catholic immigrants from Brazil and other parts of Latin America have infused new life and vigor to the Catholic Church. Along with the South Americans, there are also Catholic Korean immigrants.[73] Many dioceses along with the collaboration of various religious congregations are actively involved in catering to the pastoral needs of the immigrants. Besides pastoral work, many missionaries are also involved in providing social and legal help to the immigrants. The renewal movement within the various Christian denominations is gathering momentum. In the 1990s the Pentecostals or Charismatics numbered 1,760,000 (3% Pentecostals, 9% Charismatics and 88% Independents).[74] Japan has sent around 500 missionaries to different countries on all the six continents of the world.[75]

Christianity went through many difficult times in Japan. Initially Japan welcomed the missionaries and accepted the Church as no other country in Asia, but it is ironical that the same country also persecuted missionaries and Christians so harshly that not even a single priest or missionary could survive the persecutions and there were no priest or missionaries left in Japan for around two hundred years. However, in spite of all the difficulties, hardships and the persecutions that the Christians in Japan faced, some never abandoned their faith but rather kept the flame burning until the appropriate time when Japan opened herself again to the foreign missionaries. There are many martyrs in Japan; among them are the 26 martyrs. The Japanese government killed them in Nagasaki in 1597. Pope Pius IX canonized them in Rome on June 8, 1862. Pope Pius beatified a group of another 205 Japanese martyrs in Rome in 1867. Pope John Paul II beatified another group of 16 Japanese martyrs on February 18, 1981 and later canonized them on October 18, 1987. Again, Pope John Paul II beatified two Augustinian priests, Martin Lumbreras Peralta and Melchor Sanchez Perez on April 23, 1989. In addition, Pope Benedict XVI beatified Peter Kibe Kasui

73 Moffett, A History of Christianity in Asia, Vol. 2, 415.

74 Ibid., 416.

75 Ibid.

and his 187 companions on November 24, 2008. The blood of the martyrs on the Japanese soil is continuing to bear fruit. Even though presently the Catholic Church in Japan is a miniscule community, it has a bright future. In spite of the various challenges to the faith in Japan, the Christian community in Japan can look upon the martyrs as models of faith and ask their intercession to continue their journey ahead.

2.2 The History of the Catholic Charismatic Renewal Movement in Japan

Japan does not have a significant populatin of Christians. However, the CCRM reached Japan within 5 years of birth in the USA. The Charismatic Renewal Movement began in 1972 in Japan. Apart from the global influence of the CCRM, Protestant Pentecostalism strongly influenced the CCRM in Japan.

As there is no adequate literature available on the history of Pentecostalism in Japan it is very difficult to make an accurate account of the beginning of the Pentecostal movement in Japan. However, it seems that the pioneer Pentecostal missionaries entered Japan well before most Pentecostal denominations were organized. They were men and women of goodwill who set out of their countries with the zeal of spreading the Gospel. The exact chronological order of their entry is not certain as there are no official records. Nevertheless, there are some sources like *Mikotoba ni Tachi, Mitama ni Michibikarete*,[76] which was published by the Japan Assemblies of God (JAG) in 1999, and covers their history of the post-war section. However, there is very little about the pre-war history in this book. Another helpful resource is the *Japan Christian Yearbook* (JCY), an annual publication that tries to put together the data of all the church denominations, pastors, groups and the work done by them. It is in publication since 1903. However, the Protestant Churches published this book under different titles in the following years. They published the Japanese version of this book *Kirisutokyo Nenkan* (*KN*) since 1916. There are

76 Japan Assemblies of God, *Mikotoba ni Tachi, Mitama ni Michibikarete: Nihon Assemburizu ob Goddo Kyodan Soritsu Goju Nenshi* [Standing on the Word of God, Guided by the Holy Spirit: The Fifty Years History of the Founding of Japan Assemblies of God] (Tokyo: Japan Assemblies of God, 1999).

many discrepancies found in the listing of the chronological events of the Pentecostal missionary activities.

Historians consider Martin L. Ryan as the earliest known Pentecostal missionary. He arrived in 1907 in Yokohama, Japan. A group of 14 missionaries accompanied him. Out of these 14 missionaries, 12 of them went along with him to Japan and two proceeded to Hong Kong.[77] Protestant missionaries named the group led by Ryan as Apostolic Light and later referred their apostolate as Apostolic Faith Movement. Ryan and his companions had a very tough start in Japan. Neither the Japanese nor the missionaries present in Japan welcomed their activities. They had to face financial difficulties too. No one supported them. As time passed by, their work started to yield some fruit. Their work was concentrated mainly around Yokohama and Tokyo. They had a small boat to ferry them across the bay of Tokyo to do their mission work.[78] Due to increasing financial constraints, they were finding it very difficult to carry on their missionary work and to publish the newsletter *Apostolic Light*, which highlighted their work. As the going on became tough, they changed their mission strategy and started an English training center for the Japanese youth. They had little success in their work. They could influence only a few Japanese youth to receive the baptism in the Holy Spirit. Besides the Japanese youth, this group also influenced two British missionaries, and Mrs. Taylor.[79]

Mr. William Taylor and Mrs. Mary Taylor were from Britain and came to Japan in 1905. They started working with the destitute women and gave them training in vocational fields. In 1908, Mrs. Taylor met Cora Fritsch, a member of the group led by Ryan. Her

77 Masakazu Suzuki, "A New Look at the Pre-War History of the Japan Assemblies of God," *Asian Journal of Pentecostal Studies* Vol. 4, No.2 (2001): 242-243. See also Paul Tsuchido Shew, "A Forgotten History: Correcting The Historical Record of the Roots of Pentecostalism in Japan," *Asian Journal of Pentecostal Studies* 5, No.1 (2002): 29-30. See also Allan Anderson, *An Introduction to Pentecostalism* (Cambridge: Cambridge University Press, 2004), 140. See also Allan Anderson, *Spreading Fires: The Missionary Nature of Early Pentecostalism* (New York: Orbis Books, 2007), 138.

78 Shew, "A Forgotten History: Correcting The Historical Record of the Roots of Pentecostalism in Japan", 31.

79 Ibid., 32.

associations with Cora led her to seek baptism in the Holy Spirit in 1911. Mrs. Taylor received the baptism in the Holy Spirit in the prayer meetings led by this group and later she started the missionary work as a Pentecostal. Mr. and Mrs. Taylor were initially part of the Japan Evangelistic Band, but later cut ties with them and a joined Pentecostal Missionary Union (PMU) based in Britain.[80] Their name appears in the JCY from 1915 to 1918, so it indicates that their association with Assemblies of God during that period. However, it is surprising that their names are missing in the official records of the Assemblies of God. There is no known reason for this deletion. Their thirty-five year ministry in Japan had a significant impact on the early Pentecostal community in Japan. Historians consider the Taylors as instrumental in influencing Leonard Coote, who later started the Japan Pentecost Church or Japan Apostolic Mission.[81]

Another foreign missionary, Estella Bernauer after her encounter with Yoshio Tanimoto in 1910, a Japanese Pentecostal, decided to dedicate her life to do mission work in Japan. She arrived in Japan in late April 1910. She had to ask the help of local people for interpreting her messages as she had very little knowledge of the Japanese language. She engaged herself in English language ministry with students and ran a Sunday school for children. However, her efforts were not having a great influence on the people as her knowledge of Japanese was very limited and she had to depend on the local interpreters.[82] There are very few records of her missionary work in Japan.

Yoshio Tanimoto, who had influenced Bernauer to go to Japan for mission work, returned to Japan and began a new mission center. He arrived in Hiroshima, in 1910 and began his missionary work, but had several problems mainly due to lack of funds. He had to take a job of an English teacher and work for 6 days a week. A full time job plus the ministry work put a great physical and mental pressure

80 Shew, "A Forgotten History: Correcting The Historical Record of the Roots of Pentecostalism in Japan", 33.

81 Ibid., 33-34. See also Suzuki, "A New Look at the Pre-War History of the Japan Assemblies of God", 246-247.

82 Shew, "A Forgotten History: Correcting The Historical Record of the Roots of Pentecostalism in Japan", 36-37.

on him. He was continually seeking for financial assistance from the Pentecostal denominations in USA, but to no avail. He wanted to visit USA once again for spiritual refreshment and to collect funds for his mission, but his native sponsors did not support him to make his plans come true.[83]

Some scholars consider Carl F. Juergensen and his family as the first missionaries of Pentecostal denomination in Japan. They arrived in 1913.[84] Even though Carl Juergensen initially faced financial difficulties, he tried to work hard. He established a preaching station to carry on his missionary work. He did not have much language skills, but his younger children, who did their schooling in Japan, were fluent in the language and they became his interpreters. They also translated his speeches and articles. In the mid-1920s, they began the first Pentecostal church in Japan, *Shinshou* at Takinogawa. Carl Juergensen was also the founding member of the *Nihon Seisho Kyokai* (Japan Bible Church) in 1929, which was instrumental in spreading Pentecostalism in Japan.[85]

Kiyoma Yumiyama after his close association with the Jeurgensens became a pastor himself and established the *Seirei Gakuin* (Holy Spirit School) in 1931. A lot of financial aid poured in for

---

83 Shew, "A Forgotten History: Correcting The Historical Record of the Roots of Pentecostalism in Japan", 38.

84 For reasons unknown Juergensen and his family is credited to bring Pentecostalism to Japan in 1913 though there were many other Pentecostal missionaries in Japan who arrived prior to Juergensens. Scholars like Masakazu Suzuki, "A New Look at the Pre-War History of the Japan Assemblies of God," *Asian Journal of Pentecostal Studies* 4, No.2 (2001): 242-243; Paul Tsuchido Shew, "A Forgotten History: Correcting The Historical Record of the Roots of Pentecostalism in Japan," *Asian Journal of Pentecostal Studies* 5, No.1 (2002): 29-30; Allan Anderson, *An Introduction to Pentecostalism* (Cambridge: Cambridge University Press, 2004), 140 and Allan Anderson, *Spreading Fires: The Missionary Nature of Early Pentecostalism* (New York: Orbis Books, 2007), 138, consider that M. L. Ryan was the first Pentecostal missionary to reach Japan in 1907. However, David Hymes, "Japan," in *The New International Dictionary of Pentecostal and Charismatic Movements,* 147, mentions Carl F. Jeurgensen who arrived in 1913 as the first Pentecostal missionary in Japan.

85 Shew, "A Forgotten History: Correcting The Historical Record of the Roots of Pentecostalism in Japan", 42.

the missionaries from European countries and the USA.[86] Also other Pentecostal missionaries came to Japan to spread Pentecostalism in Japan. With the break of World War II, some of the missionaries had to leave Japan, where as some opted to stay back and face all the challenges and difficulties, which the war had thrown before them.

After the end of the World War II, the Japan Assemblies of God showed signs of resurrection and formed a conglomeration of different Pentecostal ministries in Japan. This group elected Kiyoma Yumiyama as its president. As the new constitution of Japan guaranteed the freedom of religion, Christian missionaries could freely spread Christianity in Japan. Various Christian organizations sent missionaries to Japan and supported their work. This helped the missionaries, to carry out the mission work and plant their churches in different parts of Japan. Along with the foreign missionaries, a special mention must be made of some local missionaries, who started indigenous churches and had a sizeable number of followers. One of the prominent local missionary, Murai Jun founded an indigenous church, Spirit of Jesus in 1941. He called his church, "Spirit of Jesus Church" because of his wife. His wife claimed that God revealed her to name the church, "Spirit of Jesus Church."[87] Murai Jun also opened a Bible Seminary to train his followers. In 1993, the Spirit of Jesus Christ claimed to have 433,108 members, but scholars argue that the Murai's church inflated the numbers because added the dead followers. Hymes estimates that presently there are around 5,000 to 10,000 members of this church.[88]

Meanwhile, many of the other Pentecostal missionaries like Yumiyama began to hold gatherings and in April 1947, they had a first national level revival meeting. They decided to reopen their Bible College on a new campus and make it as their headquarters for the propagation of Pentecostalism.[89]

---

86 Hymes, "Japan," in The New International Dictionary of Pentecostal and Charismatic Movements, 147.

87 Ibid., 149. See also Mark Mullins, *Christianity Made in Japan: A Study of Indigenous Movements* (Honolulu: University of Hawaii Press, 1998), 97.

88 Hymes, "Japan," in The New International Dictionary of Pentecostal and Charismatic Movements, 150.

89 Paul Shew Tsuchido, "Pentecostals in Japan," in *Asia and Pentecostal: The Charismatic Face of Christianity in Asia,* eds. Allan Anderson and Edmond

Another Pentecostal missionary, Harriet Dithridge returned to Japan in 1949. He opened a church in Tachikawa with the help of the aid received from a Pentecostal denomination in the USA.[90] L. W. Coote, a Pentecostal missionary who had worked in Japan before the break of World War II also returned to Japan in 1950. He started a Bible School to train youth to become evangelists. He was one of the most successful missionaries in the post-war era, and his efforts bore tremendous fruit. He got the support of youth in his ministry.[91]

The Pentecostal churches worldwide, started sending their missionaries to Japan to establish new churches and win as many converts as possible. The post-war Pentecostal churches received massive funds and aid from the sending native mission countries. Thus, the work of the missionaries was continuing with success. In this period, the Pentecostals established the following significant churches in Japan: International Church of the Four Square Gospel (1950), Open Bible Standard Churches (1950), Church of God (1952), and Pentecostal Church of God (1954).[92] The Scandinavian organizations started their centers, which included Fellowship of Christian Assemblies (1948), Swedish Free Missionaries (1950), Finland Free Foreign Mission (1950), and Free Christian Mission Group (1950 from Norway and Denmark).[93]

One of the prominent churches of Korea, "Full Gospel Church," founded by David (Paul) Yonggi Cho started its work in Japan in 1974. This church claims to be the largest Pentecostal Church of the world with more than 620,000 members. However, one cannot trust these figures because this church counts also those people as their members, who have just visited them once. This group has opened a Bible School in Tokyo but the majority of its members in Japan are in fact Korean immigrants.[94]

Tang, (Carlisle: Regnum Books International, 2005), 499.

90 Paul Shew Tsuchido, "Pentecostals in Japan," in *Asia and Pentecostal: The Charismatic Face of Christianity in Asia,* eds. Allan Anderson and Edmond Tang, (Carlisle: Regnum Books International, 2005), 499.

91 Ibid.

92 Ibid., 500.

93 Ibid. See also Hymes, "Japan," in The New International Dictionary of Pentecostal and Charismatic Movements, 148.

94 Ibid.

The Pentecostal Churches in Japan joined the Japan Assemblies of God in 1988 and became a member of Japan Evangelical Association. Since its inception in the Japan Evangelical Association, the Pentecostals have contributed to pneumatology. They decided to encourage charismatic groups and train members to be pastors of the Pentecostal groups. During the 1970s and 80s, Japanese Pentecostals invited many Pentecostal missionaries from the USA and Canada to begin revival movements. Their aim was to increase the membership of the Pentecostal churches. They conducted large outreach programs with special emphasis on preaching and healing. In 1992, they invited a lay minister from Argentina, Carlos Anacondia to lead a healing service. Later they also invited Claudio Frazen and others to spread Pentecostalism. They also invited Benny Hinn, a prominent Pentecostal minister from the USA to hold healing services in different parts of Japan during the 1990s.[95]

Japan has produced quite a number of indigenous churches with their own theological understanding and interpretation. Some of the doctrines preached by these churches are so very different from Christianity that mainline Protestant Churches have declared them as heretic groups. However, Japanese are attracted to them, because they contain elements of Japanese folk religions, customs and practices, which are very important for them. Mark Mullins in his book *Christianity Made in* Japan (1998) mentions the following indigenous Pentecostal churches.[96]

> *Non Church Movement* founded in 1901 by Uchimura Kanzo.
> *The Way* founded in 1907 by Matsumura Kaiseki.
> *Christ Heart Church* founded in 1927 by Kawai Shinsui.
> *Glorious Gospel Christain Church* founded in 1936 by Sugita Kotaro.
> *Living Christ One Ear of Wheat Church* founded in 1939 by Matsubara Kazuhito.

95 Hymes, "Japan," in The New International Dictionary of Pentecostal and Charismatic Movements, 149.

96 Mullins, Christianity Made in Japan: A Study of Indigenous Movements, 202-216.

Christian Canaan Church founded in 1940 by Taniguchi Toku.
Japan Ecclesia of Christ founded in 1940 by Koike Tatsuo.
The Spirit of Jesus Church founded by Muria Jun in 1941.
The Holy Ecclesia of Jesus founded in 1946 by Otsuki Takeji.
Sanctifying Christ Church founded in 1948 by Konmoto Kaoru.
Original Gospel (Tabernacle) founded in 1948 by Teshima Ikuro.
Life Giving Christ founded in 1966 by Imahashi Atsushi.
Okinawa Christian Gospel founded in 1977 by Nakahara Masao.

Pentecostalism, which existed in Japan since the beginning of the 20th century influenced the beginning of the Catholic Charismatic Renewal Movement in Japan. In the following sections, we shall trace the birth and growth of the CCRM in Japan.

2.2.1 The Beginning of the Catholic Charismatic Renewal Movement in Japan

The CCRM, which began in the USA in 1967, reached Japan in 1972 with the arrival of Mother John Marie Stewart and her companion, Sr. Stephanie, nuns from USA.[97] They reached Japan in October 1972

97 Hymes, "Japan," in *The New International Dictionary of Pentecostal and Charismatic Movements,* 148. It must be noted here that the brief history of the CCRM in Japan (to be precise only two sentences) mentioned by David Hymes in the *The New International Dictionary of Pentecostal and Charismatic Movements,* edited by Stanley M. Burgess and Eduard M. Van Der Maas does not give the accurate details of the beginning of the CCRM. Hymes mentions in his article, "The Catholic Charismatic Movement began in Japan in 1972 when Hiroshi Yoshiyama of the Japan Aseemblies of God [a protestant pastor] was invited to the Hatsudai Catholic Church in Shbuya, Tokyo, for a Holy Spirit Seminar." However, our research shows that prior to Pastor Hiroshi Yoshiyama's presence, two Catholic nuns, Mother John Marie Stewart and Sr. Stephanie from USA belonging to the Religious Order, *The Disciples of the Lord Jesus Christ* came to Japan in 1972 and pioneered the work of the Catholic Charismatic Renewal Movement in Japan. Mother John Marie Stewart is the foundress of the Religious Order for Women, *The Disciples of the Lord*

to promote the CCRM in the Catholic Church.[98] The beginning was difficult, as they did not have any enough resources to begin their work. However, they trusted the presence and power of the Jesus and His Holy Spirit as an essential tool to do their mission work.[99] They got accommodation in a convent with the help of Francis Mathy, a Jesuit priest who taught at Sophia University, Tokyo. They began to search a place to begin the prayer meeting. The interdenominational "Japan Thrust Team" from Melodyland Christian Center conducted Holy Spirit Seminars for several weeks.[100] A number of Catholic missionaries, priests and religious participated in these seminars.The sisters started a prayer group at the Franciscan Chapel Center with some people who had received the baptism in the Holy Spirit in other countries before coming to Japan.[101] The only other charismatic group, which existed then in Japan, was the small English-speaking prayer group at the American Air Force Base in Yokohama.

The sisters' did their mission work on the campus of Sophia University. They met the staff and students, telling them about the renewal. In the meanwhile, the sisters also got invitations from various international schools to give talks on renewal in Tokyo and Yokohama.[102]

The sisters decided to divide the prayer meeting at the Franciscan Chapel Center into two groups. One was for those who had already received baptism in the Holy Spirit and the other for those who were interested in the renewal movement. This prayer group "became the nucleus of the first Japanese-speaking charismatic prayer group in Tokyo."[103]

Jesus Christ. It was founded in 1972 in the Diocese of Amarillo, Texas. The Sisters of this religious community have pioneered in the work of the Catholic Charismatic Renewal in Mexico, Japan, Poland etc. Their Motherhouse is in Channing Texas, USA

98 John Marie Stewart, *Laying the Foundation: A History of the Disciples of the Lord Jesus Christ* (Channing: Disciples of the Lord Jesus Christ, 2005), 38.

99 Ibid., 39.

100 Ibid.

101 Ibid.,

102 Ibid., 41.

103 Ibid., 44.

In the last week of October 1972, before they left Japan the sisters had organized their first scheduled charismatic prayer meeting at the Franciscan Chapel Center. Around 35 to 40 missionaries who were already in touch with the sisters or had experience of the CCRM attended this meeting. Prominent among them were the priests Bernadine Schneider, Matthew Vetter and Noel Lessard who had helped and encouraged the sisters in their missionary work in Japan. Besides them, there were two other priests, six lay Japanese, a Protestant minister and sisters of different religious communities from Tokyo, Yokohama and Kyoto.[104]

After the sisters left Japan, Bernadine Schneider and Lessard got together and organized a prayer meeting on November 5, 1972 at Hatsudai Catholic Church.[105] The efforts of Mother John Marie Stewart, Sr. Stephanie, along with Bernadine Schneider, Lessard and the involvement of the Protestant Canadian evangelist Les Pritchard and his team formed the basis for the beginning of the first CCRM prayer meeting. They organized this meeting at a Redemptorist Church, Hatsudai Catholic Church in Tokyo in Mid-November of 1972. Initially the CCRM prayer meetings were a forum for ecumenical gatherings as many Protestant Pentecostals were leading and attending the prayer services. Assembly of God pastor Hiroshi Yoshiyama and other Pentecostal ministers were of a great help for the spread of the CCRM in Japan.[106] As the movement started diffusing in Tokyo, the pioneers of the CCRM conducted the first "Life in the Spirit Seminar" at Tokyo in April 1973 to make more and more people aware of the power of the Holy Spirit in their lives and the existence of the CCRM. Twenty to thirty people attended the seminar: priests, religious and lay people. At the end of the seminar, the attendees received the baptism in the Holy Spirit.[107] The same year in the September, the CCRM conducted a workshop to train leaders at the retreat house at Takarazuka, Mefu. The year

104 John Marie Stewart, *Laying the Foundation: A History of the Disciples of the Lord Jesus Christ* (Channing: Disciples of the Lord Jesus Christ, 2005), 38.

105 Ibid., 45.

106 Francis Mathy, "What in the World is going on? - Japan," *Pentecost Today*, 26, No.4 (October-December 2001): 4.

107 Hymes, "Japan," in The New International Dictionary of Pentecostal and Charismatic Movements, 148.

1974 is very important for the CCRM in Japan because the Renewal Movement gave a boost to ecumenical meetings. In the latter half of the seventies, Catholic leaders conducted the prayer services at different places and in the eighties; they shifted the venue of the prayer meeting to the campus of Sophia University, Tokyo. Gradually prayer meetings were beginning in different parts of Japan, right from Hokkaido in the extreme North of Japan to Okinawa, extreme South of Japan.[108] In 1975, the CCRM sent two delegates (Francis Mathy S. J. and Ito Yoshio) to Rome to participate in the Second International Leaders' Conference, from May 16-19. The same year, the CCRM held the First National CCRM convention at the Seminar Center of Sophia Catholic University, Hadano. There were 56 participants in this convention and roughly, half of them were foreign missionaries.[109] Fischbeck, Futoda, Ito and Nakamura went as delegates of CCRJ to Manila to attend the Asian CCRM Leaders' Conference. Their participation in international level CCRM Leaders' Conference helped the CCRJ to organize themselves in Japan. The CCRJ established a National Service Committee in 1981 to facilitate its work at national level.[110]

Many gifted leaders, preachers and resource persons of the CCRM from different countries started coming to Japan to preach, promote and facilitate the work of the CCRJ. Some of the prominent international CCRM leaders and preachers who came to Japan to conduct retreats and workshops are as follows: Francis MacNutt conducted a charismatic prayer rally in February 1977. Killian McDonnell conducted a CCRM workshop in May 1978. Dennis Linn and Mathew Linn directed a retreat for priests and conducted a CCRM workshop in October 1980. Tom Forrest directed a retreat for priest in November 1981. David Geretz directed a retreat for priests in September 1982. Francis Sullivan and Briege McKenna directed

108 Tomotaro Nakamura, "Nihon ni Okeru Katorikku Seirei ni Yoru Sasshinn no Ayumi," [The History of the Catholic Charismatic Renewal of Japan] (Tokyo: Catholic Charismatic Renewal Center, 2008). 1. This paper was presented by Nakamura during the ISAO Conference held in Jakarta, Indonesia in September 9-14, 2008. Original text is in Japanese. [Translation mine].

109 Thomas Csordas, Language, Charisma & Creativity: Ritual Life in the Catholic Charismatic Renewal (New York: Palgrave, 2001), 38.

110 Nakamura, "The History of the Catholic Charismatic Renewal of Japan," 1.

a retreat for priests in November 1983. Emilien Tardif conducted a charismatic rally at Seishin Girls High School, Tokyo in July 1988. The Director of ICCRO, Ken Metz directed a retreat for priests in September 1991. Robert Degrandes conducted a charismatic rally in November 1992. Raniero Cantalamessa directed a retreat for priests in Osaka in November 1993. Gino Hendrickes was the main speaker of the fourth Kanto regional CCRM convention in September 1994. Nancy Kellar was the main speaker of the thirteenth National CCRM convention held in November 1995. She also directed a Leadership Formation Workshop in September 2000. Bart Pastor from Philippines and Anny were the main speakers on the celebration of the 25th anniversary of CCRJ. They held this National CCRM convention in Tokyo in November 1997. Bishop Vincent M. Walsh was the main speaker of the workshop, "Everyday Meditation" held in July 1998. Briege McKenna was the main speaker of the Tokyo CCRM convention held in November 1998. Tom DiLorenzo was the main speaker of the fifteenth National CCRM convention. Fio Mascarenhas from India was the main speaker of the sixteenth National CCRM convention held at Amagasaki in August 2002. CCRJ invited Fio Mascarenhas again in 2003 to be the main resource person for the seventh Kanto regional CCRM convention. He was the main speaker of the ninth Kanto regional CCRM convention held in July 2005. Raniero Cantalamessa visited Japan again in 2005 and was the main speaker of the twelfth Kansai regional CCRM convention held in May 2005. Edward John Dougherty was the main speaker of the seventeenth National CCRM convention held in August 2006. Richard McAlear was the main speaker of the thirteenth Kansai regional CCRM convention held in August 2008 and Margaritha Valappila was the main speaker of the thirteenth Kanto regional CCRM convention.[111] Late Rufus Pereira, a diocesan priest from Indian preached the 2009 Kansai regional CCRM convention. Robert Faricy, a Jesuit priest preached the 14th Kanto regional CCRM convention in 2010. Shin from Kkottonage, South Korea preached the 18th National CCRM convention in 2010. Patti Gallaher Mansfield preached the 15th Kanto regional CCRM

111 Nakamura, "The History of the Catholic Charismatic Renewal of Japan," 1-2.

convention in 2011. Cyril John led the 15th Kansai regional CCRM convention in 2011. Bart Pastor was the main preacher of the 2012, 16th Kanto regional CCRM convention. Charles Whitehead led the 16th Kansai regional CCRM convention in 2012.[112]

The CCRJ has divided itself into five regions in Japan: Hokkaido region, Northeast region, Kanto region, Kansai region and Japan West region. Each district or region conducts its own CCRM convention once in a year and once in three years there is a National CCRM convention.[113] As some regions do not have weekly prayer meetings, the annual CCRM conventions give an opportunity to all those involved in a particular region to gather for praise, worship and Bible study. The different regions arrange the conventions keeping in mind that people from different regions can also join them and thus have fellowship with people of different regions.[114] Thus, the dates do not overlap each other.

Another prominent feature in the life of CCRJ since its inception in 1972 is the Life in the Spirit Seminar. It organized the first Life in the Spirit Seminar in Yotsuya, Tokyo in April 1973 and ever since, twice a year they conduct these seminars. A Life in the Spirit Seminar consists of eight talks. The CCRJ organizes one talk per week. Those who have attended these seminars need not necessarily become members of any CCRM prayer group. The objective of these seminars is that people can get a chance to experience the power of the Holy Spirit in their life. Many Catholics experienced a spiritual renewal in their life because of these seminars. They are contributing for the growth of the Catholic Church in diverse ways.

It is very difficult to estimate the number of people attending CCRM prayer meetings in Japan because there are no fixed prayer meetings every week in some regions and there are people who do not attend regularly. Nevertheless, the number of people who have had an experience of CCRM is significant.[115]

---

112 See *Ikeru Mizu*, Nos. 94-107.

113 Francis Mathy, "What in the World is going on? Japan," *Pentecost Today*, 26, No.4 (October-December 2001): 4.

114 Ibid.

115 Nakamura, "The History of the Catholic Charismatic Renewal of Japan," 2.

The Catholic Bishops' Conference of Japan (CBCJ) has not yet given official recognition to the CCRJ. Even though in the nineties, the CCRJ attempted to get an official approval and recognition. The CBCJ rejected it. The CBCJ did not accept the application of the CCRJ stating that there was no need for a separate official recognition or approval from the CBCJ as the Holy See had already recognized and approved the CCRM in the Catholic Church. Even though there is no official recognition of the CCRJ by the CBCJ, there are some cardinals, bishops and nuncios who have attended the conventions organized by the CCRJ and have encouraged the charismatic movement on a personal level. However, presently there is no official document of the CBCJ, which encourages or recognizes the work of the CCRJ.

2.2.2 Northeast Region

The CCRM began in the Northeast region of Japan in 1975. Fr. Bernadine Schneider, Prof. Kitano, Sr. Louis and some religious sisters started a Life in the Spirit in Sendai at Sendai YBU *Bunka Centa* (YBU Culture Centre) in May 1975. On May 20, 1975 the participants of this seminar prayed over each other for the infilling of the Holy Spirit. The CCRM began in Sendai and later spread to Akita, Yamagata, Tsuruoka, Yonekawa, Aizu Wakamatsu and Fukushima.[116] The then Bishop of Sendai, late Bishop Arikata Kobayashi was moved by the address of Pope Paul VI to the members of the CCRM on May 19, 1975. The Pope said that the CCRM is indeed a 'chance for the Church and the world.'[117] Bishop Arikata Kobayashi was convinced of the potential of the CCRM. He got personally involved in the activities of the CCRM. He preached retreats, gave talks in Life in the Spirit Seminars and conventions. He encouraged people to participate in the CCRM prayer meetings to renew their spiritual lives.

116 See Andre Lachapelle, "*Hokuto Chiku ni Seirei no Atarashii Ibuki ga*," [New Breath of the Holy Spirit in Northeast Region], *Ikeru Mizu*, No. 46 (Special Edition 1997): 2. Original in Japanese. [Translation mine].

117 See "Address of Pope Paul VI to the Participants of the Third Catholic Charismatic Renewal Congress," May 19, 1975, *AAS* 67 (1975): 364-368.

The CCRM, which started in 1975 in the Northeast region of Japan, has been conducting annual CCRM conventions to bring together all those involved with it and attract new members.

2.2.3 North Region

The CCRM began in 1978 in Sapporo and Asakawa. Fr. Chikara Hashimoto encountered the CCRM at Tsuchisaki Catholic Church and got interested in their activities. He started attending the prayer meetings at Hatsudai Catholic Church in Tokyo and later received the baptism in the Holy Spirit. He had a great experience of the Holy Spirit, which transformed his priestly life. He began to experience a deep communion with the Lord during the Holy Mass and prayers. The Word of God became alive and active in his life. He began to have a great desire to serve the community. This experience led him to start a CCRM prayer meeting at Sapporo city in Hokkaido. Later the CCRM spread to different parts of Hokkaido. A number of people have experienced a tremendous grace by participating in the CCRM prayer meetings. Even though not all the members of the CCRM participate in weekly meetings, they continue to be active members of their respective parishes. In the northern part of Japan, the Catholic Church is facing lot of problems because of the lack of vocations, increase in the greying population, and the disinterest of the youth in Church activities. In such a situation, the Catholic Church looks upon the CCRM as a sign of hope to bring renewal in the Church.[118]

2.2.4 Konan Region

Ms. Hiroko Katayama attended the Life in the Spirit Seminar at Akatsutsumi Catholic Church in Tokyo in 1975. After receiving baptism in the Holy Spirit, she continued to attend the weekly prayer meetings at Akatsutsumi Catholic Church for six months. Later she moved to Kamakura (Konan region). At that time, there were no prayer groups in this region. She had a great desire to take part in the CCRM prayer meetings and so in 1976 she took part in a retreat

118 Chikara Hashimoto, "*Kita no Chi ni Seirei no Hi ga*," [The Fire of the Holy Spirit in the North], *Ikeru Mizu*, No. 46 (Special Edition 1997): 3-4. Original in Japanese. [Translation mine].

conducted at Katsuragi Kaikan in the campus of Sophia University, Tokyo. It was during this retreat she met Ms. Asanuma and decided to start a prayer meeting in the Konan region. They held the prayer meetings in their houses. Initially there were only six participants, but later with the guidance of Frs. McKay and Gerard, the CCRM spread to Yuki no Shita, Oobune, Hayama, Seibo no Sono, Obatahara and Ninomiya Catholic Churches. In some places, the parish priest and the parishioners did not welcome the CCRM, and so the leaders decided to hire public halls to conduct the CCRM prayer meetings. Even though, the CCRM had humble begins in the Konan region, it gradually spread and people accepted it as a genuine spiritual renewal movement. This region has regularly conducted retreats and the Life in the Spirit seminars in different Catholic Churches to help people to have a deep experience of the Holy Spirit and a renewal in their Christian lives.[119]

2.2.5 Nagoya Region

Mutou, a seminarian of the Nagoya diocese participated in the CCRM prayer meetings at Hatsudai Catholic Church. In order to share his experience with the people of Nagoya he started a CCRM prayer group at the Nagoya diocese's pastoral center in March 1975. Initially the CCRM prayer meeting was attended by Frs. Curiri, Guyer, Ito, 2 religious nuns, Ms. Keiko Fukuhara and some Protestants. It was ecumenical in nature as Protestants and the Catholics prayed together without any problems. Later they shifted the venue of the prayer meeting to Johokubashi Catholic Church. They also started a new prayer group at a convent of Sei Maria Mugenzai near Higashiyama Catholic Church. However, the following year the group suffered a great loss with the death of Mutou. Fr. Ito took over as the leader of this group but later even, he fell sick and could not continue to lead the group. At this time providentially, Fr. Rüthers S.V.D. who pioneered the CCRM prayer group at Tsuchisaki Catholic Church in Akita moved to Nanzan Catholic Church, Nagoya. Fr. Rüthers took over the leadership of the group in Nagoya.

119 Hiroko Katayama, "*Konan Region no Seirei no Kaze*," [The Holy Spirit's Breeze in Konan Region], *Ikeru Mizu*, No. 46 (Special Edition 1997): 3-4. Original in Japanese. [Translation mine].

These prayer groups have attracted many people. Some of them have also participated in the Life in the Spirit seminars and have received the baptism in the Holy Spirit. Those who have received baptism in the Holy Spirit have carried the fruits of the renewal to their respective parishes and homes.[120]

2.2.6 Logos Center

The CCRM influenced late Fr. Johannes Hirschmeier S.V.D. (former President of Nanzan University) in Germany. He started to attend the prayer meetings conducted by Fr. Rüthers S.V.D. at Nanzan Catholic Church, Nagoya. Formerly Fr. Hirschmeier used to take a Bible class at the Logos Center (center for Catholic campus ministry of Nanzan University) situated in a corner of the University campus. However, after his encounter with the CCRM, he decided to start a CCRM prayer meeting every Tuesday in the Logos Center chapel. He invited the participants of this Bible seminar to join the CCRM prayer meeting. This was the beginning of the CCRM prayer meeting at Logos Center in October 1982. In 1983, Fr. Hirschmeier became ill and so Fr. Robert Reimer S.V.D. took over the leadership of this group. Later that year, Fr. Hirschmeier died and the prayer group was in search of a new animator. In 1985, Mr. & Ms. Horie came from Canada to settle in Nagoya. The Hories had a good experience of leading the CCRM prayer groups in Canada. Their presence in the prayer meeting was of a great help to all. They actively took part in leading the group in praise and worship.

The group continues to meet every Tuesday in the Logos Center chapel. The group members thank the priests for their guidance and animation, which helped the group to grow numerically and reach out to Christian as well as non-Christian youth and students.[121]

---

120 Keiko Fukuhara, "*Hitori no Shingakusei ni Yotte*," [Through One Seminarian], *Ikeru Mizu,* No. 46 (Special Edition 1997):4-5. Original in Japanese. [Translation mine].

121 Aiko Hattori, "*Seirei no Hi ha*," [The Fire of the Holy Spirit], *Ikeru Mizu,* No.46 (Special Edition 1998): 5-6. Original in Japanese. [Translation mine].

2.2.7 Aichi and Gifu Region

Fr. Rüthers S.V.D. started a CCRM prayer group in 1982 at Tajimi Catholic Church in Gifu prefecture. In 1985, Fr. Ito started a CCRM prayer group at Holy Spirit College in Seito, Aichi prefecture and at Kozoji Catholic Church in Kasugai, Aichi prefecture. These prayer groups helped many people living in these prefectures to encounter the CCRM.[122] However, some of these groups have ceased to exist.

2.2.8 Osaka Region

Sr. Grent belonging to the Order of Servants of Mary received baptism in the Holy Spirit at Rome in May 1972. When she came to Japan in the summer of the same year, she began an English CCRM prayer meeting at the Passionists' Retreat House at Hibarigaoka in Osaka. Later with the help of a Protestant pastor, she started another English CCRM prayer meeting at the Abeno Monastery belonging to the Order of Servants of Mary. In June 1972, Fr. Bernadine Schneider preached a retreat at the Hibarigaoka Retreat House in Japanese. There were 62 participants in this retreat.[123]

In the autumn of 1972, Sr. Grent along with some lay Catholics started a Japanese CCRM prayer meeting at Abeno Catholic Church. In January 1973, Sr. Grent along with Sr. Jacinta belonging to the Order of Good Samaritans started the Life in the Spirit seminar at Nara. In May 1973, Fr. Mathy along with other members of the CCRM prayer group of Tokyo conducted a two-day seminar at Takarazuka. The Late Archbishop of Osaka, Yasuda, priests, religious and lay people, attended it.[124]

In April 1974, Sr. Matsuda a Passionist nun started a Japanese CCRM prayer meeting at Hibarigaoka Retreat House. Presently they organize the English and Japanese prayer meetings jointly. In 1974, Sr. Murata started another prayer group at Sakai Catholic

---

122 Mariko Ito, "*Seirei no Hi ga Tomosareta,*" [The Fire of the Holy Spirit], *Ikeru Mizu,* No. 46 (Special Edition 1997): 6. Original in Japanese. [Translation mine].

123 Mikiko Hayashi, "*Osaka ni Seirei no Hi ga,*" [The Fire of the Holy Spirit in Osaka], *Ikeru Mizu,* No. 46 (Special Edition 1997): 6-8. Original in Japanese. [Translation mine].

124 Ibid.

Church. Protestants too attended this prayer meeting and thus it was very ecumenical in nature. In December 1975, the CCRM started another prayer at Kongo Catholic Church in Osaka. Thus, the CCRM organized prayer meetings at different parishes in Osaka. Many people living in this region attended the Life in the Spirit seminar and received baptism in the Holy Spirit.[125]

2.2.9 Kyoto Region

In 1980, Fr. Armand DeMontigny moved from Tokyo to Miyazu Catholic Church in Kyoto. He started a CCRM prayed group in his parish at Kyoto, as he was involved with the CCRM in Tokyo. In 1981, Fr. Lessard became the parish priest of Miyazu Catholic Church. He took over the group started by Fr. DeMontigny. He also started CCRM prayer meetings in six other Catholic Churches. Thus, the CCRM prayer meetings started in Kyoto and its surrounding areas. The CCRM organizes Life in the Spirit seminars, workshops and retreats in this region.[126]

2.2.10 Fukuoka Region

The CCRM had a strange beginning in Fukuoka. In 1975, a Catholic asked Fr. Richard Ha, the assistant parish priest of Hikarigaoka Catholic Church, "How to pray?" Fr. Richard Ha realized that he had no answer. However, he longed to have a divine experience. His surge for prayer, led him to start a prayer meeting in Fukuoka. Later he arranged prayer meeting on Mondays at Hikarigaoka Catholic Church. He also invited many leaders of the CCRM from other parts of Japan to lead the prayer meetings. Gradually he started conducting Life in the Spirit seminars at his Church and Tedori Catholic Church in Kumamoto. The participants of these seminars were from different parishes in the Kyushu region. Some of those

---

125 Mikiko Hayashi, "*Osaka ni Seirei no Hi ga,*" [The Fire of the Holy Spirit in Osaka], *Ikeru Mizu,* No. 46 (Special Edition 1997): 6-8. Original in Japanese. [Translation mine].

126 Machiko Yano, "*Funago ni mo Seirei no Kaza ga,*" [The Wind of the Holy Spirit in Funago Too], *Ikeru Mizu,* No. 46 (Special Edition 1997): 8-9. Original in Japanese. [Translation mine].

who received baptism in the Holy Spirit returned to their parishes and started CCRM prayer groups in their respective parishes.[127]

Late Bishop Matsunaga, Bishop of Fukuoka diocese encouraged the CCRM prayer groups in his diocese. The organizers of retreats often invited him to celebrate the inaugural and concluding Holy Eucharist. With the blessings of the local bishops, the CCRM could organize many retreats and conventions in Fukuoka.[128]

2.2.11 Kumamoto Region

Fr. Macrey, a Columban priest received baptism in the Holy Spirit in 1975. He shared his experience with other Columban priests based in Kumamoto. The Columban priests decided to organize a CCRM retreat in Fukuoka. Fr. Francis Mathy preached that retreat. The retreat was a great success and the Columban priests decided to start the Life in the Spirit Seminar at Kumamoto. Initially Bishop Arikata Kobayashi helped them to conduct the seminar. As more and more people received baptism in the Holy Spirit, they started the CCRM prayer groups in their respective parishes and homes. Thus, the CCRM spread in the Kumamoto region.[129]

2.2.12 Okinawa Region

Sr. Francisca Riko Kanna belonging to the Franciscan Sisters encountered the CCRM in Tokyo in 1974. After 3 months of stay in Tokyo, she went to Okinawa to resume her job as a teacher. The power of the Holy Spirit filled her with joy and transformed her life. She was eager to participate in the CCRM prayer meetings in Okinawa but at that time, there were no prayer groups there. She participated in the CCRM retreats and workshops conducted in different parts of Japan to revive her spiritual life. In 1978, she moved to Miyakojima as a teacher of Mitsuba Kindergarten. There

---

127 Kiyoko Nakamoto, "*Fukuoka de no Seirei Sasshin ha Kono Yoni Hajimatte*," [CCRM Began in Fukuoka This Way], *Ikeru Mizu,* No. 46 (Special Edition 1997): 9-10. Original in Japanese. [Translation mine].

128 Ibid.

129 Tsuneko Hinata, "*Kumamoto no Seirei ni Yoru Sasshin no Okori*," [The Beginning of the CCRM in Kumamoto], *Ikeru Mizu,* No. 46 (Special Edition 1997): 10-11. Original in Japanese. [Translation mine].

she took the initiative to start a prayer group at Hirara Catholic Church with the permission of the parish priest. Initially very few people participated in the meetings but gradually the CCRM prayer meetings spread to other parts of Okinawa. Leaders of the CCRM like Bishop Arikata Kobayashi, Fr. Armand DeMontigny, Fr. Chikara Hashimoto and others came to Okinawa to preach retreats and organize conventions. Thus, the number of people participating in the CCRM prayer meetings increased and many people experienced a deepening of their spiritual life.[130]

2.3 The Ecclesial Authorities and the Charismatic Renewal Movement

The CBCJ has not yet issued any official document regarding the CCRM in Japan. Most priests do not take part in the CCRM prayer meetings. In general, they do not support the CCRM. However, cardinals, archbishops and bishops have sent messages to the CCRJ encouraging them to continue with their good work. Bishop Peter Arikata Kobayashi was personally involved with the CCRM. He actively participated in the various programs undertaken by the CCRJ. The CCRJ sent him as a representative from Japan, to attend the International Leaders' Conferences held in Italy and Ireland.[131] He wrote a number of articles in the newsletters published by the CCRJ. Bishop Nobuo Souma of Nagoya diocese acknowledged the CCRM as a vital movement for the growth of the Church. He mentioned in his talk to the participants of Life in the Spirit Seminar that the CCRM has brought renewal in the Church. He further said that the CCRM has helped in opening the window of the Church, as prayed by Pope John XXIII before the opening of the Second Vatican Council. He mentioned that he was extremely happy to see that through their efforts many people deepened their prayer lives and celebrated Sacraments with joy. These people also

---

130 Francisca Riko Kanna, "Okinawa ni Seirei no Hi wo Hakonde" [Carrying the Fire of the Holy Spirit in Okinawa], *Ikeru Mizu*, No. 46 (Special Edition 1997): 12-14. Original in Japanese. [Translation mine].

131 Tomotaro Nakamura, "*Nihon ni Okeru Katorikku Seirei ni Yoru Sasshin no Ayumi*," [The History of the Catholic Charismatic Renewal of Japan], 1-2. Original in Japanese. [Translation mine].

took initiative to serve others. He encouraged them to continue their good work especially to bring the good news of Jesus to all in Japan. He considered them as partners in the work of evangelization.[132] Following are some of the messages, which the cardinals, archbishops and bishops sent to the CCRJ on occasions of National conventions and other big events.

2.3.1 Message of Peter Seiichi Cardinal Shirayanagi (1997)

Following is the message of late Peter Seiichi Cardinal Shirayanagi to the CCRJ on the 25th anniversary celebration of the CCRM in Japan.

> The CCRM, which started abruptly in 1967 in one corner of USA, was a turning point for the whole world and in no time reached the land of the Far East nation, Japan in 1972. This year being the 25th anniversary of the CCRM in Japan, it is the time to evaluate the movement and it is the time to take a leap forward, a point of new departure. In these 25 years, in the midst of the confusion and hesitation seen in all new movements in the Church, I cannot be but happy to see the stabilization and growth of the CCRM. It influenced many people to open their hearts to the Spirit and work for evangelization. Thanking God for the mysterious work of His hands through the CCRM, I also thank all those who were involved in laying the foundation of the CCRM in Japan and all those who were involved in it for the last 25 years.
>
> Pope John XXIII who called the Second Vatican Council appealed to "Open the Door of the Church," but before opening the door of the Church to the society, he asked us to open ourselves, to the indwelling Spirit, the Holy Spirit who leads and guides the Church. When we recall the happenings of the Second Vatican Council, we

132 Nobuo Souma, "*Shinri no Rei ha Hito wo Jiyu ni Suru,*" [The Spirit of Truth Will Set You Free], in *Shu no Ibuki: Bassui Ban [Breath of the Lord: Excerpts],* Vol. 2, 33-36. Original in Japanese. [Translation mine].

can strongly sense the Holy Spirit powerfully guiding the Church fathers of the Council.

The Holy Spirit has been guiding the Church in all ages but in various forms and through various signs. The CCRM, which began 25 years ago in Japan, is one of them.

Presently the Church is devoting herself totally for the preparation of the 2000th birthday celebrations of Christ. It is also her focal point now. The Church calls upon us not to merely comprehend Christ in our minds but to deepen our personal relationship with Him, to receive His love and be more intimate with Him. It is not through reason but through faith, God calls us to experience the joy of the risen Christ who walks with us always.

The year 1998 focuses on God the Holy Spirit, who arouses us to respond in faith to the call of God. It is in the water and the Spirit that we are baptized and through Baptism, we have received the gift to be part of God's family as His children and become the Sanctuary of the Holy Spirit. The love of God and the outpouring of the Spirit in the Sacrament of Confirmation strengthen us to do the work of evangelization. The Spirit makes everything clear to us. He renews everything, transforms everything and deepens our thoughts and meditation infinitely.

The third year, 1999 is the year of God the Father. In this way, the Church invites us to take part in the fellowship of the Holy Trinity. Moreover, as our joy deepens, the Church welcomes the "New Pentecost" and "New Springtime."[133]

133 Peter Seiichi Shirayanagi, "*Aa, Kami no Tomi to Chie to Chishiki no Fukasa. Kami no Sadame ha Satorigataku, Sono Michi ha Kiwamegata: Roma 11:33,*" [O the depth of the riches and wisdom and knowledge of God. How unsearchable are his judgments and how inscrutable his ways: Rom 11:33], *Ikeru Mizu,* No.46 (Special Edition 1998): 1. Original in Japanese. [Translation mine].

2.3.2 Homily of Peter Seiichi Cardinal Shirayanagi (2000)

On February 2, 2000, late Peter Seiichi Cardinal Shirayanagi preached the following homily during the Eucharistic Celebration in the 15th National CCRM convention held in Tokyo.

> As I was entering this convention hall, I recollected something that Holy Father had told me many years ago. The Holy Father was returning from his visit to Africa, and he seemed to be very happy. The Holy Father mentioned to me that when he was celebrating mass over there, there were unceasing chants of Alleluia and dancing, which made him wait for a long time. I find the same joy when I saw you praising God. Again, when there was a big convention held in Germany, the loud chants of Alleluia by the youth continued for a long time during the mass. By seeing your faces, I feel that you may be having the same feelings as them.
>
> God is truly a merciful Father. He created us in His own image. Human beings turned their back to God and went far away from Him. However, according to Bible, even before the creation of this world He chose us in Christ and loved us so much that he carved our names on the palm of His hands. A mother never forgets her own child. Nevertheless, God says; even if a mother forgets her own child, I will never forget you.
>
> God's love is unconditional, infinite and inexhaustible. God communicated His love through people and prophets, but people did not comprehend it. In other words, it is difficult to comprehend the mystery of incarnation. However, nothing is impossible for God. God took the form of a human being and entered our history. Sin corrupted humanity. However, God raised humanity once again because of the incarnation of God's Son. Moreover, God became one like us in everything except sin. He took the form of a weak human being, suffered, died and rose again from the dead for each one of us. If we accept God's love, God makes us His own child. We become children of

God. This is not just artificial love. Jesus poured the Holy Spirit in the depths of our being.

St. Paul repeats a number of times. "Or do you not know that your body is a temple of the Holy Spirit within you, which you have from God, and that you are not your own?" (1 Cor 6:19). God truly dwells in us though the power of the Holy Spirit. It is the crux of our faith. The Spirit gives us the power to overcome difficulties and sufferings. We cannot see the Holy Spirit with our naked eyes. We cannot also feel Him. It is only through faith we know Him. The power of the Holy Spirit truly transforms us. We become like Christ. In a world where there is a serious lack of true love, we receive the power to love and believe others.

The Holy Year is truly the power for each one of us to live. Two years ago, the Holy Father called the Synod of Asian bishops to prepare for the Holy Year. He himself analyzed and discussed the situation of Asia with the bishops. We sensed the mighty power of the Spirit through the discourses given by the bishops during the Synod. Surely, the Holy Spirit is also working in the hierarchy of the Church. At the same time, the Holy Spirit is working through each one of us. He is working through the Church community and various groups to renew the face of the earth and transform all. It gives me joy and at the same time, a great hope. Last year in November, after listening to the discourses of Asian Bishops, Holy Father himself went to New Delhi, India for the closure of the Synod with a concrete and profound conclusion. I too participated in that Synod. He declared the third century as the millennium of Asia. In the first millennium, Christianity reached Europe through Greece. In the second millennium Christianity reached African and American continents and now in the third millennium, we cannot but preach the Gospel to Asia. For this, we are in need of a great outpouring of the Holy Spirit.

The Holy Father told us not to be worried. He further said, all the people who were involved in the history of salvation were Asians. Jesus, Himself was an Asian. Therefore, the people of Asia have the right to come in contact the Gospel. The population of Asia is around two-thirds of the population of the whole world. Statistics reveal that there are around 6 billion people on earth. Out of the 6 billion, 4 billion are Asians. Moreover, statistics also reveal that 85% of the Asian population is below the age of 25. One cannot see this phenomenon in other continents. In Japan, the population of youth is relatively small, but in other parts of Asia, it is big. In other words, Asia has a big number of youth who can experience the grace of God, accept truth and justice and make efforts to enforce it. In the history of the world, one can observe that there were revolutions in the world through the influence of the youth. It seems there are many problems revolving around Asia. However if Christians preach the Gospel to the youth then they can change Asia with the power of the Spirit. Thus, Asia will transform the world.

Now we are welcoming the Great Holy Year. We are preparing for it in these coming 3 years. In the book of Exodus and Deuteronomy we read that, every seventh year there was supposed to be no cultivation and the slaves were to be set free. People cancelled all debts and it was to be a year of Sabbath (rest). God called all to be generous in that year, just like Him. Seven multiplied by 7 equals 49. The following year, the 50th year, the Bible calls as the year of liberation, jubilee year. The blowing of the bugle would indicate the beginning of the Jubilee Year (Jubilee means a bugle made of horn), the year of liberation. In the Jubilee Year, people worked for societal equity. God expected them to love one another much more than the year of Sabbath.

Around 700 years ago, in 1300, the late Pope Boniface VIII established the Jubilee Year as the Holy Year based on the Jewish traditional feast of Jubilee Year. The Jubilee Year calls us to experience the joy of the incarnation and salvation and to respond to God's grace. The Jubilee Year is a turning point in our lives. Moreover, especially this Jubilee Year being also the 2000th year is a great turning point. When we consider the present situation, we feel that it is indeed a providential year. In the past 2000 years, we have certainly made great advances. However, there are also many black spots in our history. Before his death Jesus passionately prayed, "[T]hat they may all be one. As you, Father, are in me and I am in you, may they also be in us, so that the world may believe that you have sent me" (Jn 17:21) because He knew the fight and the division which existed among human beings. In addition, certainly, we are repeatedly having wars and divisions. Even in the Church, there is division. This is really a sad thing because it is against the will of God. It is ascandal. It blocks fruitful mission work. It is a great obstacle, which we put before others. The Holy Spirit is the Spirit of unity. When God fills you with His Spirit, all divisions among you must disappear and you must become one. God created the world and after He created it, He said that it was, "Good." However, we have maligned this world. The world, which is supposed to bring glory to God, is withering away. We have to become instruments to block this degeneration.

Again, as the Holy Father says indeed the culture of death is influencing this world. Nowadays we are not merely killing each other in war but also legally killing unborn children. The tragedy of abortion is destroying life. We also have the problem of euthanasia. Our modern society is considering life as trivial. It is our responsibility to nurture a culture of life and a culture of love. The Holy Spirit accomplishes it through us.

St. Paul mentions about a variety of charism. The Holy Spirit has given each one of us charisms. This means that the Holy Spirit has also given a particular mission to use those charisms. Charisms are not for personal edification. The Holy Spirit has given them to us to use it for the benefit of others. We must not abuse these charisms but use them to establish God's will. The year 2000 must truly become a turning point in our lives. Each one of us must repent and be filled with the Holy Spirit to renew the face of the earth. We have to pray for it and resolve in our hearts to work for it.

I have heard that when Pope uses airplane, journalists usually accompany him....Once a journalist asked the Pope if it was his influence that changed Poland and many other East European countries. The Pope answered that it was the power of the Holy Spirit. There is no other power besides the power of the Holy Spirit, which can do it. Through this, we can know that the Holy Spirit is greatly working in the Pope.

Mother Teresa who would often come to Japan, was a person moved by the power of the Holy Spirit. Her talk was always simple and most of the times, she would repeat the same things. However, it had a new vigor because she was a person filled with the Holy Spirit and would live in love. Her life style itself was a missionary work. We must live in the love of God and it is through love we can spread the Gospel.

Now I can recollect the sayings of the Pope when he visited India last year. The Pope said that Asians do not reach the truth with reasoning but grasp it through intuition. He said that Europeans and North Americans understand things through reasoning. A is B. B is C. Therefore A must be C. Syllogism is one of the ways to reach truth. However, there is another way to reach truth. That is the way of intuition. The moment one sees a thing, he or she grasps the substance of the thing through intuition. When we die, we will see God face to face and have eternal bliss. It is only through intuition we can understand this. The Pope wanted to stress that Asians have the excellent capacity of intuition. However, it is also important to explain through words. I would ask all of you to manifest God's love through your life. That is what the Asians are seeking from you.... If we do not manifest

> God's love through our lives then around 4 billion Asians will not have a chance to know Christ. The mission given to us is indeed very great. I pray that you may come in greater contact with the love of God and live in that love. I think this God's will for each one of us.[134]

2.3.3 Message of Archbishop Francis Xavier Kaname Shimamoto (2000)

Following is the message of late Archbishop Francis Xavier Kaname Shimamoto, Archbishop of Nagasaki diocese to CCRJ. He gave this message on February 2, 2000.

> I impart my blessings and good wishes on the 15th National CCRM convention, held on the 2000th year of the birth of Christ. The Word became flesh through the power of the Holy Spirit in the womb of Mary. The first step in the work of salvation was the mystery of incarnation and it is the work of the Holy Spirit. God's Son became human and being filled with the power of the Holy Spirit He spread the Kingdom of God. The Spirit works through various signs in the Church. The Holy Spirit is the principal agent of the evangelization work of the Church. I pray that you become partners and collaborators of the Holy Spirit in renewing the Church in the new century. God bless you.[135]

2.3.4 Message of Apostolic Nuncio, Archbishop Ambrose de Paoli (2000)

Following is the message of Apostolic Nuncio to Japan, late Archbishop Ambrose de Paoli to CCRJ on the 15th National CCRM convention held in the year 2000.

134 Peter Seiichi Shirayanagi, "*Shirayanagi Sukikyo no Kowa*," [Shirayanagi's Lecture] in Jesus 2000: Shu no Eeiko he no Maneki [Jesus 2000: Invited to Partake in the Glory of the Lord], 4-6. Original in Japanese. [Translation mine].

135 Francis Xavier Kaname Shimamoto, "Message to National CCRM Convention," in *Jesus 2000: Shu no Eiko he no Maneki [Jesus 2000: Invited to Partake in the Glory of the Lord]*, 7. Original in Japanese. [Translation mine].

> I thank you for sending me the details of the National CCRM convention held in the year 2000. I think you must have done a lot of preparation and prayed for this convention. The theme, which you have selected, "Jesus 2000" indicates your desire to be near the Lord and spend time with Him. By this, you will grow in your devotion to Him and resolve firmly to be His witnesses in the coming new millennium. I pray for the success of the convention.[136]

2.3.5 Message of Bishop Francis Keiichi Sato (2000)

Following is the address of Late Bishop Francis Keiichi Sato, Bishop of Niigata diocese, to the participants of the 15th National CCRM convention held in 2000 in Tokyo. Late Bishop Sato himself participated in this convention.

> I request you to respect, love and obey the Church. Indeed the Second Vatican Council was a great wonder and it gave a lot of importance to the work of the Holy Spirit. According to *Lumen Gentium,* Dogmatic Constitution on Church, "It is not only through the Sacraments and the ministries of the Church that the Holy Spirit sanctifies and leads the people of God and enriches it with virtues but, allotting his gifts to everyone according as He wills, (1 Cor 12:11) He distributes special graces among the faithful of every rank." (*LG* 12). It refers here to faith, hope and love. The document conveys to us that Sacraments and ministries are an essential medium for salvation. The Holy Spirit also distributes charisms to us so that we can use them for the good of the Church. The Holy Spirit gives them for the edification, renewal and development of the whole Church. Therefore, even if the Church gives you cold shoulder treatments please do not abandon her.[137]

---

136 Ambrose de Paoli, "Message to National CCRM Convention," in *Jesus 2000: Shu no Eiko he no Maneki [Jesus 2000: Invited to Partake in the Glory of the Lord]*, 7. Original in Japanese. [Translation mine].

137 Francis Keiichi Sato, "*Niigata Kyouku: Sato Keiichi Shikyou no Kotoba*," [Niigata Diocese: Words from Bishop Keiichi Sato], in *Jesus 2000: Shu no Eiko he no*

2.3.6 Message of Peter Seiichi Cardinal Shirayanagi (2001)

Following is the message of late Peter Seiichi Cardinal Shirayangai to the CCRJ on occasion of the Kanto regional CCRM convention given on August 15, 2001.

> I saw the following words written on a beautiful poster. "A ship in harbor is safe but that is not what ships are built for." If we remain stagnant after receiving the joy and the enlightenment from the Holy Spirit, then we are like the ship in the harbor. We need to move out. No one builds a ship as a showpiece to anchor it in the harbor but one builds it to ferry people or cargo across ports. During the voyage, there is a possibility of facing storms. However, if one fears the possible dangers in the sea and prefers to anchor it perpetually in the harbor, then there is no sense in building that ship. The Great Holy Year is also like it. Just recollecting the great number of events of the Great Holy Year and doing nothing would amount to the loss of sense of the Great Holy Year. The Holy Father strongly calls us to "put out in the deep." There may be dangers of storms. However, there is no reason to fear. Because Jesus has assured us that, He will be with us until end of the age (Mt 28:20). I pray that you may renew the Church through your work. I also pray for the intercession of Mother Mary, the Mother of Church.[138]

2.3.7 Message of Archbishop Peter Takeo Okada (2001)

Following is the message of Archbishop Peter Takeo Okada, Archbishop of Tokyo Archdiocese to CCRJ on occasion of Kanto regional CCRM convention in 2001.

Maneki [Jesus 2000: Invited to Partake in the Glory of the Lord], 11. Original in Japanese. [Translation mine].

138 Peter Keiichi Shirayanagi, "*2001 Nen Seirei Ni Yoru Sasshin Kanto Taikai ni Yosete*," [On the Occasion of Kanto Regional CCRM Convention 2001] in *2001 Seirei ni Yoru Sasshin Kanto Taikai: Dai Rokkai Hokokusho, Oki ni Kogidase* [Sixth Catholic Charismatic Renewal Convention, 2001: Put Out Into the Deep], (Tokyo: Catholic Charismatic Renewal of Japan, Kanto Region, 2001), 4. Original text in Japanese. [Translation mine].

> "The Spirit of the Lord is upon me, because he has anointed me to bring good news to the poor. He has sent me to proclaim release to the captives and recovery of sight to the blind, to let the oppressed go free, to proclaim the year of the Lord's favor" (Lk 4:18-19). God the Father sent His Son, Jesus Christ to give good news and joy to the poor. Moreover, the Holy Spirit dwelt in Jesus. The Holy Spirit is the Spirit of the Father and the Spirit of the Son. The work of Jesus the evangelizer was the work of the Holy Spirit. Through the event of Pentecost, the Church was born to proclaim the Gospel. The Church was born and commissioned for mission work. I as the Archbishop of Tokyo welcomes you all gathered for the convention. Presently in Tokyo Archdiocese, we are working on a plan to renew the parishes. I earnestly ask for your prayers, support and cooperation so that led by the Spirit our efforts yield rich fruit. I have already published a document regarding this matter. I request all the participants of the convention to read it and help us to put it into practice. Through the intercession of Mother Mary, I pray that the Spirit fills each one of you with His charisms. I impart my blessings on you all.[139]

2.3.8 Message of Archbishop Peter Takeo Okada (2003)

Following is the message of Archbishop Peter Takeo Okada to the CCRJ on occasion of Seventh Kanto regional CCRM convention held in Tokyo on October 28, 2003.

> On the occasion of the Seventh Kanto regional CCRM convention, I greet all the participants of the convention. As a bishop, I often administer the Sacrament

---

139 Peter Takeo Okada, "*2001 Nen Seirei Ni Yoru Sasshin Kanto Taikai ni Yosete,*" [On the Occasion of Kanto Regional CCRM Convention 2001] in *2001 Seirei ni Yoru Sasshin Kanto Taikai: Dai Rokkai Hokokusho, Oki ni Kogidase* [Sixth Catholic Charismatic Renewal Convention, 2001: Put Out Into the Deep], (Tokyo: Catholic Charismatic Renewal of Japan, Kanto Region, 2001), 4. Original text in Japanese. [Translation mine].

of Confirmation. I earnestly pray that the recipients may receive the gifts of the Holy Spirit: Wisdom, Understanding, Counsel, Fortitude, Knowledge, Piety and Fear of God. I am sure God will certainly answer my prayers. In spite of the gifts why there is lack of the lively works of the Holy Spirit in our Church? Why we cannot see the abundance of fruits of the Holy Spirit in our Church? Is it because we lack the work of the Holy Spirit? Certainly, the fault does not lie on the part of the Holy Spirit. The fault lies on our part, the receivers of the Holy Spirit. The Holy Spirit is bestowing graces on us but we lack preparation to receive it. There are many people living around the venue of the convention in Tokyo who have stress. They are hurt both, physically and mentally. They are seeking peace and healing. The important mission of the Church is to teach and preach the healing and peace, which the Holy Spirit gives. The Holy Spirit truly heals and gives repose to all. I pray that you may preach this truth to many people. In addition, for this, our Church needs to profusely preach and share its deep healing experience. I hope that this convention and your presence may contribute greatly in spreading this message. I request you to pray that human beings may become aware of the work of the Holy Spirit. Moreover, for that, I request you to share and discuss about the ways to spread this message and pass on the fruits of your deliberations to the parishes. I earnestly request your cooperation regarding this. As I conclude, I request you to pray for peace and healing for the bishops and priests of Tokyo Archdiocese. I too assure my prayers for the success of the convention.[140]

140 Peter Takeo Okada, "*Dai Nana Kai Seirei ni Yori Sasshin Kanto Taikai Sankasha no Minasama he*," [7th Kanto Regional CCRM Convention: To All the Participants], *Ikeru Mizu*, No. 71(Winter 2004): 3. Original in Japanese. [Translation mine].

2.3.9 Message of Peter Seiichi Cardinal Shirayanagi (2003)

Following is the message of late Peter Keiichi Cardinal Shirayanagi to the CCRJ on occasion of seventh Kanto regional CCRM convention held in Tokyo Archdiocese in 2003.

> I am extremely happy to see the powerful presence of the Holy Spirit in different parts of the world. When Christians, who are the sanctuaries of the Holy Spirit, realize anew that the Holy Spirit dwells in them, then everything starts becoming new and truly the renewal in the Holy Spirit begins. As the renewal, which begins at the individual level, diffuses to the entire Church community, one can see the true nature of the Church. The CCRM is the power to renew the Church. I expect that all those who participate in this convention may become instruments to spread faith, hope and love. I pray may signs and wonders accompany your work. I pray for God's abundant blessings on you all.[141]

History teaches us that the Christianity had a turbulent journey in Japan. However, the Spirit strengthened the Christians to keep their faith. The CCRM in Japan has a trivial presence when compared with the activities of the CCRM in other nations. Nevertheless, the Spirit continues to comfort the Charismatics to surge ahead with His power and strength.

---

141 Peter Keiichi Shirayanagi, "*Kanto Taikai ni Goshusseki no Kyodai, Shimai no Minasama,*" [To All the Participants, Brothers and Sisters, of Kanto Regional CCRM Convention], *Ikeru Mizu,* No.71 (Winter 2004):3-4. Original in Japanese. [Translation mine].

Chapter 3

The Progress of the Catholic Charismatic Renewal Movement in Japan

The CCRM reached Japan in 1972, within five years of its birth. However, it does not have a massive growth rate as in other nations of Africa and South America. Nevertheless, it is steadily growing. In Japan Christianity is a minority religion. Moreover, the Catholic Church is numerically much smaller to the Protestant denominations. In spite of these harsh realities, the CCRM organizes various programs to attract people to faith. In the following sections, besides examining the various programs of the CCRM, we shall also study the statistical data of the growth of the CCRM in Japan.

3.1 The Growth of Catholic Charismatic Renewal Movement in Japan

It is indeed a Herculean task to measure quantitatively the growth of a social movement. This same difficulty also applies to the CCRM. Nevertheless, we shall try to trace the growth by examining the statistics available on the CCRM. We shall also take into account the surveys done in Japan regarding the CCRM.

The CCRM began in 1972 in Japan with a handful of people at the Redemptorist Church, Hatsudai Catholic Church. It had a very humble beginning but with the involvement of some priests, religious and lay people, the CCRM started gradually showing signs of growth. Even though, there are no official statistics published by the CCRJ about the growth of the CCRM in Japan, David Barrett's statistics shows that 12% of the Catholic population in Japan is involved with it. Table 3.1 enumerates the percentage wise involvement of Catholics with CCRM in 2000.

Table 3.1: Percentage of Catholics Involved with CCRM in 2000[142]

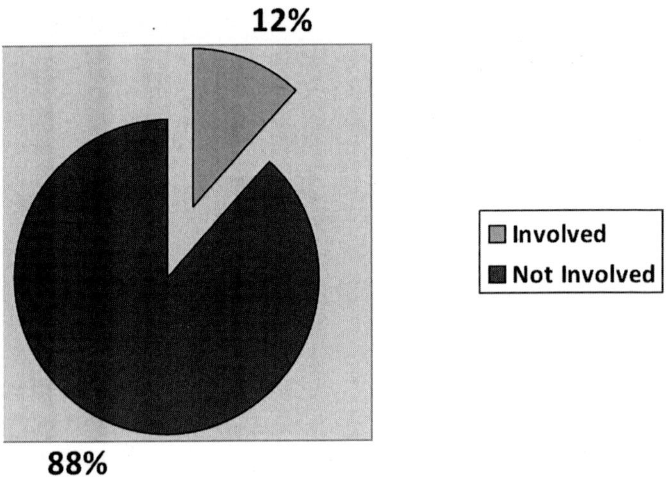

Source: David Barrett and Todd Johnson, "The Catholic Charismatic Renewal, 1959-2025.

Table 3.2: Renewal Participants in 2000[143]

Weekly	Monthly	Yearly	Involved	Familial	Community
5,000	8,083	13,067	21,124	34,148	55,200

Source: David Barrett and Todd Johnson, "The Catholic Charismatic Renewal, 1959-2025."

142 David Barrett and Todd Johnson, "The Catholic Charismatic Renewal, 1959-2025," in *Then Peter Stood Up*, 120.

143 Ibid.

Table 3.2 enumerates the six categories of participants associated with the CCRM in 2000. The first category is the basic head count, which is of weekly-attending adults who regularly attend their charismatic prayer group. The following five categories are then derived from it; the first four categories (weekly, monthly, yearly, involved) refers to adults only (over 15 years old); the last two categories (familial and community) are demographic totals including children and infants. These last two are important because it includes the family. CCRM seeks renewal not only of individuals but also of families.

Weekly-attendees are those adults who attend (involved in/enrolled in/participating in) the CCRM prayer meetings regularly every week. The CCRM calls them the 'shock troops' of the movement. Barrett estimates that there are 5,000 adults actively involved in their charismatic prayer groups. Monthly-attendees are those adults who attending CCRM prayer meetings once in a month. Barrett puts their figure to around 8,000 people. Yearly-attendees are those adults who attend less regularly, often only for a convention. Barrett notes that there are around 13,067 people participating, at least once in a year in CCRM prayer meetings, conventions or rallies in Japan. Involved or self-identifying involved adult Charismatics are those who identify themselves in public-opinion polls either as Catholic Charismatics or as otherwise involved in the Renewal in some way or the other. Barrett estimates that this category has around 21,124 adults Catholics. Familial is the category that includes all active or involved adults in Renewal plus their children and infants. Barrett puts their figure to around 34,148 people. The category Community includes all the family members of the category Familial plus a large fringe of Catholic Post-Charismatics (formerly active Charismatics but presently are less active, inactive, or elsewhere active). This category had around 55,200 people in Japan in 2000.[144]

144 David Barrett and Todd Johnson, "The Catholic Charismatic Renewal, 1959-2025," in *Then Peter Stood Up*, 120.

Table 3.3: The Influence of CCRM on the Parishes in Japan in 2000[145]

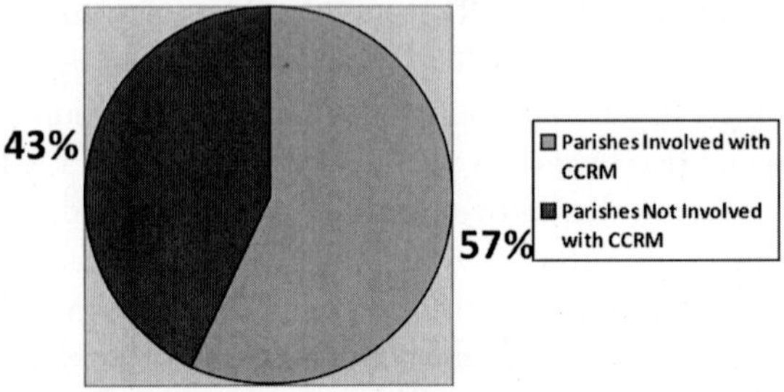

Source: David Barrett and Todd Johnson, "The Catholic Charismatic Renewal, 1959-2025."

Table 3.3 enumerates the influence of the CCRM on the parishes in Japan. Barrett estimates that out of the 869 parishes, 500 parishes have CCRM prayer groups. It means that the CCRM has influenced 57% of the Catholic parishes. In other words, 43% have no presence of the CCRM prayer groups.

Table 3.4: Percentage of Priests Involved with the CCRM in 2000[146]

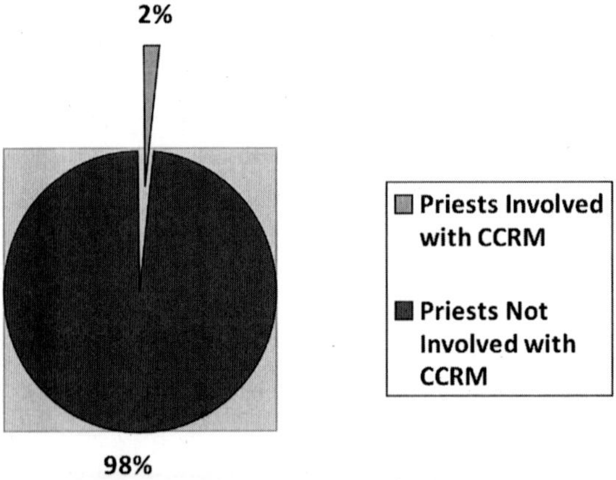

Source: David Barrett and Todd Johnson, "The Catholic Charismatic Renewal, 1959-2025."

145 David Barrett and Todd Johnson, "The Catholic Charismatic Renewal, 1959-2025," in *Then Peter Stood Up*, 120.

146 Ibid.

Table 3.4 enumerates the percentage of the priests involved with the CCRM. Out of 1,828 priests, only 40 priests (2%) are actively involved with the CCRM. 98% of the priests are not involved with it directly.

Table 3.5: Growth of CCRM in Japan from 1972-2000[147]

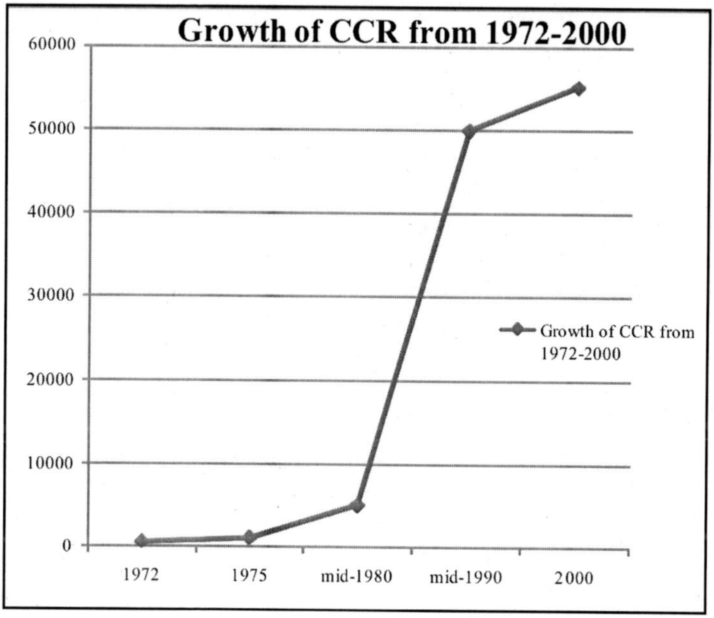

Source: David Barrett and Todd Johnson, "The Catholic Charismatic Renewal, 1959-2025."

Table 3.5 enumerates the percentage of Catholics involved from 1972 to 2000. In 1972 when the CCRM began, around 500 Catholics (0%) out of 365,662 were involved with the CCRM. In 1975, the figure rose to 1,000 (0.1%) out of 395,000. In mid-1980, the number of Catholics involved with the CCRM was 5,000 (1.1%)

147 We took the data from 1970 to 1990 from David Barrett, *World Christian Encyclopedia: A Comparative Study of Churches and Religions in the Modern World AD 1900-2000* (New York: Oxford University Press, 1982), 419. We took the data from 1990-2025 from David Barrett and Todd Johnson, "The Catholic Charismatic Renewal, 1959-2025," in *Then Peter Stood Up*, 120.

out of 420,000 Catholics. In the mid-1990 the number of Catholics involved in CCRM rose to 50,000 (11.3%) out of 439,000 Catholics. In 2000, Barrett estimates that there were 55,200 Charismatic Catholics (12%) out of 460,000 Catholics. Table 3.5 depicts the growth of the CCRM in Japan since its beginning in 1972. Even though, initially only a handful of Catholics were involved with the CCRM, the movement had a steep increase from the mid-1980s. The percentage of Catholic Charismatics grew from 1.1% in mid-1980 to 11.3% in 1990 and further rose to 12% in 2000. In spite of its phenomenal growth, Barrett estimates that the CCRM will not have more than 12% of the Catholics as its members until 2025. He predicts that in 2025, the Catholic population will increase to 600,000 and around 70,227 people (12%) may involve with the CCRM. This implies that the percentage of Catholics involved with the CCRM will remain same as in the year 2000.

From the above statistical data, we can deduce the following aspects about the CCRM in Japan. Initially the CCRM in Japan had a slow growth rate. However, it accelerated up in the mid-1980. In 1972, the percentage of Catholics involved with the CCRM was almost 0% but by 2000, the figure has shot to 12%. However, Barrett projects that the percentage of Charismatics Catholics will remain same, as it was in 2000. These figures point out that the CCRM has peaked in Japan. Further, the involvement of priests with the CCRM is very low. Only 2% of the priests are associated with the CCRM. It is a matter of concern. This is because even though the CCRM is a laity-centered group it needs the guidance and encouragement of ecclesial authorities and pastors.

3.2 The Various Activities of the Catholic Charismatic Renewal Services of Japan

The CCRJ is primarily responsible for organizing various programs to spread the CCRM. Organizing prayer meetings, conventions, retreats and Life in the Spirit seminars are some of the main activities of the CCRJ. In the following sections, we shall examine each program in detail.

3.2.1 Prayer Groups

One of the prominent forums to spread the CCRM is prayer group. The prayer group is the smallest and basic unit of the CCRJ. The first prayer group began in 1972 at Hatsudai Catholic Church, a Redemptorist Church at Tokyo. Since then as the CCRM spread in Japan, the number of prayer groups kept on increasing. The CCRJ estimates that there are around 500 prayer groups in different parts of Japan. Some of the prayer groups meet in the Church premises. Some groups borrow public auditoriums to conduct praise and worship meeting. Some Charismatics organize prayer groups at their homes. The numerical strength of the prayer group varies from group to group. There are prayer meetings with a membership of as little as 2 members coming together to pray together, while there are some prayer groups like the Yotsuya prayer group in Tokyo which claims to have a membership of over a hundred people participating in its weekly meetings. The frequency of the prayer meetings also varies from group to group. There are some groups, which meet on weekly basis, but there are also prayer groups, which find it difficult to meet once in a month. There are also some smaller groups, which meet a couple times in a year.[148]

The existence of a prayer group is of paramount importance to the CCRJ. A prayer group provides an excellent opportunity to the people to pray together, praise and worship the Lord as an extended family of God. Prayer groups help like-minded Christians to form a true praying community united in the Spirit. They also provide a platform for different people to listen to each other and share with each other, joys and sorrows. The prayer groups are also instruments in accepting new members from different occupations and introducing them to the CCRM activities. The CCRJ rules mandate that each prayer group must elect a leader and core group members. It is the responsibility of the leader and the core group members to organize the prayer meeting and if possible, announce

148 Catholic Charismatic Renewal of Japan, *2001 Seirei ni Yoru Sasshinn Kanto Taikai: Dai Rokkai Hokokusho, Oki ni Kogidase* [Sixth Catholic Charismatic Renewal Convention, 2001: Put Out into the Deep.] (Tokyo: Catholic Charismatic Renewal of Japan, Kanto Region, 2001), 38. Original text in Japanese. [Translation mine].

the time and the day in the parish or put up some posters so that many can participate. The Holy Spirit is the ultimate animator of the prayer meetings, but the leader and his or her team must work out a plan for the prayer meeting, so that there is order in the prayer meeting. It is very important to have an order in the prayer meetings. The CCRJ warns to avoid excesses because it can discourage people. The leaders must create an ambience of prayer, where people can relax and feel the presence of God in the community.[149]

The duration and the format of the prayer groups largely depend on each individual group. However, the CCRJ issues certain guidelines for the smooth functioning of the prayer groups. The CCRJ follows all the guidelines laid down by the ICCRS regarding the conducting of prayer meetings. The CCRJ, National Committee has published a small booklet, *Inori no Tsudoi he no Tebiki* [A Manual for the Prayer Meetings] in 1994. The CCRJ has borrowed the content of this manual from a book, *Participating in Prayer Meeting* (1974) by Jim Cavnar.[150] In addition to these guidelines, the CCRJ also recommends some other guidelines, which are particular for Japan.

The duration of the prayer meeting is flexible but it recommends the leaders to have a certain fixed time, ranging from one and half hour to a maximum of two hours. Occasionally the prayer meetings may tend to stretch over two hours, but as a norm, the CCRJ suggests to limit it to a maximum of two hours. In addition, the CCRJ suggests the leaders to fix a particular day and a time in a week or month to organize meetings. Leaders must strictly follow the opening time. Japanese are usually punctual and so the leaders must be punctual with the time to give a good impression to everyone.[151]

---

149 Catholic Charismatic Renewal of Japan, *2001 Seirei ni Yoru Sasshinn Kanto Taikai: Dai Rokkai Hokokusho, Oki ni Kogidase* [Sixth Catholic Charismatic Renewal Convention, 2001: Put Out into the Deep.] (Tokyo: Catholic Charismatic Renewal of Japan, Kanto Region, 2001), 38. Original text in Japanese. [Translation mine].

150 Jim Cavnar, *Participating in Prayer Meetings* (Ann Arbor: Word of Life, 1974).

151 Catholic Charismatic Renewal of Japan, *2001 Seirei ni Yoru Sasshinn Kanto Taikai: Dai Rokkai Hokokusho, Oki ni Kogidase* [Sixth Catholic Charismatic Renewal Convention, 2001: Put Out Into the Deep.], 39.

The prayer meeting begins with extemporary praise and worship session along with lively worship music. The CCRJ also recommends choosing the hymns and practicing before hand, so that the praise and worship session are done without any interruption. It also highly recommends the leader and the members of the core group to prepare a list of praise and worship songs. The CCRJ expects the leader and the core group members to read the lyrics of the hymns so that people understand the meaning of the hymns before they sing. The CCRJ encourages leaders to make the prayer meetings lively.[152]

The CCRJ suggests the leaders to observe a period of silence after the praise and worship session. It is very important to maintain a brief period of silence, because in these quiet moments one can deeply worship God and feel His mighty presence in one's life. People with charisms of prophecy, can use this time to discern the divine messages, which the Lord wants to give to the group. After the pause, leaders can ask some people to pray extemporarily and thus lead all in a spirit of prayer. During this time, as the Spirit leads one can read passages from the Bible or give a prophecy or a word of encouragement.[153]

With this, the first half of the prayer meeting ends and the second half begin. The second half begins with an exchange of sign of peace, followed by testimonies, sharing, study session, or preaching. After this, there are intercessory prayers, especially praying for the community, the Church and other intentions.[154]

The CCRJ cautions that sharing sessions or extemporary prayer sessions should not be occasions to criticize or hurt others. If someone does so, it is the duty of the leader to immediately stop them and lead the group back to prayer. It also suggests proper divisions between different sessions of the prayer meeting. People should not mix prayer sessions with personal sharing or testimony. The purpose of a testimony or sharing is to make known to others

---

152 Catholic Charismatic Renewal of Japan, *2001 Seirei ni Yoru Sasshinn Kanto Taikai: Dai Rokkai Hokokusho, Oki ni Kogidase* [Sixth Catholic Charismatic Renewal Convention, 2001: Put Out Into the Deep.], 39.

153 Ibid. See also Catholic Charismatic Renewal of Japan, *Inori no Tsudoi he no Tebiki* [A Manual for Prayer Meetings] (Tokyo: Catholic Charismatic Renewal of Japan, 1994), 4. Original text in Japanese. [Translation mine].

154 Ibid.

the goodness of the Lord. It is a sharing of the personal experience of the Lord, which one shares or testifies to edify others. Sharing or testimonies are for the greater glory of God. They are not forums for sharing one's personal problems, or display one's acts of piety or devotion. The testimony or sharing must be brief and concise. As far as possible, the CCRJ suggests not using personal interpretation of the Bible or using bombastic language or jargons. This is because use of such language could be misleading and some may not understand the real message or content of the testimony or sharing. Sharing must be objective and sound. People should avoid expressing subjective interpretations of the Bible during sharing. Sharing is also not a time for discussion or an occasion to settle an old score. Such acts would be detrimental for the growth of the whole community. In order to use sharing and testimonies for the growth of the community the leader and core group members must take care that people are encouraged to do sharing and give testimony of their personal encounter with the Lord. Leaders must request people to prepare before hand the content of their testimony so that they can effectively communicate it.[155]

It is also important to discern the use of various charisms. Charisms are very important. The leader must encourage all the members to use them prudently, following the promptings of the Holy Spirit. Especially people having the gift of prophecy must exercise it with prudence and restrain. As Paul says: "those who prophesy speak to other people for their up building and encouragement and consolation" (1 Cor 14:3). The person who prophesies must be loud enough so that everyone can hear him or her, but must not resort to dramatics to scare others. The person prophesying must use simple language. A prophecy must always be consistent with the Word of God and the doctrines of the Church. The Holy Spirit will never contradict the revelation in the Bible. People must not prophesize to condemn, criticize, accuse, or embarrass anyone. After receiving the prophecy, generally there must be an atmosphere of calm and peace in the prayer group. However, if the content of the prophecy leads to uneasiness or disputes, then it is the responsibility of the leader

155 Ibid. See also Catholic Charismatic Renewal of Japan, *Inori no Tsudoi he no Tebiki* [A Manual for Prayer Meetings], 8-9.

and the whole prayer group to evaluate prayerfully the content of the prophecies.[156]

3.2.2 Conventions

The CCRJ organized conventions every year, from 1975 to 1985. However, as the movement started growing and spreading to various parts of Japan, the CCRJ decided to hold annual conventions in respective zones and organize a National CCRM convention once in 3 years. Since then the CCRJ has organized several regional and national conventions.[157]

National CCRM conventions and regional CCRM conventions offer an excellent chance to all to gather as one large community to praise and worship the Lord. It also offers a platform for mutual sharing, exchange of opinions and time to study the Bible. Usually every convention has a theme and the CCRJ invites experts in that field as resource persons. The conventions span out for 2 or 3 consecutive days. The program of the convention includes the daily celebration of the Holy Eucharist, adoration of the Blessed Sacrament, praise-worship sessions, lectures based on the theme, sharing in groups, praying over the participants for healing and infilling of the Holy Spirit.

These conventions have helped many people to live authentic Christian life. The CCRJ National Committee conducted a survey during the 15th National CCRM Convention held in 2000. Two hundred and sixty people responded to the questionnaire prepared by the CCRJ National Service Committee. The CCRJ has tabulated the data collected to know the effects of the National CCRM Convention.

156 See Catholic Charismatic Renewal of Japan, *Inori no Tsudoi he no Tebiki* [A Manual for Prayer Meetings], 16-17.

157 Nakamura, "The History of the Catholic Charismatic Renewal of Japan," 2.

Table 3.6: The regional division of the respondents[158]

Total	Hokkaido	Northeast	Kanto	Shinetsu	Chubu	Kinki	Shikoku	Kyushu	Okinawa	Not Acquired
260	8	13	122	19	16	38	8	16	6	14
%	3.1	5	46.9	7.3	6.2	14.6	3.1	6.2	2.3	5.4

Table 3.7: Gender division of the respondents[159]

Total	Men	Women	Not Acquired
260	32	153	75
%	12.3	58.8	28.8

Table 3.8: Have you participated in the Life in the Spirit Seminars?[160]

Total	Yes	No
260	121	139
%	46.5	53.5

Table 3.9: The age groups of the respondents[161]

Total	10s	20s	30s	40s	50s	60s	70s	80s	Not Acquired
260	0	9	29	25	78	78	29	12	0
%	0	3.5	11.2	9.6	30	30	11.2	4.6	0

158 Catholic Charismatic Renewal of Japan, National Service Committee, *Jesus 2000: Shu no Eiko he no Maneki* [Jesus 2000: Invited to Partake in the Glory of the Lord] (Tokyo: Catholic Charismatic Renewal of Japan, National Service Committee, 2000), 68-71.

159 Ibid.

160 Ibid.

161 Ibid.

Table 3.10: Impressions about 15th National CCRM Convention, 2000.[162]

Excellent	214	82.3%
Good	36	13.8%
Fairly Good	2	0.7%
Poor	0	0%
No response	8	3.1%
Total	260	100%

Table 3.11: Impressions about the talks given during the 15th National CCRM Convention, 2000.[163]

Excellent	211	81.2%
Good	41	15.8%
Fairly Good	2	0.7%
Poor	0	0%
No Response	6	2.3%
Total	260	100%

Table 3.12: Graces received during the 15th National CCRM Convention, 2000[164]

Many Graces	112	43.1%
Encouragement	114	43.8%
Healing of Heart (emotional healing)	69	26.5%
Physical Healing	31	11.9%
Did not experience anything special	9	3.5%
Total	260	100%

162 Catholic Charismatic Renewal of Japan, National Service Committee, *Jesus 2000: Shu no Eiko he no Maneki* [Jesus 2000: Invited to Partake in the Glory of the Lord] (Tokyo: Catholic Charismatic Renewal of Japan, National Service Committee, 2000), 68-71.

163 Ibid.

164 Ibid.

Table 3.13: In which sharing subcommittee did you participate during the 15th National CCRM Convention, 2000[165]

Subcommittees	Total	%	Men	Women	Not Acquired
Children's Subcommittee	12	4.6	0	11	1
Explanation about the CCRM	28	10.8	2	16	10
Priests' Subcommittee	2	0.7	2	0	0
Intercessory	35	3.5	2	19	14
Healing Services	53	0.4	5	29	19
Youth	4	1.5	1	1	2
Every Bible Meditation	33	12.7	5	25	13
Social Welfare	18	.9	2	11	5
Free Sharing	6	2.3	1	4	1
Not Acquired	34	13.1	8	11	15
Did not participate	35	13.5	6	22	7

Table 3.14: Impressions about participation in the subcommittees

Excellent	80	31%
Good	68	26%
Fairly Good	32	12%
Poor	6	0.2%
No Response	74	28.4
Total	237	100%

Table 3.6 enumerates the region to which the respondents belong. It is clear from the data that the respondents come different parts of Japan. It clearly implies that CCRM has spread all over Japan. Table 3.7 enumerates the gender division of the respondents. The number of women is very high. Around 58% of the respondents are women. Table 3.8 enumerates the data about the prior participation of the respondents in the Life in the Spirit

165 Catholic Charismatic Renewal of Japan, National Service Committee, *Jesus 2000: Shu no Eiko he no Maneki* [Jesus 2000: Invited to Partake in the Glory of the Lord] (Tokyo: Catholic Charismatic Renewal of Japan, National Service Committee, 2000), 68-71.

Seminars. Table 3.9 enumerates the age group of the respondents. Table 3.10 enumerates the general impression of the respondents about the CCRM convention. It is remarkable to know that 214 respondents (82.3%) had an excellent impression about the convention, 36 respondents (13.8%) rated it as good and no one rated it as poor. Table 3.11 enumerates the impression about the talks given in the convention. Two hundred and eleven respondents (81.2%) rated the talks as excellent; 41 respondents (15.8%) rated the talks as good and 2 respondents (07%) rated the talks as fairly good. None of the respondents rated the talks as poor. Table 3.12 enumerates about the graces received during the convention. Hundred and twelve respondents (43.1%) said that they received many graces, 114 respondents (43.8%) said that they received a special grace of encouragement, 69 respondents (26.5%) received the grace of healing, 31 respondents (11.9%) received the grace of physical healing and only 9 respondents (3.5%) did not experience anything. The CCRJ then requested the respondents to specify the graces received in detail. Table 3.15 mentions the details.

Table 3.15: Responses about the specific graces during the 15th National CCRM Convention, 2000[166]

Gift of Tongues		2
Physical Healing	Back Pain	3
	Fingers	1
	Body ache	11
	Hump back pain	1
	Joint pains	1
	Respiratory disorder	1
	Chest pain	1
	Stomach	1
	Dermatological problems	1

166 Catholic Charismatic Renewal of Japan, National Service Committee, *Jesus 2000: Shu no Eiko he no Maneki* [Jesus 2000: Invited to Partake in the Glory of the Lord] (Tokyo: Catholic Charismatic Renewal of Japan, National Service Committee, 2000), 68-71.

	Influenza, cough	1
	Eyes	1
	Debility	1
Encouragement	To serve as a community	4
	To work for evangelization in Japan	2
	To be convinced that all people will be saved	1
	To be encouraged by a brother	1
Confession		2
Healing of Heart (Emotional healing)	Deliverance from negative thoughts	7
	Peace and joy	5
	Transformation in the behavior of husband (he was very aggressive but became very gentle)	3
	Prayed for others, but was healed	1
	Feeling refreshed	3
	Deliverance from a heavy burden on heart	7
	Got deliverance from something	6
	Cannot say distinctively, but to get a feeling of being healed	3
	Transformation of body and mind, internally prepared to surrender to everything to God	6
Thanksgiving	Thank God at all times	2
	Received true freedom	1
	To know the mercy of God	1
To have an experience of God's love	For the first time	5
	To experience the grace of God	1

Praise	To praise from whole heart	4
	To know the power of praise	2
	To experience the presence of God	5
	To receive gold dust	3
	To get gift of smile	2
	To get the fragrance of rose	2

From the above data, it is evident that the National CCRM convention 2000 was a grand success. It did indeed achieve its goal of gathering many people involved with the CCRM under one roof. It was also equally successful in introducing CCRM to many new comers. Most of the participants appreciated the talks and the sessions of the convention. They were very happy with the overall program of the convention. The convention also yielded rich fruits in terms of the renewal it brought in the lives of the people. The survey indicates that the people received graces and a deeper urge to love God during the convention.

We shall examine another survey conducted by the Catholic Charismatic Renewal of Japan, Kanto region at the 6th Kanto regional CCRM convention, 2001. Eighty-seven participants took part in the survey. Out of the 87 participants, 63 (72%) were women and the rest men.

Table 3.16: General Impressions about the Sixth Kanto CCRM Convention, 2001.[167]

Excellent	57	65.5%
Good	20	23.1%
Fairly good	5	5.7%
Poor	0	0%
No response	5	5.7%
Total	87	100%

167 Catholic Charismatic Renewal of Japan, Kanto Region, *2001 Seirei ni Yoru Sasshinn Kanto Taikai: Dai Rokkai Hokokusho, Oki ni Kogidase* [Sixth Catholic Charismatic Renewal Convention, 2001:Put Out Into the Deep.], 52.

Table 3.17: Impressions about the subcommittee [168]

Name of Subcommittee	Number of respondents	Excellent	Good	Fairly Good	No Response
About CCRM	5	2	2	1	1
Praise and Worship	14	10	1	0	3
Prayer	13	3	8	2	0
Charisms	18	5	10	0	3
Life in the Spirit Seminars	12	10	2	0	0
Organizing Prayer Meeting	13	6	0	0	1
Leading a Prayer Group	8	2	5	0	1
One day participants	3	0	3	0	0
No Response	1				1
Total	87(100%)	38(43.7%)	36(41.4%)	3(3.6%)	10(11.5%)

Table 3.18: Impressions about the Holy Eucharist, Prayer Sessions and Praise and Worship Sessions during the Sixth Kanto Regional CCRM Convention, 2001.[169]

	Total	Excellent	Good	Fairly Good	No Response
Prayer Sessions	87 (100%)	44(50.6%)	17(19.5%)	2(2.3%)	24(27.6%)
Praise and Worship Sessions	87(100%)	45(51.7%)	20(23%)	4(4.6%)	18(20.7%)
Holy Eucharist	87(100%)	42(48.3%)	16(18.4%)	3(3.4%)	26(29.9%)

168 Catholic Charismatic Renewal of Japan, Kanto Region, *2001 Seirei ni Yoru Sasshinn Kanto Taikai: Dai Rokkai Hokokusho, Oki ni Kogidase* [Sixth Catholic Charismatic Renewal Convention, 2001:Put Out Into the Deep.], 53.

169 Ibid.

Table 3.19: Graces received during the Sixth Kanto Regional CCRM Convention, 2001.[170]

Name of subcommittee	Number of Respondents	Excellent	Encour-agement	Gained a lot	Healing of heart	Physical healing	Nothing special
About CCRM	5	1	2	1	3	0	0
Praise and Worship	14	4	9	5	4	1	0
Prayer	13	3	6	3	1	2	0
Charisms	18	4	10	11	2	2	0
Life in the Spirit Seminars	12	9	2	2	4	1	0
Organizing Prayer Meetings	13	6	6	5	1	0	1
Leading a Prayer Group	8	4	4	1	2	0	0
One day participants	3	0	0	0	0	0	0
No response	1	0	0	0	0	0	0
Total	87 (100%)	31 (35.6%)	39 (44.8%)	28 (32.2%)	17 (19.5%)	6 (6.9%)	1 (1.2%)

Table 3.16 enumerates the data about the general impressions of the respondents regarding the overall organizing and functioning of the Sixth Kanto regional CCRM convention. Fifty-seven respondents (65.5%) said they were extremely happy with the convention. Twenty respondents (23.1%) said they were happy with the convention. This shows that a majority of the respondents felt the convention was well organized and they gained by attending it.

Table 3.17 enumerates the impressions about the various subcommittees of the Convention. Thirty-eight respondents (43.7%) found the subcommittee in which they participated as excellent. Thirty-six respondents (41.4%) found the subcommittee in which they participated as good. We can deduce from this data that most of

170 Catholic Charismatic Renewal of Japan, Kanto Region, *2001 Seirei ni Yoru Sasshinn Kanto Taikai: Dai Rokkai Hokokusho, Oki ni Kogidase* [Sixth Catholic Charismatic Renewal Convention, 2001:Put Out Into the Deep.], 54.

the respondents were happy with the various subcommittees of the convention.

Table 3.18 enumerates the impressions of the respondents about the celebration of the Holy Eucharist, the prayer sessions and the praise-worship sessions. Forty-four respondents (50.6%) said that the prayer sessions were excellent, while 17 (19.5%) said that they were good. Forty-five respondents (51.7%) said that the praise-worship sessions were excellent, while 20 (23%) said that they were good. Forty-two respondents (48.3%) had excellent impression about the celebration of the Holy Eucharist and 16 respondents (18.4%) said they felt it was good.

Table 3.19 enumerates the graces received during the Sixth Kanto regional CCRM convention. Thirty-one respondents (35.1%) said that they received many excellent graces. 39 respondents (44.8%) said they received encouragement, 28 respondents (32.2%) said that they gained a lot through this convention, 17 respondents (19.5%) received healing of heart (emotional healing) and 6 respondents (6.9%) received physical healing.

From the above analytical data, it is clear that the Sixth Kanto regional CCRM convention was successful in bringing renewal in the life of the participants in various forms and ways. In general, the participants were very happy with the organizing of the convention and got grace to lead a fruitful Christian life.

3.2.3 Charismatic Retreats

The CCRJ organizes regularly retreats to attract many people to the CCRM. In addition, these retreats aim the spiritual growth of a person. The CCRJ also organizes retreats for priests and religious. The CCRJ aims to spread the Charismatic spirituality among the pastors, because it considers their assistance as indispensable in Church's renewal. The CCRJ invites international preachers and leaders to direct the retreats.

The retreats also aim to train people to work for the CCRM. A priest who had participated in the retreat conducted by Rufus Pereira, a Catholic priest from Bombay Archdiocese India, at Nagoya, Japan in 1998, said that as a priest he always considered being devout, rational, wise and kind were the qualities essential for priestly ministry. However, he realized that these qualifies alone would not help a priest to carry out all his responsibilities as a pastor. More than these qualities, one needs the guidance of the Holy Spirit. A priest must be open to the Holy Spirit and allow Him to work through all his projects. Some of the other priests who participated in this retreat mentioned that they learned practical skills to work for the healing of memories.[171]

As there are many non-Japanese Catholics living in Japan, these retreats provide them a good opportunity to integrate with the Japanese Catholics. The CCRJ organized an international retreat at a Catholic Church in Osaka in 2000 to bring both the Japanese and the non-Japanese Catholics together. The CCRJ reported that many Korean and Japanese Catholics attended this retreat as a family united in Christ. They praised and worshiped God in both Korean and Japanese. The participants experienced the presence of God amongst them. The Holy Spirit helped them to pass over their cultural differences and work towards unity.[172]

Each retreat has a particular theme. The CCRJ invites preachers specialized in the area of the theme to direct the retreats. These retreats have been providing a wonderful opportunity to priests and religious to renew their spiritual commitment to the Lord and work energetically in their respective ministries. They have also helped many lay people to learn many new things like organizing prayer meetings, intercessory prayer groups and healing sessions. These retreats continue to attract many people from all occupations to seek peace, joy and a renewed strength in their lives.

3.2.4 Life in the Spirit Seminars

Life in the Spirit Seminar has been a prominent feature of the CCRJ right from its inception in 1972. The Yotsuya prayer group organizes twice, each year Life in the Spirit Seminars of 8 weeks each. The

---

171 Noel Lessard, "*Futsu no Shisai*" [Ordinary Priest], *Ikeru Mizu,* No.47 (Special Edition 1998): 10-11. Original text in Japanese. [Translation mine].

172 Shinsuke Akimoto, "*Ikuno Katorikku Kyoukai no Shijiunsetsu: Mokusokukai wo Testudatte*" [Lent at Ikuno Catholic Church: Helping to Conduct the Retreat], *Ikeru Mizu,* No.56 (Spring 2000): 7-8. Original text in Japanese. [Translation mine].

format of these seminars is the same as that used by ICCRS and many of the prayer groups around the world. The two main sources of these seminars are *Life in The Spirit Seminars: Participants Booklet* published by ICCRS (formerly known as ICCRO) in 1993 and *The Life in the Spirit Seminars Team Manual* published by the Word of God Community, Ann Arbor (USA).[173] HSRO the renewal office of CCRJ in Tokyo has published a book *Shinnsei he no kadode* [The Entrance to New Life] in 2006. This book is a translated adaptation of the books published by ICCRS and the Word of God Community in Ann Arbor. The goal of the Life in the Spirit Seminars is fourfold: (1) To help the participants to have a personal relationship with Jesus Christ. (2) To experience the dynamic power of the Holy Spirit in one's life. (3) To help the participants become active members of a Christian community. (4) To share their faith with others and to love Jesus Christ more.

The format of the Life in the Spirit Seminars is as follows: Every week there is a 2-hour seminar. 1 hour of praise and worship session, followed by 30 minutes of talk on the theme as mentioned in the Life in the Spirit Seminar booklet and finally 30 minutes of sharing. The organizers expect that each participant spend daily, at least 15 minutes in personal prayer and prayerfully read the suggested biblical passages. Each week has a fixed theme. The themes are: (1) God's Love (2) Salvation (3) The New Life (4) Receiving God's Gift (Call for Conversion) (5) Praying for baptism in the Holy Spirit (6) Growth in the Holy Spirit (7) Transformation in Christ. During the eight week, the CCRJ usually organizes a one-day retreat for the participants. The leaders of the CCRJ lay their hands over the participants and pray. They also suggest ways for the continual growth of their life in the Holy Spirit. The CCRJ expects that each participant attend all the seminars and the retreat without any absence.[174]

The contents of the Life in the Spirit seminar are as follows:

---

173 See International Catholic Charismatic Renewal Office, *Life in the Spirit Seminars* (Rome: International Catholic Charismatic Renewal Office, 1993). See also The Word of God, *The Life in the Spirit Seminars Team Manual* (Ann Arbor: Servant Books, 1979).

174 Catholic Charismatic Renewal of Japan, Kanto Region, *2001 Seirei ni Yoru Sasshinn Kanto Taikai: Dai Rokkai Hokokusho, Oki ni Kogidase* [Sixth Catholic Charismatic Renewal Convention, 2001: Put Out Into the Deep.], 34-35.

3.2.4.1 Week One: God's Love

The purpose of this seminar "God's Love" is to make the participants aware that God is not someone who lives far away in a place where no one can reach Him. Nor is He like a police officer who is keeping an eye over all. He is not waiting to punish the sinners. On the contrary, God is a loving father, Abba, as Jesus called Him. Every person in this world has the capacity to know God and know how much God loves him or her. God wants to be in a personal relationship with everyone. He wants to make everyone His son and daughter. He longs to be in communion with all. He loves everyone because He cares for everyone and wants to give everyone the fullness of life. Because God loves the whole humanity, He sent His only Son Jesus Christ to save the humanity (Jn 3.16). The suggested biblical passages for reading during this week of seminar are. Jer 31:3; Jer 31:33-34; Ez 34:14-16; Jn 3:16; Is 55:1-3; Jer 29:11-13; Ps 145:18.[175]

3.2.4.2 Week Two: Salvation

We find ourselves in a world that has something seriously wrong with it. We read daily about wars, murders, poverty, racial conflicts and exploitation of the poor and the weak. There is loneliness, depression, anxiety, boredom, hatred and all other negative emotions, which are burdening us in our daily lives. At times, we find ourselves very confused and seek a way out. The world tries to offer many solutions in the forms of technological progress, advancement of science, psychological techniques and skills to get rid of the stress. There are also many new religions, which try to advocate a quick fix solution to all the problems. The effects of secularization challenge our Christian faith. There are people who think that Christ and His message are no longer relevant for this world. They rely on human capabilities alone. Nevertheless, Christians believe, in spite of all these human-made solutions, there is something lacking. There is a vacuum, which we need to fill. It is only Christ, who can fill our empty lives. God sent

175 See Arikata Kobayashi, *Shinsei he no kadode* [Entrance to New Life] (Tokyo: Catholic Charismatic Renewal of Japan HSRO, 2006), 11-16. Original text in Japanese. [Translation mine]. See also International Catholic Charismatic Renewal Office, *Life in the Spirit Seminars*, 2-7. See also The Word of God, *The Life in the Spirit Seminars Team Manual*, 83-94.

His Son, Jesus into the world to save us. Jesus has freed us from all the bondages and has offered us life in abundance. Jesus gave us true life through His death on the cross. Through His resurrection, He has offered us a hope of a new life. Jesus has saved us; we need to accept it in faith. The Scriptural texts recommended for this week of the seminar are as follows: Mi 4:1-6; Is 55:9; Eph 6:12; Jn 11:21-27; Rom 5:6-8; Is 53:4-6; Col 1:13.[176]

3.2.4.3 Week Three: The New Life

The prophets of the Old Testament predicted that the day would come when God would send His Spirit on all. Those who would turn to Him and receive His Spirit would change. They would be new people of God with a new life. Jesus promised His followers that He would send the Holy Spirit upon them when He ascends to the Heaven. He promised to them the Paraclete, who would be with them and teach them. On the day of Pentecost, Jesus fulfilled His promise. The Holy Spirit mightily descended on the apostles and disciples of Jesus gathered in the Upper Room in Jerusalem (Acts 2:1-4). The promise, which Jesus made to His disciples, is also valid to every one of us. As Christians, we have received the Holy Spirit through the Sacraments of initiation. We need to grow in faith and pray to the Holy Spirit, to experience His mighty presence in our life and that He may use us as instruments for the glory of God and for the up building of the Church. When we do so, the Holy Spirit equips us with all the necessary gifts and charisms needed to live our life as Christians and work for the glory of God. God has given us the Holy Spirit so that we unite with each other as the Body of Christ, the Church. The new life in the Holy Spirit will lead us to have a deeper fellowship with our brothers and sisters in the Church and to reach out to all the people with love. The scriptural texts suggested for meditation are as follows: Ez 36:22-28; Jn 14:15-18; Acts 2:1-4; 19:5-7; 1 Cor 12:7-11; Eph 2:19-22.[177]

---

176 Ibid., 17-25. See also International Catholic Charismatic Renewal Office, *Life in the Spirit Seminars*, 8-13. See also The Word of God, *The Life in the Spirit Seminars Team Manual*, 95-105.

177 Ibid., 26-32. See also International Catholic Charismatic Renewal Office, *Life in the Spirit Seminars*, 14-19. See also The Word of God, *The Life in the Spirit*

3.2.4.4 Week Four: Receiving God's Gift (Call for Conversion)

The Lord expects we turn away from sins and come back to Him. He wants that we must receive the gift of new life in the Holy Spirit. We may have confusion or fear about the uncertainty of the future. However, we need not fear or worry because Jesus loves us. He wants that we receive the gift, which He is offering to every one of us. Jesus wants to give us the fullness of life in the Holy Spirit. We may feel we are sinners and not worthy of receiving Jesus' gift. However, the fact is that we do not receive the gift because we are worthy or holy people, we receive Jesus' gift gratuitously. Jesus loves us and He freely gives us of His Holy Spirit. When we make a commitment to follow His ways, He changes our lives radically. He gives us His Holy Spirit who leads us in all truth. He equips us with the charisms needed to work for the glory of God. Once we are in relationship with the Holy Spirit, we will find that our life is no longer the same. Our prayer life will improve dramatically. There will be deep surging within us to be with the Lord in silence. As we grow in faith, we will see the Holy Spirit will activate His charisms in our lives. We must be open to these charisms and must not be afraid or ashamed to use them for the good of the Church. Above all, we need to learn to entrust our lives into the hands of the Almighty.

The model of the prayer of commitment used in these seminars is as follows: Lord Jesus Christ I want to belong to you from now on. I want to be freed from the dominion of darkness and the rule of Satan. I want to enter into your kingdom. I will turn away from all wrongdoing and I will avoid everything that leads me to wrongdoing. I ask you to forgive all my sins. I offer my life to you and I promise to obey you as my Lord. I ask you to baptize me in the Holy Spirit and give me the gift of tongues.[178]

After this prayer of commitment is made, the leaders pray over the participant for the infilling of the Holy Spirit. The suggested

---

Seminars Team Manual, 106-122.

178 Arikata Kobayashi, *Shinsei he no kadode* [Entrance to New Life] (Tokyo:Catholic Charismatic Renewal of Japan HSRO, 2006), 36. Original text in Japanese. [Translation mine].

Scriptural texts for prayer are Tit 3:4-6; Jn 7:37-38; Mk 1:15; Acts 2:38-39; 1 Cor 6:9-10; Rom 4:20-21; Lk 11.9-13.[179]

3.2.4.5 Week Five: Praying for Baptism in the Holy Spirit

After the leaders pray over the participants, they experience joy and peace in their lives. They realize the importance of having close relationship with Jesus. They begin to spend more time in praising and adoring Him. On the other hand, there may be some doubts and confusions, which may loom over them. They may feel that they have made a fool of themselves by believing in the things told to them in the past seminars. However, at this stage of advancement, they must be undeterred by all doubts and confusions. They must resolve to walk ahead with full faith and confidence in the Lord. The Holy Spirit begins to work in them in a new way as they allow Him to take over the reins of their lives. Receiving the Holy Spirit does not make them insulated from the troubles and problems of routine life. They remain as before, fragile human beings, but equipped with the power of the Holy Spirit. Therefore, even if they face any problem or discouragement they must not allow it to be obstacle in their relationship with Jesus. They must believe that the Holy Spirit is always present among them especially in difficult times. They need to take time to read the Bible and meditate on it daily. They also need to fix a time for personal prayers. The Scriptural texts suggested for this week are as follows: 1 Pt 5:7-9; Mt 25:23; Eph 6:18; Rom 8:26; 1 Cor 3:1-3; 14:1; 2 Cor 4:16; 5:1-5.[180]

3.2.4.6 Week Six: Growth in the Holy Spirit

The new life, which Jesus offers, is to be lived fully. One needs to grow perennially in faith. Baptism in the Holy Spirit is only the beginning of a long spiritual journey. It is not the crux of spiritual life. If one has the flame of the Holy Spirit within then he or she needs to fan it

179 Ibid., 33-43. See also International Catholic Charismatic Renewal Office, *Life in the Spirit Seminars*, 20-26. See also The Word of God, *The Life in the Spirit Seminars Team Manual*, 123-137.

180 Ibid., 44-55. See also International Catholic Charismatic Renewal Office, *Life in the Spirit Seminars*, 27-32. See also The Word of God, *The Life in the Spirit Seminars Team Manual*, 138-151.

continuously. Just as a person who sows seeds in fertile ground, takes proper care so that it yields maximum fruit, so too the seeds of spiritual life that are planted by the Holy Spirit needs to be nurtured.

The following diagram below explains the new life in the Triune God. The rim of the wheel is the life of the Triune God, the Father, the Son and the Holy Spirit, which becomes the center of a person's life. The spokes of Prayer, Fellowship, Service and Word of God are essential to remain in contact with God. The more one grows in these four areas of life; the more he or she will grow in faith. The Triune God plants the new life but one needs to nurture it. The growth of our Christian life is not automatic and at times it may be painful, but one needs to go ahead by regular prayer life, fellowship with other Christians, service to all, daily meditation and study of the Bible. The suggested Scriptural texts for this week are as follows: Jn 4:14; 15:5-6; Eph 4:22-23; Lk 5:15-16; 2 Tm 3:15-17; Acts 2:41-47; Col 4:5-6.[181]

3.2.4.7 Week Seven: Transformation in Christ

The new life needs to grow. The Holy Spirit helps one in all our weaknesses and leads one to live a better life. One begins to change

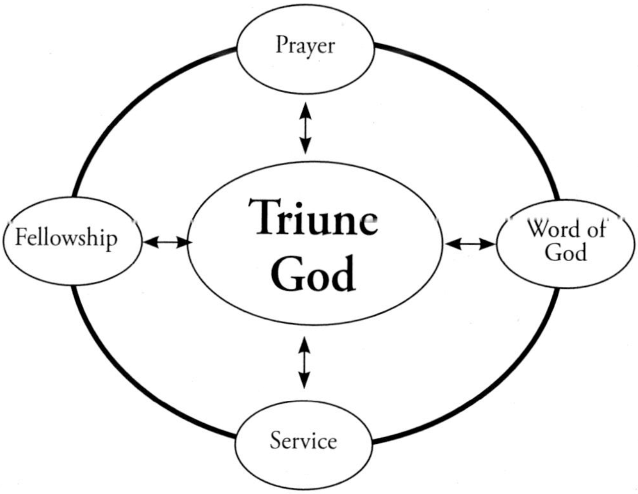

181 Ibid., 56-64. See also International Catholic Charismatic Renewal Office, *Life in the Spirit Seminars*, 33-39. See also The Word of God, *The Life in the Spirit Seminars Team Manual*, 152-163.

for good. One finds the greatest treasure of life is Christ and he or she is ready to give up everything to follow Him more closely. One begins to nurture the new life in him or her. However one's life as a human person continues as usual. There are times of joy and there are times of sorrow. There are occasions when people encourage and acknowledge, but there are times when criticize. The baptism in the Holy Spirit does not change the chores of daily life. Neither is it the aim of the new life. The new life within is to make one aware of the tremendous and dynamic power of the Holy Spirit, which is in work. God is always present and He never abandons anyone. God is ever faithful and He loves everyone. All things work for good. The Lord brings good out of evil (Rom 8:28). In order to remain united with Jesus, one needs to connect with His Body, the Church. Jesus works in one's life through the Church and through other Christians. He wants him or her to take care of the Christian community and help other Christians. The suggested biblical passages for this week are as follows: Phil 2:13; 3:8-9; Jas 1:2-4; 1 Cor 10:13; Rom 8:28; 12:4-5; Heb 10:24-25.[182]

---

182 Ibid., 65-72. See also International Catholic Charismatic Renewal Office, *Life in the Spirit Seminars*, 40-45. See also The Word of God, *The Life in the Spirit Seminars Team Manual*, 164-170.

Chapter 4

The Renewal Brought by the Charismatic Renewal Movement in Japan

The statistical data reveals that 12% of the Japanese Catholics are Charismatics.[183] Even though, the numerical strength of Charismatics is very low, the CCRM has made a good impact on the Catholic Church in Japan. Statistical data is not enough to measure the fruits of the renewal. Renewal is concerned with the lives of persons.[184] We can see the fruits of the renewal by observing the lives of the Charismatics. We can assess the role of the CCRM in the renewal of the Church by studying the testimonies of Charismatics. In the following sections, we shall study the fruits of the CCRM in Japan. In addition, we shall also examine its drawbacks. The intention to study the drawbacks is not to criticize the movement but rather, help this movement to reform itself to serve the people better.

183 See David Barrett and Todd M. Johnson, "The Catholic Charismatic Renewal, 1959-2025," in *Then Peter Stood Up*, 120.

184 See Peter Hocken, "The Impact of the Charismatic Movement on the Roman Catholic Church," in *Journal of Beliefs & Values*, Vol. 25, No. 2 (August 2004): 205-216.

4.1 The Fruits of the Baptism in the Holy Spirit in Japan

The CCRM has touched and is continuing to touch the lives of many people in Japan. People from all occupations have found newness in their relationship with God and the Church. The visible effects of the renewal are their lives themselves. Jesus gave us the yardstick to measure genuine holiness in a person. He said, "You will know them by their fruits... every good tree bears good fruit, but the bad tree bears bad fruit" (Mt 7:16-17). We can be measure the renewal brought by the CCRM by using Jesus' yardstick.

In his address to the Members of the Catholic Fraternity of Charismatic Covenant Communities in Rome on November 14, 1994, Pope John Paul II urged the CCRM to promote holiness among youth, preserve the sanctity of marriage and respect for family life, which are essential to uphold the dignity of a person.

> Your witness can be particularly important for young people, upon whom the ideal of holiness exerts a great fascination. I especially encourage you…to proclaim the sanctity of marriage and the family in accordance with God's plan, and to work to ensure respect for God's gift of life at every level of society.[185]

Pope John Paul II in his address of February 25, 1995 to the Bishops of Japan on their '*Ad Limina*' visit mentioned the need of the renewal of the Church of Japan and he defined renewal as a fervent conversion to Christ and a deep love for the Church. He noted that:

> An ever-present priority of your Episcopal ministry is the renewal of the Catholic community in faith and holiness of life. This renewal is nothing other than a more fervent conversion to Christ, a deeper knowledge and love

185 "Address to the Members of the Catholic Fraternity of Charismatic Covenant Communities, November 14, 1994," *Insegnamenti di Giovanni Paolo II*, 17.2 (1994): 775-777.

> of his person and message, an ever-increasing fidelity of the Church's members to the demands of the Gospel.[186]

Fr. Francis Mathy, a Jesuit missionary priest and leader of the CCRJ has summarized the role CCRM has been playing in the renewal of the Catholic Church of Japan in his article published in *Pentecost Today.* Following is an excerpt of the same.

> [F]rom the beginning the leaders have encouraged those receiving baptism in the Holy Spirit to use their gifts in helping, unobtrusively, to revitalize their parishes, especially by contributing to the formation of genuine Christian community there. We have had some success in this: many of our people are active in parish pastoral committees, religious education programs, music ministry, evangelical outreach, social welfare programs, care of the sick, etc. And their help is much appreciated. The Holy Spirit has been drawing us into more intensive prayer in private and into greater praise at our prayer meetings. The praise often leads to deep adoration in the strongly felt presence of the Lord. The charisms, especially prophecy and the other word gifts, have become more and more manifest. There is a growing devotion to our Lord in the Blessed Sacrament and many quiet hours are spent before the tabernacle.[187]

The CCRM emphasizes on the phenomenon of baptism in the Holy Spirit. The CCRJ organizes Life in the Spirit Seminars all over Japan to teach about this phenomenon. Baptism in the Holy Spirit is not the climax but the point of new departure in a Christian's life. St. Paul says, "If we live by the Spirit, let us also be guided by the Spirit" (Gal 5:25). A person baptized in the Spirit begins to live his or her Christian life with greater joy, love and peace. He or she rediscovers the beauty of being a Christian. The CCRM does not

---

186 "Address to the Bishops of Japan on their 'Ad Limina' Visit on February 25, 1995," *AAS* 88.1 (1996) 1026.

187 Francis Mathy, "What in the World is going on?- Japan," *Pentecost Today*, 26, No.4 (October-December 2001): 4, 15.

consider the baptism in the Holy Spirit as a Sacrament like Baptism or Confirmation. The CCRM has been following the guidelines and teachings of the Catholic Church in order to impart proper teaching on this phenomenon.[188] The CCRM does not claim that the phenomenon of baptism in the Holy Spirit is greater or equal to the Sacraments. Instead, it calls upon all Christians to celebrate the Sacraments meaningfully. It recognizes especially, the importance of the Sacraments of Initiation (Baptism, Confirmation and Holy Eucharist).

The CCRJ organizes seminars, conventions, retreats and workshops regularly all over Japan to teach about the baptism in the Holy Spirit from theological and biblical point of view. The CCRJ takes a lot of effort to translate books, articles and other literature published in other languages to Japanese. It especially translates as soon as possible the literature from ICCRS and other renowned leaders of the CCRM so that the Japanese people can have a regular update of all the teachings and events of the CCRM worldwide.

Apart from proper teaching about baptism in the Holy Spirit, the CCRM also stresses on the actual effects of this phenomenon. People having the experience of the power of the Holy Spirit cannot remain isolated. The CCRM insists that after having an experience of baptism in the Holy Spirit a person must have fellowship with other Christians. Fellowship is important for spiritual growth.

People participating in the CCRM prayer meetings initially find it difficult to praise God in loud voices before others.[189] However, when such a person has an experience of the baptism in the Holy Spirit, then there is a change in his or her attitude. He or she can pray longer. He or she can pray spontaneously. He or she finds it necessary to pray in a community and share with others. He or she does not act superficially, as all fears disappear. He or she feels more comfortable to drop one's guard. In such a true Christian fellowship and sharing

---

188 The Catholic Church has no official teaching on the baptism in the Holy Spirit. However, the doctrinal commission of ICCRS has published a document on it. See ICCRS Doctrinal Commission, *Baptism in the Holy Spirit* (Vatican: ICCRS, 2012).

189 Francis Mathy, "*Seirei No Mitashi Ha...*" [Baptism in the Holy Spirit is...], in *Shu no Ibuki: Bassui Ban* [Breath of the Lord: Excerpts], Vol. 1, 24. Original In Japanese. [Translation mine].

there is mutual growth. There is love and acceptance for one another. The community encourages each member to use his or her gift for the good of the Church. The words of the Bible come alive. Each member uses the gift he or she has for the building up of the Church and in service of others.[190]

When there is genuine sharing in the community, people begin to change. Even though this transformation may not be always instantaneous, definitely some change begins to happen. This transformation and conversion of one's heart, leads to the healing of a person. Thus, a person who receives baptism in the Holy Spirit continues to experience the joy of Christ deep down in his or her heart. This joy and peace are diffusive. Such a person shares the joy and peace of Christ to all those whom he or she comes across. Baptism in the Holy Spirit is not an experience to be lived only when one is in the Church; it is to be lived in one's daily life.[191] It is from the effects that one can easily judge whether a person had a real experience of the power of the Holy Spirit.

Fr. Armand DeMontigny, a Canadian Redemptorist priest ordained in 1940 came to Japan as a missionary in 1948. He was working as the parish priest of Hatsudai Catholic Church where the CCRM prayer meetings began in 1973. The assistant parish priest, Fr. Lessard, gave him the news about the first prayer meeting at Hatsudai Catholic Church. He was extremely angry with Fr. Lessard because he had not taken his permission to organize the prayer meeting in the parish hall. He wanted to cancel the meeting because he thought it would add to the problems of the parish. However, he could not do so because he heard that Fr. Bernadine Schneider would also participate in this meeting. He had a lot of respect for Fr. Schneider and thought it would be best not to cancel the prayer meeting. However, he decided not to participate in it. Fr. DeMontigny confesses that in those days he was reckless and proud. He wanted to block the working of the Holy Spirit, but in vain. Human endeavors cannot defeat the work of the Holy Spirit. Even

190 Francis Mathy, "*Seirei No Mitashi Ha...*" [Baptism in the Holy Spirit is...], in *Shu no Ibuki: Bassui Ban* [Breath of the Lord: Excerpts], Vol. 1, 24. Original In Japanese. [Translation mine], 25.

191 Ibid., 26.

though he was against the CCRM prayer meeting, the Holy Spirit had plans to change him. Within a few weeks after the beginning of the CCRM prayer meeting at Hatsudai Catholic Church, there was a transformation in him. He started attending the weekly prayer meeting. However, for around 3 months, he did not experience the power of the Holy Spirit. It was on a Sunday after the prayer meeting, that he had an experience of deep joy and peace within him. Even though he did not realize that it was the baptism in the Holy Spirit, he felt the transformation in his life. His prayer life deepened. He got a new meaning for all the things he was doing. He continued to grow in faith and love of Christ as years passed on. This experience helped him to be a dynamic priest of the Lord. He wonders what would have happened to him if the Holy Spirit had not led him to the CCRM prayer meeting. He thanks God for the all the graces he received through the CCRM.[192]

Following are the fruit (effects) of the baptism in the Holy Spirit in Japan.

4.1.1 Conversion of Heart and Renewed Interest in Spiritual Life

One of the prominent aims of the CCRM is spiritual renewal. The CCRM emphasizes on the importance of baptism in the Holy Spirit in a Christian's life.[193] Conversion of heart (*metanoia*) is a prerequisite to experience the baptism in the Holy Spirit. Cardinal Léon Joseph Suenens notes that:

> A Christian is radically a 'convert.' The first Christians, those of Pentecost morning had to undergo a complete change of mind and heart, a *metanoia* a break with

192 Armand DeMontigny, "*Are Kara Mou Juu Nen*" [Already Ten Years After It], in *Shu no Ibuki: Bassui Ban* [Breath of the Lord: Excerpts], Vol. 6 (Tokyo: Catholic Charismatic Renewal of Japan, 1993), 33-35. Original in Japanese. [Translation mine].

193 See Paul Thigpen, "Catholic Charismatic Movement," in *The New International Dictionary of Pentecostal and Charismatic Movements*, 465. Vincent Walsh, *A Key to Charismatic Renewal in the Church* (St. Meinrad: Abbey Press, 1977), 41.

> manifold ties. Baptism meant for them: death to the 'old man,' deliverance, liberation, a new life.[194]

Genuine *metanoia* leads a person to live a life of holiness. God wills that we live a life of holiness. A number of scripture passages very clearly indicate that God desires that everyone must lead a holy life. "You shall be holy to me; for I the Lord am holy, and I have separated you from the other peoples to be mine" (Lv 20:26). "For this is the will of God, your sanctification" (1 Thes 4:3). "May the God of peace himself sanctify you entirely; and may your spirit and soul and body be kept sound and blameless at the coming of our Lord Jesus Christ" (1 Thes 5:23).

What is holiness? Does holiness mean to cut off all connections with the outside world? Albert Marie DeMonléon argues that, "Holiness is not in the first place a moral perfection or the result of a planned life of asceticism. It is, above all, the complete and loving belonging to God."[195] A life of holiness does not mean following a set of rules faithfully, but being open to the Holy Spirit. It means to allow the Spirit, the Sanctifier to sanctify a person interiorly. A person must train himself or herself to know what is God's will for him or her and must continuously seek to accomplish it with God's grace. However, a person must discern every inspiration in prayer. God's inspiration can never contradict the message of the bible and the teachings of the Church.

Pope John Paul II considered holiness as an essential part of Charismatic spirituality. He noted that, "I hope that the spirituality of Pentecost will spread in the Church as a renewed incentive to prayer, holiness, communion and proclamation."[196] Further, he connected the Charismatic spirituality with holiness. He emphasizes that holiness should not be an option but a priority in every age. The

---

194 Léon Joseph Suenens, *A New Pentecost?*, (New York: The Seabury Press, 1975), 117.

195 Albert Marie DeMonléon, "The Movements as Places of a Transfigured Humanity," in *Movements in the Church* (Vatican: Pontificum Consilium Pro Laicis, 1999), 162.

196 "Celebration of the First Vespers of Pentecost on May 29, 2004," *Insegnamenti di Giovanni Paolo II*, No. 3, 27.1 (2004): 713.

CCRM must encourage people to reflect on the call of holiness. Pope John Paul II noted that:

> [H]oliness is the priority in every age, and therefore also in our own time. The Church and the world need saints, and we ourselves become holier the more we allow the Holy Spirit to configure us to Christ. This is the secret of the regenerating experience of the 'outpouring of the Spirit', a typical experience that defines the process of growth proposed for the members of your groups and communities. I hope that Renewal in the Spirit may be a true gymnasium in the Church for prayer, asceticism, virtue and holiness.[197]

Spiritual renewal and transformation are the main goals of the CCRM. It aims at the renewal of the whole Church by the renewal of individual members. Many people in Japan have experienced an inner renewal and transformation of their lives because of their contact with the CCRM. The CCRM has helped many people to renew their relationship with God, others and their own selves. Pope John Paul II noted in his address of April 4, 1998 to the leaders of the Renewal in the Spirit that the CCRM has helped many people to change their lives, have an ardent faith in God and actively engage themselves as Catholics. He noted that:

> The Catholic Charismatic movement is one of the many fruits of the Second Vatican Council, which, like a new Pentecost, led to an extraordinary flourishing in the Church's life of groups and movements particularly sensitive to the action of the Spirit. How can we not give thanks for the precious spiritual fruits that the Renewal has produced in the life of the Church and in the lives of so many people? How many lay faithful men, women, young people, adults and the elderly have been able to experience in their own lives the amazing power of the Spirit and his gifts. How many people have rediscovered the faith, the joy of prayer, the power and beauty of the Sacred Scriptures,

197 "Address to a Delegation of Members of the Renewal in the Spirit on March 14, 2002," *Insegnamenti di Giovanni Paolo II*, No. 4, 25.1 (2002) 361.

> translating all this into generous service in the Church's mission. How many lives have been profoundly changed? For all this today, together with you, I wish to praise and thank the Holy Spirit.[198]

Again, in his address of March 14, 2002 Pope John Paul II noted the following about the effects of the CCRM.

> Yes. The Renewal in the Spirit can be considered a special gift of the Holy Spirit to the Church in our time. Born in the Church and for the Church, your movement is one in which, following the light of the Gospel, the members experience the living encounter with Jesus, fidelity to God in personal and community prayer, confident listening to his Word and a vital rediscovery of the Sacraments, not to mention courage in trials and hope in hardship.[199]

Leaders of the CCRM in Japan have taken efforts to teach people especially those who have received baptism in the Holy Spirit at the CCRM gatherings to know the real meaning of renewal and its effects. This is because initially people having an experience of the baptism in the Spirit, may have a conversion of heart and thus transform their spiritual lives. However, with the passage of time, they loose their initial zeal. If there is no growth in spiritual life then there is a strong possibility that they can regress. Therefore, it is necessary that all those who have experienced the power of the Holy Spirit in their lives must make efforts to grow in holiness and in their spiritual lives. The CCRM in Japan has been constantly emphasizing that a genuine renewal in the Holy Spirit is not only a spiritual renewal but also a total renewal of a person, which covers all the facets of his or her life.[200] In 1 Thes 5:23, St. Paul prays for the total sanctification

198 Address to the Eight Meeting of the Catholic Confraternity of Charismatic Covenant Communities and Fellowships, *Insegnamenti di Giovanni Paolo II*, 21.1 (1998): 1262-1265.

199 "Address to the National Congress of the Italian "Renewal in the Holy Spirit," *Insegnamenti di Giovanni Paolo II*, No. 2, 25.1 (2002): 359-361.

200 Francis Mathy, "*Rei ni Okeru Deai: Jibun to Hito to Kami*" [Encounter in the Spirit: Self, Others and God], in *Shu no Ibuki: Bassui Ban* [Breath of the Lord: Excerpts], Vol. 3, 85. Original in Japanese. [Translation mine].

of body, soul and spirit of the Thessalonians. "May the God of peace himself sanctify you entirely; and may your spirit and soul and body be kept sound and blameless at the coming of our Lord Jesus Christ" (1 Thes 5:23). Renewal must bring total sanctification in the body, mind and spirit of a person.

The renewal and sanctification in the Holy Spirit leads a person to have a renewal of relationship with self, others and God. After the baptism in the Holy Spirit, a person begins to experience the power of the Holy Spirit in his or her life. He or she becomes more humane. He or she also begins to have deeper self-knowledge, which eventually leads a person to have a better self-image and at the same time to humbly accept one's weaknesses and shortcomings.[201]

The new life that the Holy Spirit plants in a person's life is like a seed. Such a person needs to sow it in a fertile ground in order to nurture it. He or she needs to take care of the sapling so that it grows and becomes fruitful. For this, a person needs to spend time in prayer and silence. A person must root his or her faith in God and not on emotional gratifications or consolations received during prayer. At the same time, a person must be aware of the fact the transformation and renewal that has begun in one's life is a life-long process. No one can reach the stage of perfection in a spur of the moment.[202]

A person who begins to grow in his or her spiritual life begins to let go egoism and self-centeredness. He or she becomes more other-centered. He or she finds meaning in the fellowship with other Christians, united through the Sacraments of Baptism and Confirmation. He or she realizes the meaning of being members of the body of Christ. "We who are many, are one body in Christ, and individually we are members one of another" (Rom 12:5). He or she begins to appreciate the good in others and begins to serve others. The Holy Eucharist becomes an essential part of such a person's life because it becomes the summit of thanksgiving to God, the Father through Jesus Christ in the Holy Spirit and binds all the faithful in love and unity.[203]

---

201 Francis Mathy, "*Rei ni Okeru Deai: Jibun to Hito to Kami*" [Encounter in the Spirit: Self, Others and God], in *Shu no Ibuki*: *Bassui Ban* [Breath of the Lord: Excerpts], Vol. 3, 86. Original in Japanese. [Translation mine].

202 Ibid., 87.

203 Ibid., 88.

Following are the testimonies of people who have experienced renewal and transformation in their lives through the power of the Holy Spirit. Fr. Chikara Hashimoto, a diocesan priest of Sapporo diocese mentions about his renewal of life as a priest because of his involvement with the CCRM.

> There was no CCRM prayer meeting in Hokkaido. I had absolutely no idea of the contents of the CCRM. I did not know that the CCRM organizes prayer meetings at Tokyo. I consider it God's grace in spite of my ignorance He brought me in contact with the CCRM. I think it is mysterious. Every year I would go with my priest friend to different Churches to spend some time in relaxation. One particular year we went to Akita (Northeast region of Japan) city and incidentally we went into Tsuchisaki Catholic Church to make a quick visit. After visiting the Blessed Sacrament, Fr. Rüthers, the parish priest who belongs to the Society of Divine Word (SVD) invited us for a cup of coffee. He mentioned to us about the activities of the CCRM. I had absolutely no interest in the CCRM at that time. However, before we left, Fr. Rüthers handed me a list of books about the CCRM. When I returned to my diocese in Sapporo, I was inspired to buy one of the books mentioned in the list to know something about the works of the Holy Spirit. I ordered Dennis J. Bennett's book called *Nine O'clock in the Morning* (1970). As I started reading this book, I was fascinated. I continued to read it. I read about the marvelous works that the Holy Spirit is doing in this age. I was astonished to read that the effects of Pentecost, which occurred 2000 years ago, are continuing even in our age. With all theological studies and faith life, I had no explanation for these things. On the other hand, I started doubting about these things. I was keen to know how the Catholic Church has responded to the happenings of the CCRM. There was no one around to clarify my doubts. I started to read all the available material on the CCRM. Moreover, as I was reading by the inspiration of

> the Holy Spirit, all my doubts disappeared. The address of Pope Paul VI given to those associated with the CCRM in Rome in 1975 impressed me. All my doubts completely disappeared after I read the Pope's address.... When the Vicar of Christ, the guide of the Catholic Church, the Holy Father himself spoke words of encouragement about the CCRM, all my doubts about the CCRM disappeared. I had a strong urge to receive baptism in the Holy Spirit and so I started attending the prayer meeting held at Hatsudai Catholic Church in Tokyo. I used to travel all the way from Sapporo to Tokyo to attend the prayer meetings to prepare myself to surrender to the Lord. The following year in 1978, I attended the Leaders' Workshop and asked the core group members of the CCRM prayer meeting belonging to Hatsudai Catholic Church to pray over me for baptism in the Spirit. That day became the turning point of my priestly life. I began to have a profound taste for the Holy Eucharist and prayer, which I had never experienced before. The Bible became alive to me. It became the source of life. Again, even in the smallest thing I found a deep joy to serve the community. Besides these blessed gifts, I have received countless graces from the Lord. The spirit led me to start the first CCRM prayer group at Sapporo. The Lord used a poor and powerless instrument like me to ignite the flame of the Holy Spirit in the far north, Hokkaido region of Japan.... Once the Holy Spirit renews a person, he or she witnesses to his or her faith at their respective parishes and place of work.... The Church in Japan is weak and so is in great need of renewal.[204]

Fr. Clement Painter, a Passionist priest testifies that the CCRM changed his life. He was convinced that the CCRM was for the good of the Church. He introduced the CCRM to a Catholic priest

204 Chikara Hashimoto, "*Kita no Chi ni Seirei no Hi ga*" [The Fire of the Holy Spirit in the North], *Ikeru Mizu*, No. 46 (Special Edition 1997): 3-4. Original in Japanese. [Translation mine].

in Philippines, Fr. Bart Pastor who later became a very famous international charismatic preacher.

> The first time I encountered the Charismatic Renewal was in 1970 at the Meifu Retreat House where a group of Pentecostals were doing a retreat. I heard this group singing and praying in tongues. However, at that time I did not know anything about the Charismatics. I thought that they have gone mad. The pastor wanted to pray over me for baptism in the Spirit, but I refused because I did not want to become crazy like them. After that, I went to the USA for vacations in 1972 and stayed with my cousins at California. My cousins were leaders of a CCRM prayer group. I stayed in their house for 5 days and during these days, I had a chance to go through many books and tapes about the renewal. However, more than the books and tapes what struck me more was the life of my cousins. They witnessed their faith, prayer and joy through their life. I was highly impressed by this and had a deep desire to be like them. Before leaving them, I attended a prayer meeting. The leaders there prayed over to receive baptism in the Spirit. Though I did not receive the gift of tongues that time, I felt a tremendous joy and liberation in my life.... In 1973, the Archbishop of Cebu, Philippines invited me to preach four retreats for the diocesan priests. I wanted to refuse but since the Cardinal himself requested me, I accepted the offer. In the first two retreats, I never spoke directly about the CCRM but indirectly spoke about it using Merlin R. Carothers' book *Power in Praise*. In the third week, I shared my experience of the CCRM and all appreciated it. Therefore, the following week for the fourth retreat too I decided to share my experience of the CCRM...During the fourth retreat I spoke passionately about the CCRM. I felt that the Holy Spirit had kindled His fire at least in one priest. The next day I returned to Japan. Twenty-five long years have passed since I gave those four retreats in Philippines

> and I forgot about it. Last year the CCRJ invited Fr. Bart Pastor a charismatic priest to preach a retreat for priests and to lead the Kansai regional CCRM convention. This year when Fr. Bart met Fr. Motoyuki Hata (from Japan) in Philippines, he told him that he came in contact with the CCRM 25 years ago because a Passionist priest who came from Japan introduced the CCRM during the retreat for the priests. In fact, Fr. Bart had attended the fourth retreat, which I preached 25 years ago in Cebu, Philippines. That retreat had a tremendous effect on his life. He had a radical transformation in his life and he became a great instrument of God. Presently he is the leader of the CCRM in the Philippines. This happening shows that God can use anyone to work great wonders. All that the Lord needs is our *Yes.*[205]

Kenji Iwabuchi testifies that Jesus transformed and renewed his life. *Ikeru Mizu*, newsletter of the CCRJ published his testimony. It is as follows:

> Right from my childhood, I was seeking something. I realized it when I was going to the Middle School. However, I did not know what it was that I was seeking. I did many bad things like fights, smoking, blackmail, setting fire and refusing to go to school. My heart was always restless. I wanted to go to High School but, I told the teacher that I did not want to continue studies. I expected the teacher to coax me to reconsider my decision but to my surprise, the teacher told me to return to my home. After that, I went to a training school and got a government job. I had a good job. If I had continued to work at the same place then I could have led a stable life as a government official. However, in my youth I hated stable life. I wanted to start a music band group and show off. Therefore, I gave up my job and started a band with my

205 Clement Painter, "*Seirei no Hi ha Firipin Ni*" [The fire of the Holy Spirit in Philippines], *Ikeru Mizu*, No. 46 (Special Edition 1997): 14-15. Original in Japanese. [Translation mine].

friends. I continued this job for 20 years as an entertainer. However, even my passion for music did not satisfy me. My heart was seeking something else. I got married and had a child. I quit the night entertainment job and took up a daytime job to take care of the child. However, as I was used to night work, I could not adjust myself to daytime jobs and I could not continue daytime job for long. At that time, I also stood as a guarantee for a bad loan, which my friend had taken. I became a debtor. I had no proper job and to add to my problems, the debt of my friend made my life a hell and I became mentally ill. I had to go to the hospital for treatment. My married life was in doldrums and I took custody of my son. There was no other way but to return to the night job. However, times had changed and there was no place for music bands. So, I worked at host clubs (adult entertainment bars in Japan) and at the end as a pimp. I could not take care of my son and asked my elder sister to take care of him. On a New Year's Day my parents, siblings and myself came together for a gathering. All were busy with their spouses and children. Nobody was concerned about me. I felt very lonely and felt nobody has any interest in me. I thought there is no point in living. I took the month's dose of medicines to commit suicide. Then I slit my wrist repeatedly. As I was getting unconscious, I felt I was dying. However, before dying, I wanted to hear my son's voice so I called my son who was with my elder sister. My elder sister understood that something was wrong with me and immediately called for help. When I regained consciousness, I was in hospital. I wanted to change my life so I joined a designing school at the age of 36. There I met a Protestant friend who gave a Marian medal. He told me to keep it close to me. I do not know why a Protestant was carrying a Marian medal. It is mysterious. A few years later, I went to a departmental store. I saw that the Catholic bookstore had put up many books for sale. When I went there, someone recommended me to go to Yamahana Catholic Church. The next Sunday

> I went to the Church and at that time, the Holy Mass had just begun. At that time, it suddenly dawned on me that this is the thing, which I was seeking from my childhood. All these years I was searching for Jesus. That day I met Jesus and my life changed.[206]

Kana Haruta attended the Life in the Spirit Seminar in 1998 and received baptism in the Holy Spirit. She says that after the infilling of the Holy Spirit she could experience God in her heart. Prior to the infilling she would try to know God through her reason alone. Her experience in the Life in the Spirit Seminar helped her to have a personal relationship with God, which she never had before.[207]

Sachie Joumori along with her family attended the 14th Hokkadio regional CCRM convention held in May 1999. She testifies that the convention helped her family to take renewed interest in family prayers. Every evening the family gathers for prayer, praise and worship. She is happy that her family is growing in the love of the Lord.[208]

Haruyo Koguma in her testimony published in *Ikeru Mizu*, newsletter of the CCRJ shares her experience of God in the midst of suffering and pain. Haruyo Koguma had a miscarriage when she was in the twelfth week of pregnancy. She got married at the age of 36 and so she was thinking to raise a family as soon as possible, but sadly, she lost her unborn child. This brought a lot of suffering and sorrow in her life. In this time of pain, the CCRM prayer group of Shibuya Catholic Church supported her and gave her a strong spiritual support. Weeks later, she realized that she always had her plans and she never cared for God's plan. What was lacking on her part was a total surrender to God's plan. She quotes Is 55:8 where the Lord says, "For my thoughts are not your thoughts, nor are your

---

206 Kenji Iwabuchi, "*Iesu to no Deai*" [Encounter with Jesus], *Ikeru Mizu*, No. 49 (Summer Edition 1998): 2-3. Original in Japanese. [Translation mine].

207 Kana Haruta, "*Hajimete no Seirei no Mitashi*" [Being Filled with the Holy Spirit], *Ikeru Mizu*, No. 50 (Fall Edition 1998): 4. Original in Japanese. [Translation mine].

208 Shirou Ishii, "*Dai JuuYon Kai Seirei ni Yoru Sasshin Hokkaido Taikai Hirakareru*" [14th Hokkaido Regional CCRM Convention Opens], *Ikeru Mizu*, No. 53 (Summer Edition 1999): 2. Original in Japanese. [Translation mine].

ways my ways, says the LORD." She believed that in all her suffering and pain God was with her. Her unborn child was enjoying heavenly bliss and praying for her family. She further says that in spite of the sufferings, her family has grown in love for one another. There is unity in the family. She thanks the CCRM for helping her build close relationship with God as her Father.[209]

Hideko Nishiyama received Baptism when she was a youth. She tried to involve herself with the Church activities. However, she felt that she never cared for the Lord's will. She felt the Lord is telling her that she is missing something in her faith life. With this struggle going on within her, she participated in the Life in the Spirit Seminar and spiritual exercises preached by Fr. Francis Mathy. This spiritual experience changed her. She testifies that before her encounter with the CCRM, she would try to understand God through her reason alone, but after her conversion, she realized the importance of surrender and the power of the Holy Spirit in her life.[210]

Misa Shimada attended the National CCRM convention held in 2000. She testifies that it was very difficult for her to leave her children with her 80-year-old mother. However, God made it possible for her to participate in the convention. The talks and prayer at the convention healed the dryness and bitterness within her. After the convention, she felt there had been a great change in her. She was able to praise God even when things did not work out well. She was able to relate to those whom she avoided before. She used to be a short-tempered person but after the convention, she found that she became much sober and could surrender all her problems and worries to the Lord.[211]

---

209 Haruya Koguma, "*Ikiru ni Shite Mo Shinu ni Shite Mo, Watashi ha Shu no Mono Desu*" [Whether we Live or Die We Belong to the Lord], *Ikeru Mizu*, No. 54 (Fall Edition 1999): 9-10. Original in Japanese. [Translation mine].

210 Hideko Nishiyama, "*Dai Seinen ni Itadaita Megumi*" [Graces Received During the Great Holy Year], *Ikeru Mizu*, No. 56 (Spring Edition 1999): 1-2. Original in Japanese. [Translation mine].

211 Misa Shimada, "*Samariajin no You ni Shougenshitai*" [I Want To Testify Like Samaritan] in *Jesus 2000: Shu no Eiko he no Maneki* [Jesus 2000: Invited to Partake in the Glory of the Lord], 47. Original in Japanese. [Translation mine].

Haruya Murai had many familial problems. Her husband was not taking care of her and her second son used to beat her and her younger son. She had to leave her home because of the escalation of domestic violence. Her eldest son was also not interested in the family matters. With all these problems and sufferings, she attended the Kanto regional CCRM convention held in 2001. It was during the convention she got the grace to forgive her husband and the two sons. God liberated her from all heavy burdens in her heart. She could praise and thank God freely. There was also a change in her elder son's attitude. He repented for his bad behavior toward her.[212]

Sachiko Kamiya had difficulty in relating to God as a loving Father. This was because in her childhood she did not receive much love from her father. After receiving Baptism, she started attending the Life in the Spirit Seminar held in Fujisawa Catholic Church. She changed her attitude after encountering Jesus in the CCRM Seminar. When the leaders prayed over her for the infilling of the Spirit she could forgive her father and experience God as loving father.[213]

The editorial board of the *Ikeru Mizu* published a testimony of a recent convert to Catholicism. This person faced lot of difficulties in her life. It was in such a situation she started participating in Life in the Spirit Seminar. Her life started changing gradually. She understood that the trials she is facing in life are graces, which she has to accept. She thanks God for the Seminar because through it she could deepen her prayer life and have a firm faith in the Lord.[214]

A person, who is truly seeking to do the will of God, finds a tremendous progress in his or her prayer life (personal and

212 Haruya Murai, "*Kokoro no Kaihou Kara Hajimatta Kami no Miwaza*" [God's Grandeur Began with the Liberation of My Heart] in *2001 Seirei ni Yoru Sasshin Kanto Taikai: Dai Rokkai Hokokusho, Oki ni Kogidase* [Sixth Catholic Charismatic Renewal Convention, 2001: Put Out Into the Deep], (Tokyo: Catholic Charismatic Renewal of Japan, Kanto Region, 2001), 45-46. Original in Japanese. [Translation mine].

213 Masaaki Terada, "*Yokohama, Shounan Chiku no Hataraki*" [The Happenings at Yokohama and Shounan Region], *Ikeru Mizu*, No. 79 (Fall Edition 2006): 9. Original in Japanese. [Translation mine].

214 Editorial Board of *Ikeru Mizu*, "*Seirei ni Yoru Sasshin Semina wo Ukete*" [Participating in Life in the Spirit Seminar], *Ikeru Mizu*, No. 86 (Fall Edition 2007): 9-10. Original in Japanese. [Translation mine].

communitarian) and a genuine transformation of one's personal life. Further, growth in prayer life is one of the most common effects of baptism in the Holy Spirit. Those who have experience of baptism in the Holy Spirit begin to spend time in personal as well as communitarian prayer. Some make special efforts to spend time in meditation before the Blessed Sacrament every day. While others pray the breviary, rosary and intercessory prayers in small groups either daily or on regular basis. Apart from communitarian prayer, the CCRM encourages people to spend time in personal prayer. Personal prayer is the backbone of the spiritual and interior life. Pope John Paul II in his General Audience of April 17, 1991 noted that,

> The first and the most excellent form of the interior life is prayer. The teachers and masters of the spiritual life are so convinced of this that they often present the interior life as a life of prayer. The principal author of this life is the Holy Spirit, as he was already in Christ.[215]

In his address of March 14, 2002 to the members of the renewal in the Spirit, Pope John Paul II noted that,

> In a special way continue to love and spread love for the prayer of praise, the form of prayer that recognizes more immediately that God is God; praises him for his own sake, gives him glory for who he is, long before thinking of what he does .[216]

Further, Pope John Paul II in his address of May 20, 1980 to the Bishops of Japan on their '*Ad Limina*' visit noted that prayer is an essential part of the Church's life. He commended the Japanese Church because of the increase of vocations to contemplative religious life. He noted that:

> Precisely by reason of the central dimension of faith we see the great value that prayer has in the Church: faith

215 "General Audience of April 17, 1991," *Insegnamenti di Giovanni Paolo II*, 14.1 (1991): 785-789.

216 "Address to a Delegation of Members of the Renewal in the Spirit on March 14, 2002," *AAS* 25.1 (2002): 361.

> is kept alive and is fortified by prayer. By prayer, hearts are opened to the promptings of the Holy Spirit and to the message and action of Christ's Church. Hence, we know that fidelity to prayer is an essential element of the Church's life.
>
> In this regard Japan has been blessed with contemplative vocations, with religious who carry on Christ's loving praise of his Father. And in this contemplative aspect of the Church's life in Japan is there not an excellent element of dialogue with your non-Christian brethren, who in their own ancient traditions have given a place of prominence to contemplation? Is not the desire to be united with God in purity of heart one of those elements in which the teaching of our Saviour Jesus Christ is so naturally inculturated into the lives of so many of your people?[217]

Pope Benedict XVI in his message of May 22, 2006 to the participants of the Second World Congress of Ecclesial Movements and New Communities told the members of the CCRM that they could use the Liturgy of the hours (breviary) as part of their prayers. "May you be sustained by participating in the prayer of the Church, whose liturgy is the most exalted expression of the beauty of God's glory, and in a certain way a glimpse of Heaven upon the earth."[218]

Pope Benedict XVI said that prayer is the most important thing in the life of Christians. He noted that that it is through prayer we can attune ourselves to the promptings of the Holy Spirit.

> The Acts of the Apostles stresses that '[a]ll these with one accord devoted themselves to prayer' (1:14). Prayer, therefore, is the principle activity of the nascent Church through which she receives her unity from the Lord and lets herself be guided by his will, as shown by

217 "Address to the Bishops of Japan on their '*Ad Limina*' Visit on May 20, 1980," *AAS* 72.1 (1980): 400.

218 "Message to the Participants of the Second World Congress of Ecclesial Movements and New Communities, May 22, 2006," *Insegnamenti di Benedetto XVI*, 2.1 (2006): 662-665.

> the decision to cast lots in order to elect the one who would take Judas' place (cf. Acts 1: 26).[219]

Leaders of the CCRM in Japan have always insisted the need for a strong prayer life for all, especially the Charismatics. The CCRM encourages people to base their prayer on the Trinitarian spirituality. As the prayers of the Catholic Church are Trinitarian in nature, generally in CCRM prayer meetings all the prayers are addressed to God, the Father through Jesus in the Holy Spirit.[220]

The CCRM insists on a strong prayer life because without prayer it is not possible to advance in the spiritual life. After receiving the baptism in the Holy Spirit, one experiences a deep thirst for prayer and holiness, but as time passes there is a possibility of backsliding unless one makes prayer a part of one's life. Baptism in the Holy Spirit is not a magical thing. Christians who have the experience of the baptism in the Spirit continue to be human persons with all the possibilities of being tempted to sin. There is a constant bombardment of secular ideas from this world and the society that surrounds them, therefore in such a situation prayer is an essential means to nurture their spiritual life and a powerful shield to guard and protect them from all forces that are opposed to the Kingdom of God.[221]

Jesus told His disciples a parable about "their need to pray always and not to lose heart" (Lk 18:1). Again, St. Paul mentions about the necessity of praying unceasingly. "Pray without ceasing" (1 Thes 5:17). St. Paul's advice to pray unceasingly seems very difficult to practice, especially for the Japanese who are usually busy with their work the entire day. In Japan, one may not easily find time for prayer.

---

219 "Homily on the Solemnity of Pentecost, May 11, 2008," *Insegnamenti di Benedetto XVI*, 4.1 (2008): 763-767.

220 Armand DeMontigny, "*Inore Taezu Inore*, 2" [Pray Unceasingly Pray, 2], in *Shu no Ibuki: Bassui Ban* [Breath of the Lord: Excerpts], Vol. 2 (Tokyo: Catholic Charismatic Renewal of Japan, 1992), 1-3. Original in Japanese. [Translation mine].

221 Armand DeMontigny, "*Inore Taezu Inore*, 1" [Pray Unceasingly Pray, 1], in *Shu no Ibuki: Bassui Ban* [Breath of the Lord: Excerpts], Vol. 1 (Tokyo: Catholic Charismatic Renewal of Japan, 1992), 83-84. Original in Japanese. [Translation mine].

However, the CCRM in Japan recommends all the participants of prayer meetings, retreats and conventions to spend time in prayer and meditation.

The CCRM encourages people to first prepare themselves for prayer and to put themselves before the Almighty God. Secondly, they advice them to find some time, if possible a particular time everyday, which is most suitable for them for prayer. About the method of prayer, the CCRM encourages each person to follow the guidance of the Holy Spirit. The CCRM asks people to prayer relaxedly. The CCRM also teaches people to pray the *Liturgy of Hours*, which is full of praise and thanksgiving to God. In the CCRM meetings, people also pray the Rosary. They do not consider the Rosary as a mechanical prayer, but a prayer about the mystery of salvation.[222] The CCRM encourages people to use both formal and informal prayers, as the Spirit leads them. The Spirit's guidance is of paramount importance for a fruitful prayer life.

Apart from fixed time for prayer, the CCRM also asks people to seek the guidance of the Spirit in all the activities of their life.[223] St. Paul says, "Likewise the Spirit helps us in our weakness; for we do not know how to pray as we ought, but that very Spirit intercedes with sighs too deep for words" (Rom 8:26).

In the CCRM prayer meetings, leaders use different methods of prayer. They use the prayers of different schools of spirituality. They also use the Jesus prayer (repeating the name of Jesus) or repeating any phrase from the Holy Bible meditatively and slowly. The leaders request people to prayer for those who are suffering. They also recommend prayers asking for physical, emotional and spiritual healing. They highly recommend praying for healing of memories, deliverance from resentment and for the grace to forgive.[224]

---

222 Armand DeMontigny, "*Inore Taezu Inore,* 1" [Pray Unceasingly Pray, 1], in *Shu no Ibuki: Bassui Ban* [Breath of the Lord: Excerpts], Vol. 1 (Tokyo: Catholic Charismatic Renewal of Japan, 1992), 84-86. Original in Japanese. [Translation mine],

223 Haku Sasaki, "*Seirei ni Ikasareta Atarashii Seikatsu*" [A New Life in the Holy Spirit], in *Shu no Ibuki: Bassui Ban* [Breath of the Lord: Excerpts], Vol. 1, 93-94. Original in Japanese. [Translation mine].

224 Martin Lafont, "*Inori de Kami no Koe wo Kiku*" [To Listen to God's Voice Through Prayer], in *Shu no Ibuki: Bassui Ban* [Breath of the Lord: Excerpts],

One of the important forms of prayer in the CCRM is prayer of praise and thanksgiving. A considerable part of the CCRM prayer meetings is praise and thanksgiving. The leaders consider it as very important because through praise and thanksgiving one acknowledges the sovereignty, greatness and the beauty of God. Praising God also means that one acknowledges His presence in one's life and activities. True praise comes out of a heart that is convinced of God's goodness. Prayer of praise and thanksgiving also reflects the depth of one's faith in God, who works all things for good for those who love him (See Rom 8:28).[225]

Leaders of the CCRM in Japan have always insisted on a balanced prayer life. By balanced prayer life, they mean that every person must find enough time for personal as well as communitarian prayer. The CCRM cautions the Charismatics not to neglect their daily tasks in order to spend time in prayer or attending prayer meetings. At the same time, the CCRM urges Charismatics to take care about the spiritual dryness in their lives. When people receive the baptism in the Holy Spirit, initially they have a great desire for prayer, but gradually as time passes, they lose fervor. This happens because many people focus on emotions and consolations, which they receive in prayer. When they do not find emotional gratification or consolation in prayer, they begin to doubt about the real presence of the Holy Spirit in their lives and tend to give up prayer. Again, if people come across sufferings and difficulties in their lives, they begin to doubt about God's existence. Therefore, the CCRM leaders have always insisted that people should not seek consolations from God during prayer, but rather God Himself. Prayer must spring not out of emotions but out of absolute faith and trust in God.[226]

Some people can pray easily in a prayer group. They think praying must include singing loudly, praising God in tongues and

---

Vol. 2, 4-6. Original in Japanese. [Translation mine].

225 DeMontigny, "Mottomo Sugureta Inori Ha Sanbi Desu" [The Best Prayer is Praise], in *Shu no Ibuki: Bassui Ban* [Breath of the Lord: Excerpts], Vol. 2, 37-40. Original in Japanese. [Translation mine].

226 George Fischbeck, "*Baransu no Aru Inori no Seikatsu wo*" [Balanced Prayer Life], in *Shu no Ibuki: Bassui Ban* [Breath of the Lord: Excerpts], Vol. 5 (Tokyo: Catholic Charismatic Renewal of Japan, 1993), 71. Original in Japanese. [Translation mine].

thanking God publicly. If any of these elements are lacking then they not consider it as true prayer. Leaders of the CCRM in Japan have rejected such thinking because it is not a part of the Christian spirituality. There is no fixed form or methodology, which the CCRM imposes. Again, every person is free to decide the amount of time for prayer according to his or her life pattern. The CCRM calls upon people to pray fervently as the Holy Spirit leads them. The CCRM has a great respect for the traditional forms of prayer of the Church and in fact recommends them as important means for building a healthy spiritual life.[227]

Following are some of the testimonies of people who have experienced a deepening of their desire to pray and are spending more time in personal and communitarian prayer.

Sr. Francisca Riko Kanna mentions about the deepening of her prayer experience after participating in the CCRM prayer meetings.

> The first time I attended the CCRM meeting was around the last week of July 1974 at Hatsudai Catholic Church. Initially I was shocked to see that a protestant like prayer meeting in a Catholic Church. However, slowly my prejudices about the CCRM disappeared and I too began to praise and thank God with songs and free praises. As I was singing praise and worship songs I felt a tremendous joy and peace in my heart. My heart was full of gratitude and praises were flowing out of my mouth. I thanked God for His strong presence within me. It was the first time in my life I had a deep experience of prayer. I began to pray from my heart.[228]

Abiko Tamasaki testifies that after attending Life in the Spirit seminar, she experienced the infinite love of Jesus. She strongly feels

---

227 George Fischbeck, "*Baransu no Aru Inori no Seikatsu wo*" [Balanced Prayer Life], in *Shu no Ibuki: Bassui Ban* [Breath of the Lord: Excerpts], Vol. 5 (Tokyo: Catholic Charismatic Renewal of Japan, 1993), 72. Original in Japanese. [Translation mine],

228 Francisca Riko Kanna, "*Okinawa ni Seirei no Hi wo Hakonde*" [Carrying the Fire of the Holy Spirit in Okinawa], *Ikeru Mizu*, No. 46 (Special Edition 1997): 13. Original in Japanese. [Translation mine].

His presence in her daily life. She says her spiritual life has deepened and she can spend long time in prayer and worship.[229]

Keiko Kyono participated in the National CCRM convention held in 1998. She testifies that she learnt in the convention, the way to surrender all her worries to the Lord. She notes that being a very timid person, small worries would easily disturb her, but the talks given by the priest during the convention helped her to understand the importance of surrender.[230]

Sadami Ri received the grace of Baptism at the CCRM meetings. She testifies that by participating in the CCRM workshops and retreats her faith and prayer life has deepened. "I received Baptism last year and till today that is the most important thing for me. I am convinced of the Holy Spirit's constant guidance. Prayer has changed my life."[231]

Toshiko Imashiro is a member of the CCRM from a long time. She notes that she begins her day every morning with prayer. The first thing, which she does every morning, is to pray the following, "Good Morning heavenly Father, Jesus Christ and Holy Spirit. Anoint me today afresh. Fill me with the Holy Spirit and lead me."[232]

Shinichi Sasaki became a member of the CCRM in 1992. He notes that the CCRM is ever fresh even though, it began in Japan in 1972. He says that usually a movement loses its initial vigor and vitality with time. It becomes structured. However, in the case of the CCRM it is not so because renewal, refreshment and vitality are its basic elements. The CCRM would mean nothing without freshness and vitality. He says that for him the source of his renewal has been prayer and the Word of God. He testifies that before coming in contact with the CCRM, he was not able to pray or read Sacred

229 Abiko Tamasaki, "*Seirei ni Yoru Seikatsu Sasshin Semina ni Sankashite*" [Participating in the CCRM Life in the Spirit Seminar], *Ikeru Mizu*, No. 46 (Special Edition 1997): 15. Original in Japanese. [Translation mine].

230 Keiko Kyono, "*Shu no Ibuki ga Fuku*" [The Breath of the Lord], *Ikeru Mizu,* No. 47 (Special Edition 1998): 6. Original in Japanese. [Translation mine].

231 Sadami Ri, "*Michibikareru Mama Ni*" [To Be Led], *Ikeru Mizu*, No. 50 (Fall Edition 1998): 3. Original in Japanese. [Translation mine].

232 Toshiko Imashiro, "*Inochi wo Kaetekudasaru Seirei*" [The Holy Spirit Who Changes Lives], *Ikeru Mizu*, No. 50 (Fall Edition 1998): 3. Original in Japanese. [Translation mine].

Scriptures. Nevertheless, his life changed after his contact with the renewal. He notes that:

> If I had not heard the testimonies of brothers and sisters associated with the CCRM then I would not open myself to receive the Holy Spirit. I would not be able to praise God. I would not be able to listen to the Word of God or pray. It is because of the CCRM I am able to serve and love though not adequately. I am very happy that my association with the CCRM has helped me to relate intimately to the Lord.[233]

Shouko Irei participated in the Okinawa regional CCRM convention in September 2000. She notes that in spite of the family problems she decided to attend all the days of the convention. Her participation in the convention gave her much joy and peace. She realized that God is her loving Father. He has forgiven all her sins and accepted her as His child. This realization of God's love deepened her relationship with God.[234]

A 31-year-old woman testified about her experience after participating in the 15th Hokkaido regional CCRM convention in *Ikeru Mizu*. She writes that her father was Catholic but a very strict person. Her father died when she was in high school. She had always harbored rancor against her father because he used to beat her for being naughty. Her image about God as Father was very poor because of her poor image of her own earthly father. Her participation in the CCRM convention gave her an altogether new understanding of the love of the heavenly Father. She was also able to forgive her earthly father and thank him for his timely suggestions, which eventually led her to receive Baptism.[235]

---

233 Shinichi Sasaki, "*Seirei Sasshin to Watashi*" [CCRM and Me], *Ikeru Mizu,* No. 50 (Fall Edition 1998): 7-8. Original in Japanese. [Translation mine].

234 Shoko Irei, "*Okinawa Taikai ni Sankashite*" [Participating in Okinawa Regional CCRM Convention], *Ikeru Mizu,* No. 55 (Winter Edition 1998): 6. Original in Japanese. [Translation mine].

235 Machiko Ishii, "*Dai Juugo Kai Seirei ni Yoru Sasshin Hokkaido Taikai wo Oete*" [Finishing 15th Hokkaido Regional CCRM Convention], *Ikeru Mizu,* No. 57 (Summer Edition 1998): 11. Original in Japanese. [Translation mine].

Yuuko Nakadai has three small children. She has a full time job. She used to be extremely busy with her work in the office and at home. Even though she was a Catholic, she could hardly find time for prayer or Church services. In such a situation, she decided to attend the Kanto regional CCRM convention held in October 2000. Bishop Mizobe's sermon on prayer moved her. The bishop mentioned in his sermon that unless a person faithfully continues in his or her prayer life, he or she would find it difficult to continue their lives as Christians. To neglect prayer would extinguish the flame of the Holy Spirit. Her experiences of the convention lead her to find more time in prayer. She realized that if she had time for reading newspaper, then she could certainly find time for prayer.[236]

Soshi Hosoi participated in the 10th Kansai regional CCRM convention and realized the relation between the need to pray and the purification from sins. She realized that prayer cleanses all the accumulated sins in a person. It is like rubbing smoky glasses. Prayer washes clean and polishes a person. Such a person begins to understand the plan of God in his or her life.[237]

Keiko Sakai participated in the 12th Kansai regional CCRM convention held in May 2005. Fr. Raniero Cantalamessa was the main speaker at the convention. Keiko Sakai praises God for the innumerable graces received during this convention. One of the realizations, which she received, is that, as a person experiences the power of the Holy Spirit in his or her life, the power of evil tries all the more to disturb and tempt that person. Prayer of praise and worship delivers a person from evil influence. She testifies about her struggles after the convention. However, she thanks God for being with her and leading her out of all the difficulties.[238]

---

236 Yuuko Nakadai, "*Inori no Tsudoi ha Ikiteiru*" [Prayer Meetings are Alive], *Ikeru Mizu,* No. 59 (Winter Edition 1998): 6. Original in Japanese. [Translation mine].

237 Soshi Hosoi, "*Dai Juu Kai Kansai Taikai ni Sankashite*" [Participating in 10th Kansai Regional CCRM Convention], *Ikeru Mizu,* No. 73 (Winter Edition 2003): 6. Original in Japanese. [Translation mine].

238 Keiko Sakai, "*Dai Juuni Kai Seirei ni Yoru Sasshin Kansai Taikai*" [12th Kansai Regional CCRM Convention], *Ikeru Mizu,* No. 77 (Summer Edition 2005): 6-7. Original in Japanese. [Translation mine].

Naoe Fujisaki attended Life in the Spirit seminar organized at Fujisawa Catholic Church and realized that her life was dry without prayer. Initially she found it difficult to praise and thank God from her heart but gradually she realized the power of praise. She testifies that the seminar had a great impact on her life, especially her prayer life. She thanks God for deepening her prayer life and leading her to meditate on the Word of God.[239]

One of the first time participants of the 23rd Hokkaido regional CCRM convention testifies the dramatic growth in her prayer life.

> When I evaluated my prayer life, I realized that it was a dry. I never had the experience of a lively prayer. At the convention for the first time, I prayed with all my heart. Hereafter I wish to continue a strong prayer life.[240]

Nigo Yuriko attended the Life in the Spirit Seminar in 2010. She had a spiritual transformation during this seminar. She realized the importance of being open to God. She started reaching out to others in love. She started reading the Bible meditatively. She thanked God for these graces.[241]

The CCRM has been emphasizing the renewal in the Spirit for every Catholic and the whole Church. The graces received during the Life in the Spirit Seminar, convention and prayer meeting are meant not only for an individual's personal growth and renewal but also for the renewal of the whole Church.[242] The renewal, which the CCRM

---

239 Naoe Fujisaki, "*Shounan Chiku no Seirei ni Yoru Seikatsu Sasshin Semina*" [Life in the Spirit Seminar at Shounan Region], *Ikeru Mizu,* No. 83 (Fall Edition 2005): 7. Original in Japanese. [Translation mine].

240 Editorial Board of *Ikeru Mizu*, "*Dai Nijuusan Kai Seirei ni Yoru Sasshin Hokkaido Taikai no Hokoku*" [Report of the 23rd Hokkaido Regional CCRM Convention], *Ikeru Mizu,* No. 90 (Fall Edition 2008): 5. Original in Japanese. [Translation mine].

241 Nigo Yuriko, "*Seirei ni Yoru Sasshin Semina ni Sankasareta Katagata no Kansobun kara*" [Reflections from the Participants of the Life in the Spirit Seminar] *Ikeru Mizu,* No. 98 (Fall Edition 2010): 9-10. Original in Japanese. [Translation mine].

242 See Haku Sasaki, "*Dai Seinen ni Ibuki wo Ukete*" [Receive the Breath During Great Holy Year], *Ikeru Mizu*, No. 56 (Spring Edition 1999): 1-2. Original in Japanese. [Translation mine].

focuses, is the inner renewal of a person. St. Paul writes in the letter to Ephesians about the inner renewal as follows: "To be renewed in the spirit of your minds and to clothe yourselves with the new self, created according to the likeness of God in true righteousness and holiness" (Eph 4:23-24). The above testimonies prove that many people who have attended the prayer meetings or retreats organized by the CCRM had a radical transformation in their lives. They have developed a close relationship with Jesus. They could forgive and accept others through the power of the Holy Spirit. God liberated some people from their bad habits and behaviors. Their experience of the power of the Holy Spirit has led them to deepen their prayer life. People involved with the CCRM realize the importance of having a strong prayer life in order to serve God and others. Thus, we can conclude that the CCRM has indeed brought a spiritual renewal and transformation in the lives of the people in Japan.

4.1.2 Relishing the Word of God

The Second Vatican Council encouraged all to meditate on the Word of God. The CCRM too, gives importance to the Word of God. It insists on the prayerful reading of the Bible. The Bible helps a person to grow in faith. It is very powerful. It can purge away all sins. It brings forth the truth in the lives of those who welcome it. The author of the letter to the Hebrews notes that, "Indeed, the word of God is living and active, sharper than any two-edged sword, piercing until it divides soul from spirit, joints from marrow; it is able to judge the thoughts and intentions of the heart (Heb 4:12)." The Dogmatic Constitution on Divine Revelation (*Dei Verbum*) notes that:

> The sacred synod earnestly and especially urges all the Christian faithful... to learn by frequent reading of the divine Scriptures the excellent knowledge of Jesus Christ (Phil.3:8). For ignorance of the Scriptures is ignorance of Christ. Therefore, they should gladly put themselves in touch with the sacred text itself, whether it be through the liturgy, rich in the divine word, or through devotional reading, or through instructions suitable for the purpose and other aids which, in our time, with approval and active

> support of the shepherds of the Church, are commendably spread everywhere. And let them remember that prayer should accompany the reading of Sacred Scripture, so that God and man may talk together; for we speak to Him when we pray; we hear Him when we read the divine saying. (*DV* 25)

The Bible is an essential part of a Christian's life. It gives spiritual strength to a person at all times. The baptism in the Holy Spirit arouses in a person a deep interest for the Word of God. People associated with the CCRM meditate on the Bible to deepen their relation with God. The Word of God becomes "the food of the soul, the pure and everlasting source of spiritual life," (*DV* 21) in the life of the Christians who meditate it. The CCRM in Japan gives importance to the meditative reading of the Bible. It organizes workshops at regular intervals all over Japan to teach people various methods of reading the Bible.[243]

Fr. Bernadine Schneider, a scripture scholar and one of the pioneer leaders of the CCRM in Japan suggested the following four methods of Bible reading in an article published in *Shu no Ibuki*, newsletter of CCRJ.[244] The first method was to pray the *Liturgy of Hours*. The *Liturgy of Hours* or the *Prayer of the Church* is composed of psalms of praise and thanksgiving, along with several passages from the Bible, writings of saints and treatises of the doctors of the Church. Thus, the *Liturgy of the* Hours helps the spiritual growth of a Christian. Even before the birth of the CCRM, the Catholic Church has been using these texts to offer thanks and praise to God. The Church encourages people to use the *Liturgy of Hours* as a means of prayer and meditation.[245] The second method, which he suggested was to read the Word of God, during the prayer meetings, especially

---

243 Lafont, "Inori de Kami no Koe wo Kiku" [To Listen to God's Voice Through Prayer], in *Shu no Ibuki: Bassui Ban* [Breath of the Lord: Excerpts], Vol. 2, 4. Original in Japanese. [Translation mine].

244 Bernadine Schneider, "*Sanbi ni Inori ni Tsuite: Seisho to Tomoni Inori*" [About Prayer of Praise: To Pray with the Sacred Scriptures], in *Shu no Ibuki: Bassui Ban* [Breath of the Lord: Excerpts], Vol. 3 (Tokyo: Catholic Charismatic Renewal of Japan, 1992), 47. Original in Japanese. [Translation mine].

245 Ibid.

passages that, can help the group to grow.[246] The third method was the reading and sharing of the Bible in small groups. He suggested group members to share the text, which inspired them.[247] The fourth method was first, to read a passage of the Bible during one's personal prayers and then listen to the message, which God wants to give the person through it.[248]

Again, the CCRM invites people to make the Word of God a part of their lives. The CCRM further suggests one's daily life must reflect the inspiration and grace received by meditating on the Sacred Scriptures. People must not read the Bible as a book to increase knowledge alone. The Bible gives more than knowledge. It gives direction to a person's life. It changes a person's interior life.[249]

St. Paul says, "All scripture is inspired by God and is useful for teaching, for reproof, for correction, and for training in righteousness, so that everyone who belongs to God may be proficient, equipped for every good work" (2 Tm 3:16-17). The CCRM encourages people to read the Bible to get inspiration, reproof, and correction. However, the CCRM asks people not to interpret the Biblical tects subjectively. The CCRM agrees with the Dogmatic Constitution on Divine Revelation, *Dei Verbum*, which notes that it is the Church, which gives authentic interpretation of the Sacred Scriptures.

> But the task of authentically interpreting the word of God, whether written or handed on, has been entrusted exclusively to the living teaching office of the Church, whose authority is exercised in the name of Jesus Christ. This teaching office is not above the word of God, but serves it, teaching only what has been handed on, listening to it devoutly, guarding it scrupulously and explaining it

246 Bernadine Schneider, "*Sanbi ni Inori ni Tsuite: Seisho to Tomoni Inori*" [AboutPrayer of Praise: To Pray with the Sacred Scriptures], in *Shu no Ibuki: Bassui Ban* [Breath of the Lord: Excerpts], Vol. 3 (Tokyo: Catholic Charismatic Renewal of Japan, 1992), 48. Original in Japanese. [Translation mine].

247 Ibid.

248 Ibid.

249 Akira Mizoguchi, "*Kami no Mikotoba to Inori no Sekatsu*" [Sacred Scriptures and Prayer Life], in *Shu no Ibuki: Bassui Ban* [Breath of the Lord: Excerpts], Vol. 2, 49-50. Original in Japanese. [Translation mine].

> faithfully in accord with a divine commission and with the help of the Holy Spirit, it draws from this one deposit of faith everything which it presents for belief as divinely revealed. It is clear, therefore, that sacred tradition, Sacred Scripture and the teaching authority of the Church, in accord with God's most wise design, are so linked and joined together that one cannot stand without the others, and that all together and each in its own way under the action of the one Holy Spirit contribute effectively to the salvation of souls. (*DV* 11)

The CCRM encourages people to read, meditate and take inspiration from the Bible for personal spiritual growth as well as for the good of the community. However, the CCRM cautions people about the subjective interpretation of the Bible. The CCRM is against using one's private revelation or inspiration as basis of interpretation of the Word of God during prayer meetings. It urges all to subject themselves to the teachings of the Church in matters of the interpretation of the Bible. Following are the testimonies of people who relish the Word of God. The CCRM helped them to discover the richness of the Word of God:

Reiko Kato a Catholic convert took part in the Life in the Spirit Seminar organized at Fujisawa Catholic Church, Shounan region from May to June 2003. She quit her job to spend time in prayer. She registered for the Life in the Seminar. She says that formerly she thought that to read prayers from books is the right way to pray. However, after attending the Seminar she learnt how to pray in the Spirit. She understood the importance of praise, which forms an essential part of prayer. She also learnt that prayer does not mean asking favors only for oneself but also to pray for others' needs. Formerly she had no interest to read the Bible, but after the infilling of the Holy Spirit her attitude changed. She started taking more interest in reading the Word of God.[250]

Mikiko Itou participated in the 26th northeast regional CCRM convention held in September 2004. The talks given during the

---

250 Reiko Kato, "*Shu no Heian*" [Peace of the Lord], *Ikeru Mizu,* No. 70 (Fall Edition 2003): 10-11. Original in Japanese. [Translation mine].

convention inspired her. She learnt the way to read the Bible. Moreover, she also learnt to pray with the Bible.[251]

Yuko Sugiura, a protestant was deeply disturbed with her faith life. She decided to participate in the Life in the Spirit Seminars organized at Yukinoshita Catholic Church. This seminar transformed her whole life. She testifies that the Spirit gave her many graces. She also testifies that after attending the seminar she could relish the Word of God. She has a greater longing to read the Bible. She feels the Holy Spirit is guiding her as she reads the Bible.[252]

Midori Iizuka testifies that she had received Baptism because of the influence of a nun. However, even after Baptism she had no interest in spirituality. She would occasionally attend the mass but found it difficult to study the Bible. She started attending the Life in Spirit Seminars organized at Harajuku Catholic Church. It was in this seminar that she got the conviction of the Lord's presence within her. She was a sickly person and during her childhood, she did not receive proper love from her mother. By attending the seminar, the Holy Spirit filled her with joy. She received a new desire to meditate on the Word of God. She desires to be close to the Lord and to know more about Him.[253]

Wakako Kaseman attended a workshop organized by Sr. Margarita and received grace to read the Bible meditatively. She notes that,

> Before participating in this seminar whenever I read the Bible, it was as if I were reading just words, they did not mean anything to me. Now, after participating in this workshop I feel the Bible, is the Word of God. It is alive and active. The Word of God speaks strongly to me.[254]

---

251 Mikiko Itou, "*Sankasha no Koe Kara*" [Participants Testimonies], *Ikeru Mizu,* No. 71 (Winter Edition 2003): 6. Original in Japanese. [Translation mine].

252 Yuko Sugiura, "*Kakuchi no Inori no Tsudoi no Hataraki Kara*" [The Happenings in Each Region], *Ikeru Mizu,* No. 78 (Fall Edition 2003): 12. Original in Japanese. [Translation mine].

253 Midori Iizuka, "*Seirei ni Yoru Seikatsu Sasshin Semina wo Ukete*" [Participating in Life in the Spirit Seminars], *Ikeru Mizu,* No. 83 (Winter Edition 2003):6. Original in Japanese. [Translation mine].

254 Wakako Kaseman, "*Doitsu no Seirei Sasshin Kara: Shisuta Marugarita no Hataraki*" [CCRM in Germany: Activities of Sister Margarita], *Ikeru Mizu,*

Keiko Kyono testified that she relishes reading the Word of God. After attending the Koinonia Seminar, she realized the importance of the Word of God.[255] From the above testimonies, we can conclude that the CCRM is giving importance to the Bible. It urges all the Christians to make the Bible, as the book of their lives.

4.1.3 Meaningful Celebration of Sacraments

Many Catholics have rediscovered the beauty and richness of the Sacraments of the Catholic Church through their involvement in the CCRM. Many Catholic Charismatics worldwide testify to the deepening of their devotion to the Sacraments especially the Holy Eucharist, Sacrament of Reconciliation, Sacrament of Baptism and Confirmation. In Japan too, the CCRM has a similar effect on the lives of the Catholics. Sometimes there is a danger among those involved in the CCRM to give more importance to prayer meetings than the Holy Eucharist. The leaders of the CCRM in Japan have cautioned people about this danger. They have always insisted that the Sacraments of the Church are important sources to receive graces and to have a living encounter with God. The *Catechism of the Catholic Church* notes the relevance of the Sacraments in a Christian's life. "The seven Sacraments touch all the stages and all the important moments of Christian life: they give birth and increase, healing and mission to the Christian's life of faith" (CCC 1210). The leaders of the CCRM in Japan make it clear that prayer meetings can never replace the Sacraments. Genuine renewal in the Holy Spirit never impels a person to lose love for the Sacraments of the Church; it rather increases one's love for them.[256]

Following are the testimonies of people who have actually received this grace of an increase in love for Sacraments through their involvement in the CCRM.

No. 89 (Summer Edition 2008): 6-7. Original in Japanese. [Translation mine].

255 Keiko Kyono, "*Koinonia Tsukuri no Reshipi*" [Recipie for Kononia], *Ikeru Mizu*, No. 106 (Fall Edition 2012): 6. Original in Japanese. [Translation mine].

256 Akira Mizoguchi, "*Karisuma to Hiseki*" [Charisms and Sacraments], in *Shu no Ibuki: Bassui Ban* [Breath of the Lord: Excerpts], Vol. 2, 79. Original in Japanese. [Translation mine].

Fr. Jeremiah Cassidy a Capuchin priest wrote in an article about the 14th National CCRM convention held in 1998. He notes that the preacher's from Philippines made an impact on the Japanese people. One of the preachers, Annie in her testimony mentioned that she always had resentment against the Japanese for their aggression and torture during the World War II. However, when she came to Japan she had a conversion of heart. She publicly forgave the Japanese soldiers for the violence they did during the war. Her testimony touched many people. They too felt the need to make a good confession. Fr. Cassidy notes that, "In this convention the CCRM has become instrumental in calling people to love the Sacrament of Reconciliation and have deeper experience of the forgiveness from the Lord."[257]

Fr. Jean Raymond Girard a Redemptorist priest participated in the 14th National CCRM convention. He shared his experience in an article of *Ikeru Mizu*.

> This year I participated in the 14th National CCRM convention. It has been 32 years since I came to Japan, but I feel this is the best convention I have ever attended. There was a general atmosphere of prayer and praise in the convention. The impressive talks given by Fr. Bart from Philippines along with Annie's testimony had a great impact on all. It was a heavenly experience. I had the chance to hear life transforming confessions. I am convinced that many people made a radical change in their lives. Inspired by hearing life transforming confessions from many people, I myself received the grace to have a deep change of heart. I pray that I may faithfully respond to the grace received at the confessional box.[258]

Tsue Watanabe attended a Life in the Spirit Seminar earlier but gradually lost interest in the CCRM. She became a backslider.

257 Jeremiah Cassidy, "*Yurushu no Saiten*" [Festival of forgiveness], *Ikeru Mizu,* No. 47 (Special Edition 2003): 3. Original in Japanese. [Translation mine].

258 Jean Raymond Girard, "*Yurushi no Hiseki ha Kijun Desu*" [Sacrament of Reconciliation is the Base], *Ikeru Mizu,* No. 47 (Special Edition 2003): 4. Original in Japanese. [Translation mine].

However, when she attended the 14th Hokkaido regional CCRM convention in May 1999 she had a great experience of the Lord.[259] She testified that:

> The talks and the grace of God helped me to do a sincere confession. Confession helped me to remove all the blocks in my life, which were not allowing me to grow closer to the Lord. Now I have tranquility in my heart. I feel that there is flowing stream of water in my heart. Now I am emptying myself so the Holy Spirit can fill me and work through me. The Sacrament of reconciliation brought a true renewal in my life.[260]

Kuniko Kitamura attended the 14th Hokkaido regional CCRM convention. She wrote about the importance of the Sacrament of Reconciliation.

> I received Baptism 10 years ago but I always had a difficulty in doing confessions. I used to think that if there were no confessions in Catholicism, it would be a wonderful religion. God loves us and forgives us, then why do we need to confess. If we do something wrong, we can directly ask pardon from the Lord. It is something between God and the person who sins. I came to the convention with these negative thoughts about the Sacrament of Reconciliation. After the talk, we had sharing and somebody shared that I confess once in a month and always tears flow down my cheeks. I shared that I do not have such experience and I told them about my thoughts about confession. After the sharing, it was time for receiving the Sacrament of Reconciliation. I

259 Tsue Watanabe, "*Dai JuuYon Kai Seirei ni Yoru Sasshin Hokkaido Taikai Hirakareru*" [14th Hokkaido Regional CCRM Convention Opens], *Ikeru Mizu*, No. 53 (Summer Edition 1999): 3. Original in Japanese. [Translation mine].

260 Kuniko Kitamura, "*Dai JuuYon Kai Seirei ni Yoru Sasshin Hokkaido Taikai Hirakareru*" [14th Hokkaido Regional CCRM Convention Opens], *Ikeru Mizu*, No. 53 (Summer Edition 1999): 3. Original in Japanese. [Translation mine].

> still had reservations about confessions in my mind and I did not want to go to the priests because they knew me. However, I decided to go a priest whom I knew in order to discuss some spiritual things. Then I went to the confessional box of Fr. Hashimoto. However, no sooner I reached there than tears started flowing through my eyes. I do not know why tears came out of my eyes. I shared with my younger sister this experience and told her that God has delivered from all the negative thoughts towards the Sacrament of Reconciliation. I think it is God's grace and work. After that confession, I felt a deep peace and serenity in my heart. I thank God for His marvelous work in my life.[261]

Riko Ashio attended the Life in the Spirit Seminar in June 2003. She notes that she used to be a very reserved and egoistic person. She would always justify herself. She was very self-righteous person. However, she soon realized that she is spiritually dry and dying. She needed deliverance from her egoism. It is in this condition she attended the Life in the Spirit Seminar and found a dramatic change in her life. She testifies as follows:

> This year I attended the Life in the Spirit Seminar. I made it a goal to complete successfully all the seminars. Had I not done it I would remain in my tiny hole as before. I had strong desire to get out of my world. Now I experience a deep joy and peace in my heart as I have completed the seminar. From childhood, the self-defense mechanism would work very strongly in me and even for silly things, I would try to justify myself. I thought faith is human made concept. I need not care about it. Soon I realized that my spiritual life is dry and dying. I wanted to deliver myself with my own power. I had a great difficulty in doing a genuine surrender to Jesus Christ. It was during

261 Kuniko Kitamura, "*Dai JuuYon Kai Seirei ni Yoru Sasshin Hokkaido Taikai Hirakareru*" [14th Hokkaido Regional CCRM Convention Opens], *Ikeru Mizu*, No. 53 (Summer Edition 1999): 4. Original in Japanese. [Translation mine].

> the seminar that I received the infilling of the Holy Spirit and a tremendous grace to make a good confession....I was delivered from egoism and I restarted the service towards the sick. All my sufferings and worries disappeared. I thank God for His graces.[262]

Tetsuko Kawaoka attended the 14th Kansai regional convention held in 2009. She got the grace to confess her sins. She accepted her sinfulness. She prayed for her genuine conversion.[263]

The CCRM has been promoting devotion to the Holy Eucharist. The CCRM organizes Eucharistic Adorations especially during conventions and workshops. Many people attending these CCRM prayer meetings and conventions have received the grace for more devotion to the Sacraments. Many have started participating daily in the Holy Eucharist and receiving the Sacrament of Reconciliation frequently. Both these Sacraments have brought healing in the lives of many people. People involved in the CCRM discover the power of the Sacraments. They realize the importance of receiving the Sacraments to nourish their Christian lives. Some also get the grace to respond to the call of God by offering their lives in His service as priests and religious. The CCRM in Japan has been emphasizing the real transformation that takes place in a person when he or she receives a Sacrament. Many people through their association with the CCRM have rediscovered the importance and the beauty of the Sacraments of the Catholic Church.[264]

4.1.4 Healing and the Use of Charisms

The CCRM encourages Christians to use the charisms of the Holy Spirit. The CCRM relates the phenomenon of baptism in the Holy Spirit with the use of charisms. Baptism in the Holy Spirit makes a

262 Riko Ashio, "*Inori no Tsudoi ha Ikiteiru*" [The Prayer Meetings are Alive], *Ikeru Mizu*, No. 70 (Fall Edition 2003): 10. Original in Japanese. [Translation mine].

263 Testuko Kawaoka, "*Shu ha Ima Ikiteorareru*" [The Lord is Living], *Ikeru Mizu*, No. 94 (Fall Edition 2009): 5. Original in Japanese. [Translation mine].

264 Keiko Kyono, "*Shu Yo, Inochi no Pan wo Kudasai*" [Lord Give Us the Bread of Eternal Life], *Ikeru Mizu*, No. 79 (Winter Edition 2006): 11. Original in Japanese. [Translation mine].

person aware of the power of the Holy Spirit working within him or her. St. Paul notes the following about the charisms in his first letter to the Corinthians.

> Now there are varieties of gifts, but the same Spirit; and there are varieties of services, but the same Lord; and there are varieties of activities, but it is the same God who activates all of them in everyone. To each is given the manifestation of the Spirit for the common good. To one is given through the Spirit the utterance of wisdom, and to another the utterance of knowledge according to the same Spirit, to another faith by the same Spirit, to another gifts of healing by the one Spirit, to another the working of miracles, to another prophecy, to another the discernment of spirits, to another various kinds of tongues, to another the interpretation of tongues. (1 Cor 12:1-10)

The above list of charisms is not exhaustive. The Bible contains other lists of spiritual gifts too.[265] The Holy Spirit is free to grant new spiritual gifts relevant for a particular age. Thus, the Church recognizes charisms or spiritual gifts as graces from the Holy Spirit. The Holy Spirit gives these charisms for the good of the community.

The CCRM encourages people to exercise their charisms during the prayer meetings. However, in the context of Japan it is very important to stress that charisms, especially extraordinary charisms are not magic. The episode of Simon the magician in the Acts of Apostles can help us to know how people who have a deep attraction for magic can easily mistake the gift of God for cheap magic and sorcery.

> Now a certain man named Simon had previously practiced magic in the city and amazed the people of Samaria, saying that he was someone great. All of them, from the least to the greatest, listened to him eagerly, saying, 'This man is the power of God that is called Great.' And they listened eagerly to him because for a long time he had amazed them with his magic. But when

265 See Rom 12:6-8; 1 Cor 12:28.

> they believed Philip, who was proclaiming the good news about the kingdom of God and the name of Jesus Christ, they were baptized, both men and women. Even Simon himself believed. After being baptized, he stayed constantly with Philip and was amazed when he saw the signs and great miracles that took place. Now when the apostles at Jerusalem heard that Samaria had accepted the Sacred Scriptures, they sent Peter and John to them. The two went down and prayed for them that they might receive the Holy Spirit (for as yet the Spirit had not come upon any of them; they had only been baptized in the name of the Lord Jesus). Then Peter and John laid their hands on them, and they received the Holy Spirit. Now when Simon saw that the Spirit was given through the laying on of the apostles' hands, he offered them money, saying, "Give me also this power so that anyone on whom I lay my hands may receive the Holy Spirit." But Peter said to him, 'May your silver perish with you, because you thought you could obtain God's gift with money. You have no part or share in this, for your heart is not right before God'. (Acts 8: 9-21)

Just like Simon the magician, in Japan too there is a possibility that people who attend the CCRM prayer meetings without proper knowledge about Christianity may misunderstand the charisms as magic. Charisms are not the propriety of the person who has them; they belong to the Holy Spirit. The person is merely an instrument. In Japan, there are various new religious movements and cults, which emphasize healings, divination and supernatural phenomena. People can misunderstand the use of charisms among the Charismatics. They may think it is similar to Shamanism. They may think of Charismatics as Shamans.[266] This particular problem has been of concern among the people involved in the CCRM. The bishops

---

266 See Alena Govorounova, "Pentecostalism and Shamanism in Asia and Beyond: An Inter-disciplinary Analysis," in *Pentecostalism and Shamanism in Asia*, ed. Paul Swanson, (Nagoya: Nanzan Institute for Religion and Culture, 2013), 58-59. See also Reginald Alva, "The Dangers of Overstressing on Healing in Japan," in *Church + Society in Asia Today*, 16, No. 3 (December 2013): 175-185.

and pastors too recognize this danger. Therefore, it is of paramount importance to give proper place to charisms in the CCRM prayer meetings.

The community needs charisms for the growth. However, they are not signs of holiness. The Holy Spirit gives them for service. St. Paul cautioned the community at Thessalonica to "test everything; hold fast to what is good" (1 Thes 5:21). Similarly, the bishops, priests and the leaders of the CCRM must encourage the use of charisms but stop every abuse. The leaders of the CCRM need to discuss regularly about the role of proper discernment of their ministries. Fr. Francis Mathy, a Jesuit priest and a leader of the CCRM in Japan, gives importance to the discernment of spirits because it forms the backbone of a healthy spiritual life.[267]

Discernment of spirits is indeed a difficult task, yet important. Leaders in Japan have issued certain common guidelines for discernment. They ask the members of the CCRM not to base their discernment on anyone's private opinion. They insist that the community must pray and then discern together. The community must especially discern the prophecies. Any prophecy which accuses someone, brings division and dissension in the community cannot be from the Holy Spirit because St. Paul says, "For God is a God not of disorder but of peace" (1 Cor 14:33). Moreover, the prophecy must not contradict the Word of God or the teachings of the Church. It must not lead people to break away from the Church and to fight against each other.[268]

The exercise of spiritual charisms brings joy in the community. There is no place for egoism. The person who has charisms is not special. He or she is not otherworldly. He or she continues with the routine of life. The possession of spiritual gifts does not separate a person from his or her daily chores or does not make a person superhuman. It only helps the person to perform his or her duties and

267 Francis Mathy, "*Rei no Shikibetsu no Sho Mondai*" [Problems in Discernment of the Spirits], in *Shu no Ibuki: Bassui Ban* [Breath of the Lord: Excerpts], Vol. 2, 66. Original in Japanese. [Translation mine].

268 Lafont, "*Yogen ni Tsuite*" [About Prophecy], in *Shu no Ibuki: Bassui Ban* [Breath of the Lord: Excerpts], Vol. 2, 68-70. Original in Japanese. [Translation mine].

obligation with love and zeal.[269] However, spiritual transformation is more important than the use of charisms. One of the common effects of spiritual transformation is deepening of prayer life. St. Paul mentions, "The fruit of the Spirit is love, joy, peace, patience, kindness, generosity, faithfulness, gentleness, and self-control. There is no law against such things" (Gal 5:22-23). These fruits of the Holy Spirit are clearly visible in a person's life that has spiritual transformation. It is impossible that a person who claims to have deep spiritual experience can fail to love his or her neighbors. St. John writes,

> Whoever says, 'I am in the light,' while hating a brother or sister, is still in the darkness. Whoever loves a brother or sister lives in the light, and in such a person, there is no cause for stumbling. But whoever hates another believer is in the darkness, walks in the darkness, and does not know the way to go, because the darkness has brought on blindness. (1 Jn 2:9-11)

Again, the Holy Spirit leads a person to become genuinely meek and humble. He or she does not consider oneself as someone special or different from others.[270] The following biblical texts teach about the importance of humility. "Humble yourselves before the Lord, and he will exalt you" (Jas 4:10). "Humble yourselves therefore, under the mighty hand of God, so that he may exalt you in due time" (1 Pt 5:6).

The leaders of the CCRJ recognize the need of prudence and restrain in using spiritual charisms in Japan. Based on the teachings of the Catholic Church, the spiritual teachings of saints and doctors of the Church, the leaders of the CCRJ advise the people not to concentrate too much only on extraordinary charisms like healing, working miracles or prophecy.[271] They hold that simple ministries

---

269 Mathy, "*Rei no Shikibetsu no Sho Mondai*" [Problems in Discernment of the Spirits], in *Shu no Ibuki: Bassui Ban* [Breath of the Lord: Excerpts], Vol. 2, 71. Original in Japanese. [Translation mine].

270 Ibid., 72.

271 Mathy, "*Rei no Shikibetsu no Sho Mondai*" [Problems in Discernment of the Spirits], in *Shu no Ibuki: Bassui Ban* [Breath of the Lord: Excerpts], Vol. 2, 71.

like welcoming people to the CCRM meetings, cleaning, arranging the prayer hall or serving are also gifts from the Holy Spirit. Both the extraordinary as well as the ordinary gifts are from the Holy Spirit. A person must gratefully receive gifts for the good of the community.

The leaders of the CCRJ have also cautioned against spiritual dictatorship.[272] A leader of the prayer group is not supposed to be a dictator. He or she cannot impose his or her decisions on all the members. The leader must encourage every member of the group to discuss a matter. The group must take decisions in prayer. The leader must not force anyone to do a particular task. There must be absolute freedom. St. Paul writes about the importance of freedom in a community. "Now the Lord is the Spirit, and where the Spirit of the Lord is, there is freedom" (2 Cor 3:17). The Holy Spirit does not bind anyone; rather the Spirit leads to true freedom. The core group members of a prayer group have a great responsibility to constantly evaluate and discern the happenings at the prayer meeting. There should be no space for disunity, unhealthy criticisms and resentment among the group members.[273] St. Paul's advice to the Ephesians can be of great help to the members of the CCRM.

> I therefore, the prisoner in the Lord, beg you to lead a life worthy of the calling to which you have been called, with all humility and gentleness, with patience, bearing with one another in love, making every effort to maintain the unity of the Spirit in the bond of peace. There is one body and one Spirit, just as you were called to the one hope of your calling, one Lord, one faith, one Baptism, one God and Father of all, who is above all and through all and in all. But each of us was given grace according to the measure of Christ's gift. (Eph 4:1-7)

Original in Japanese. [Translation mine].

272 Mathy, "*Rei no Shikibetsu no Sho Mondai*" [Problems in Discernment of the Spirits], in *Shu no Ibuki: Bassui Ba*n [Breath of the Lord: Excerpts], Vol. 2, 73. Original in Japanese. [Translation mine].

273 Atsu Kobayashi, "*Korinzu Shinpu ni Yoru Dai Seinen wo Mukaeru Mokusokai*" [Retreat by Fr. Collins: To Prepare for the Great Holy Year], *Ikeru Mizu,* No.55 (Winter Edition 2000): 9-10. Original in Japanese. [Translation mine].

St. Paul calls on the Christians of Ephesus to maintain unity of the Spirit. He also writes about the grace, that Christ gave to each one. Thus, it is apt that all must receive the charisms gratefully and exercise them for the growth of the Church. Genuine charisms lead to a greater unity and love among the members of the community.

People involved in the CCRM use regularly the charisms of healing. The Gospels have many passages about the healings and miracles of Jesus. Jesus commanded His disciples to cure the sick (see Mt 10:8). Jesus has commanded the Church, to continue the ministry of healing through the celebration of Sacraments.

> The Lord Jesus Christ, physician of our souls and bodies, who forgave the sins of the paralytic and restored him to bodily health, has willed that his Church continue, in the power of the Holy Spirit, his work of healing and salvation, even among her own members. This is the purpose of the two Sacraments of healing: the Sacrament of Penance and the Sacrament of Anointing of the Sick. (CCC 1421)

The Church recognizes the charisms of healing (See 1 Cor 12: 9). However, she knows that the charisms of healing are not magic. All genuine healing comes from the Lord. However, there may be cases where there is no healing in spite of fervent prayers. It is difficult to know the exact reason behind it.

> The Holy Spirit gives to some a special charism of healing so as to make manifest the power of the grace of the risen Lord. But even the most intense prayers do not always obtain the healing of all illnesses. Thus St. Paul must learn from the Lord that 'my grace is sufficient for you, for my power is made perfect in weakness,' and that the sufferings to be endured can mean that 'in my flesh I complete what is lacking in Christ's afflictions for the sake of his Body, that is, the Church.' (CCC 1508)

Healing is a basic desire of any human person. If someone claims to have supernatural powers to heal, people flock around such a person. Even in Japan, there are many new religious movements, which emphasize supernatural healing. In this context, people can misunderstand the healings in the CCRM prayer meetings as magic or occult. The CCRM in Japan has already realized this danger and has taken care to follow the directives of the bishops and the *Catechism of the Catholic Church* to impart sound teaching on healing. At the same time, the CCRM also recognizes that healing can be an effective instrument in evangelization. Thus, the CCRM has taken a balanced view with regard to healings; it neither emphasizes them nor discourages the practice of praying for healing. The CCRM in Japan invites prominent international leaders involved in the healing ministry to give teachings on healing. Apart from it, the leaders of the CCRM in Japan have regularly published articles in the newsletter of the CCRJ to keep the people updated about the Catholic Church's official stand and teaching on healing.

The tradition of the Catholic Church classifies healing into three categories: spiritual healing, physical healing and psychological healing. A human person is made of body, mind and spirit. Therefore, the healing, which Jesus offers, covers all the aspects of a human person.

Spiritual healing refers to the healing of the wounds and disorders in a person's spiritual realm. In religious language, people consider sin as the cause of these disorders. Repentance, inner transformation, conversion and forgiveness are essential elements for spiritual healing. The Catholic tradition relates spiritual healing to Sacrament of reconciliation. The CCRM refers to spiritual healing as inner healing. Inner healing is very important for the holistic well-being of a person. Development in psychology has also ascertained that deep-seated wounds, painful memories, lack of acceptance and lack of love can lead to disorders in a person. The consequences of one's habitual sins also distort one's relationship with self, others and God.[274]

God is love. He wills that every human person come to Him. Spiritual healing begins when one becomes aware of God's love for

274 See Francis Macnutt, *Healing* (Notre Dame: Ave Maria Press, 1974), 169-178. See also Barbara Leahy Shlemon, *Healing the Hidden Self* (Mumbai: Asian Trading Corporation, 1987), 9-28. See also Benedict Heron, *Praying for Healing: The Challenge* (Mumbai: St. Paul's Press, 1989), 81-89.

him or her. The CCRM in Japan organizes workshops on inner healing to teach people about the need for spiritual healing and to pray for the same. Leaders especially blessed with charisms of healing lead prayer services pleading for the grace of the Holy Spirit to heal all the wounds in the spiritual realm of a person. Spiritual healing leads a person to have a renewed relationship with God and experience His profound love. The person also finds new strength to face the challenges of life and continue his or her trust-relationship with God.[275]

Spiritual healing may sometimes lead to physical and psychological healing. The CCRM has been cautious about overstressing on healings.[276] The CCRM warns against any sort of sensationalism, theatricals because these things have no relation with the process of healing.[277] Physical or psychological healings do happen in prayer groups. However, it is not compulsory that prayers must effect physical or psychological healing. God heals some people. No one must say that lack of physical healing means lack of faith. A person may have faith yet may not receive healing. The CCRM tells people not to loose hope, even if they do not receive physical or psychological healings. The CCRM also teaches on the importance of redemptive suffering. A person must not be obsessed with any form of healing. What is more important is to realize God's unfathomable love and experience deep peace in one's inner being. The CCRM encourages all to receive Sacraments, as they are instruments of God's abundant graces.[278] Following are the testimonies of people healed of their physical illness.

---

275 See Francis Macnutt, *Healing* (Notre Dame: Ave Maria Press, 1974), 169-178. See also Barbara Leahy Shlemon, *Healing the Hidden Self* (Mumbai: Asian Trading Corporation, 1987), 9-28. See also Benedict Heron, *Praying for Healing: The Challenge* (Mumbai: St. Paul's Press, 1989), 81-89.

276 See Alva, "The Dangers of Overstressing on Healing in Japan," 175-185.

277 Sometimes in Pentecostal healing services the preachers insist that those who want to receive healing must fall down on the ground or shout loudly. The CCRM must absolutely not insist on such techniques as it is God who heals and not these techniques. Moreover, it is against the teachings of the Catholic Church.

278 Fischbeck, "*Kirisuto no Onrei ni Okeru Iyashi*" [Healing Through the Spirit of Jesus], in *Shu no Ibuki: Bassui Ban* [Breath of the Lord: Excerpts], Vol. 5, 31.

Masatoshi Tsuchida was suffering from polyp for 10 years. He could not sing, as the polyp would hurt his throat. He wanted to get the polyp removed by operation but did not have time because of his busy work schedule. His condition worsened towards the end of March 1998. He decided to go to the hospital. However, he had a great desire to participate in the Hokkaido regional CCRM convention to sing praises to the Lord. He prayed for healing and got a message from the Bible, "I have seen their ways, but I will heal them; I will lead them and repay them with comfort, creating for their mourners the fruit of the lips" (Is 57:18). He was convinced of his healing and he continued to pray. On the following day, he went to the hospital. The doctor examined his throat and told him he had no polyp. After his healing, he could sing without any pain.[279]

In 1996, Kazuko Nakamura had bladder cancer. The doctors removed her cancerous bladder through endoscope surgery. They asked her to take anti-cancer medication to prevent recurrence of the cancer. Since then she would undergo regular checkups in the hospital. In April 2003, her medical tests reported that the cancer had reappeared and her condition was very grave. The doctors gave her the option of having an artificial bladder put in or getting treatment to increase her immunity. She decided to go for treatment to increase her immunity. However, her condition worsened. Further tests revealed she had blood clots (tumor) formed in many parts of her body. The doctors suggested her thorough medical checkup. However, she requested the doctors to postpone the checkup until the completion of 10th Kansai regional CCRM convention on August 18, 2003. The doctors scheduled her checkup on August 20, 2003. Before her checkup, she was praying that God might reveal His glory. On August 20, she went to the hospital and the doctors collected samples from 20 different parts of her body. She believed that God had already begun His mysterious work in her. On August 7, 2003, she had noticed that the blood clots, which she could feel in her body, had disappeared and the blood, which was passing through her

Original in Japanese. [Translation mine].

279 Masatoshi Tsuchida, "*Anata wo Shounin ni Suru*" [I Will Make You My Witness], *Ikeru Mizu*, No. 49 (Summer Edition 1998): 4. Original in Japanese. [Translation mine].

urine, had stopped. Five days later the reports of the tests revealed that, she had no cancerous cells in her. The doctors were surprised to see the reports. She firmly believes that it is the work of God. She believes that the prayers of many people especially during the 10th Kansai region CCRM convention had a miraculous effect. She thanks God, priests, religious and prayer group members who prayed for her healing.[280]

Shuko Yamaoka testifies about her daughter's healing. She participated in the CCRM convention in 1988. She prayed for her daughter who had a very poor vision. Her daughter would wear thick glasses. Her daughter did not participate in the convention but God healed her vision problem. Later in 2005, Shuko Yamaoka was suffering from herpes and dysautonomia (autonomic dysfunction). Due to dysautonomia, she had dizziness and anxiety in her. A day before the 11th Kansai regional CCRM convention she slipped and fell on the street. She had a leg sprain but the next day she went to the convention. In the convention hall her right foot had become stiff and had inflammation. The next day during the mass, the priest, Fr. Humprey gave a message that God has healed a person's wound in the right leg. When she heard it, she was shocked. It was indeed her right leg. She was so totally lost in praise and worship that she did not realize her right foot had healed. When she noticed that the wound is no more, she could not but give thanks to the Lord for her healing.[281]

Kashi Ishibashi family was Buddhist. The only Catholic in her family was her uncle. He took her once to a Catholic Church. As a child, she was fascinated to look at the Crucifix. She experienced a deep compassionate look of the Lord from the crucifix. She wanted to go to Catholic kindergarten but her parents refused. However, later she insisted on going to a Catholic High school, run by a congregation of religious nuns. The classes on the Bible

---

280 Kazuko Nakamura, "*Boukou Shuyou Gan ga Iyasareta*" [Bladder Cancer Healed], *Ikeru Mizu*, No. 70 (Fall Edition 1998): 7. Original in Japanese. [Translation mine].

281 Shuko Yamaoka, "*Kansai Taikai de no Iyashi no Akashi Kara*" [Healing Testimonies at Kansai Regional CCRM Convention], *Ikeru Mizu*, No. 75 (Winter Edition 2005): 5-6. Original in Japanese. [Translation mine].

and Christianity influenced her to receive the grace of Baptism. She married a Catholic man and lived peacefully. However, as years passed by her faith life became stagnated. She tried to solve all her problems by herself. She was gradually forgetting about Jesus and the love she had for him. She endured much stress at the work place. Her son wanted to commit suicide because his classmates bullied him at the school. During such a difficult situation, she came to know about the CCRM's plan of organizing a Life in the Spirit Seminar at Tsuchisaki Catholic Church in Akita. She decided to participate in this seminar. She heard the talks and read the scripture with a renewed interest. She realized her folly of trying to fix all her problem by herself. She realized that, she had to surrender all things to the Lord. After praying, she wrote a letter to the Principal of the school where her son was studying. She did not ask the Principal to punish the child who was bullying her son but to take care of that child. She knew that the child who was bullying her son had emotional wounds in his heart and therefore needed love and attention. The letter impressed the Principal very much. He did take necessary action to stop the bullying. All the problems of bullying disappeared and all the stress she was experiencing at the work place too disappeared. She thanks God for healing her emotionally.[282]

Kaneko Ishida participated in the National CCRM convention held in 2006. God healed her joint pains and backache. Her knees were in very bad shape. She could not climb the stairs and even while walking she felt a terrible pain in her knees since July 2005. During the Holy Eucharist in the convention, she asked for forgiveness and grace to follow sincerely God's ways. When she was returning home, she realized that she could climb up the stairs of the railway bridge without any pain. She thanks God for the healing. When she reached home, she realized that God had healed her excruciating back pain too.[283]

282 Kashi Ishibashi, "*Tsuchisaki Kyokai de no Semina ni Sankashite: Junbisareteita Michi*" [Participating in the Seminar at Tsuchisaki Church: The Way Prepared], *Ikeru Mizu*, No. 75 (Winter Edition 2005): 7. Original in Japanese. [Translation mine].

283 Kaneko Ishida, "*Taikai Jimukyoku ni Yoserareta Akashi no Naka Kara*" [Testimonies Sent to Convention Office], *Ikeru Mizu*, No. 82 (Fall Edition 2006): 3-4. Original in Japanese. [Translation mine].

Chiyoko Yoshioka had a very bad migraine headache since 2004. She attended the National CCRM convention held in 2006. During the Holy Mass, Fr. Edward the main celebrant said that God has healed a person with migraine headache. At the same moment, Yoshioka experienced healing of her migraine. She used to think that healing is only for special people. People like her are not worthy. However, God healed her. She praises God for his mercy and love.[284]

Nobuko Oouchi had detachment of the retina of her left eye in 1990. She had a surgery for rectification of this problem but it did not help her. Her eyesight kept on dwindling and she could hardly see anything with her left eye. In 1995, she had once again detachment of the retina of her left eye. Doctors decided not to operate on her, as it would be very risky. In 2005, she attended the CCRM convention and on the second day of the convention during lunch break, she realized she could see her surroundings very clearly. After a very long time she could see the beautiful blue sky. She could distinguish each leaf on the tree. Previously due to her poor vision she could see everything very hazily. She was not able to make fine distinctions. However, after God healed her, she regained her eyesight. She went to an eye specialist to confirm her healing and told him about the problem of the detachment of retina which she was suffering earlier. The eye specialist checked her eye and told her that, her eye is completely fine. Moreover, there were no marks of the previous operation which she had 15 years ago. Secondly, during the convention she prayed for her second son who was suffering from kidney stones. After the convention, she received a letter from him saying that during the second diagnosis the kidney stones disappeared. She thanks God for the healing of her eye and the kidney problem of her son.[285]

---

284 Chiyoko Yoshioka, "*Taikai Jimukyoku ni Yoserareta Akashi no Naka Kara*" [Testimonies Sent to Convention Office], *Ikeru Mizu*, No. 82 (Fall Edition 2006): 4. Original in Japanese. [Translation mine].

285 Nobuko Oouchi, "*Taikai Jimukyoku ni Yoserareta Akashi no Naka Kara*" [Testimonies Sent to Convention Office], *Ikeru Mizu*, No. 82 (Fall Edition 2006): 5. Original in Japanese. [Translation mine].

Doctors had diagnosed Yukiko Ishikawa with lung tumor. She had a son who had brain tumor. Her husband too was a sickly person. She was in distress and pain. At that time Higashi, a parishioner of Tsuchiura Catholic Church recommended her to go to the convention. Yukiko Ishikawa had no idea of the CCRM but decided to participate in the National CCRM convention held in February 2000. On February 12, 2000 Fr. Tom DiLorenzo, a diocesan priest of Boston Archdiocese, the main speaker at the convention called all the sick people to come forward in order to pray over them. Yukiko Ishikawa went forward and whispered a prayer of total surrender to the Lord. Fr. Tom DiLorenzo gave the message that God has healed a person having lung tumor. At that very moment, Yukiko Ishikawa knew that God healed her. She felt light. Instead of the tremendous pain, she experienced a tremendous joy within her. After the convention on February 26, 2000, she underwent a Computed Tomography (CT) scan and the results confirmed that the tumor had disappeared. She thanks and praises God for giving her new life.[286]

Kiyoko Matsumura was suffering from five different diseases since 1985. Her condition was very bad and her mother had lost all hope of her recovery. It was in such difficult times, members of the CCRM recommended her to join prayer meetings held at Yotsuya, Tokyo. After participating in the meetings her faith deepened. She decided to participate in National CCRM convention held in 2000. Her husband requested Fr. Tom DiLorenzo to pray over her. However, he told him that she should pray for healing after receiving the Holy Eucharist. The convention ended on February 13, 2000 but God did not heal her. However, she kept her faith and continued to read the books on renewal, which she had bought at the convention hall. On February 23, 2000 while she was continuing to praise God, her pain left her. She went to the hospital to confirm her healing. The diagnosis clearly revealed that all her organs were functioning properly and all her internal swelling disappeared. All were surprised to see her healthy again because she had been suffering for 14 long

286 Yukiko Ishikawa, "*Sono Hi Iyasareta HaiShuyou*" [Lung Tumor was Healed That Day] in *Jesus 2000: Shu no Eiko he no Maneki* [Jesus 2000: Invited to Partake in the Glory of the Lord], 47. Original in Japanese. [Translation mine].

years. She thanks God for His healing touch and above all for His love.[287]

Yonago Asanuma was suffering from severe joint pains for many years. She could not kneel down to pray. It was not possible for her to bend the knees. She participated in National CCRM convention in 2000. During the prayer services, she saw people around her kneeling and praying. She felt very bad because she wanted to kneel and pray. However, her knee pain kept her from doing so. It was at that time she felt someone supporting her to stand. After a few moments, she saw herself kneeling and praying. She was surprised to see herself kneeling. Her joint pain vanished. God healed her knee.[288]

Aiko Tsuboi received Baptism in 1995 but had no knowledge about the CCRM. Her friend recommended her to participate in National CCRM convention, 2000. For the first time Aiko Tsuboi could whole-heartedly participate in prayers especially the Holy Eucharist. She also had a very good confession, which she did not like previously. She could also pray before the Blessed Sacrament. On the third day of the convention, Fr. Tom DiLorenzo said that, God has healed a person who was receiving radiation therapy for breast cancer. She immediately knew that the message was for her. She had breast cancer and she was undergoing radiation therapy. Her physical condition had debilitated. However, after receiving healing, she regained her strength and vigor immediately. She praises God for all the graces He gave her during the convention.[289]

Mayumi Tominaga attended the 14th Kansai regional CCRM convention in 2009. She noted in her testimony that her mother did not love her. After the death of her young brother in her childhood, her mother could not overcome the grief. She neglected her. Tominaga

---

287 Kiyoko Matsumura, "*14 Nen Buri ni Iyasarete*" [14 Years Old Sickness Healed] in *Jesus 2000: Shu no Eiko he no Maneki* [Jesus 2000: Invited to Partake in the Glory of the Lord], 47. Original in Japanese. [Translation mine].

288 Yonago Asanuma, "*Watashi no Hiza ga Iyasareru to ha*" [My Knee was Healed] in *Jesus 2000: Shu no Eiko he no Maneki* [Jesus 2000: Invited to Partake in the Glory of the Lord], 47. Original in Japanese. [Translation mine].

289 Aiko Tsuboi, "*Houshasenn de Yowatteita Watashi wo*" [I was Getting Weak Because Of Radiation] in *Jesus 2000: Shu no Eiko he no Maneki* [Jesus 2000: Invited to Partake in the Glory of the Lord], 47. Original in Japanese. [Translation mine].

had ill feeling towards her mother. However, after attending the convention she experienced healing of her painful memories. In addition, even though her mother did not attend the convention, she experienced peace in her heart.[290]

The above testimonies point out that God has indeed healed many people during the various CCRM programs. Healings are not a sign of personal holiness but they are manifestation of God's unfathomable love and mercy. It is not necessary that God must heal a person during healing services. God's ways are different and inscrutable. We will never know why God heals some people. Whether God heals a person or not, the message, which the CCRM gives, is that God cares for each person. When a person realizes this great love of God for him or her, a deep inner healing already starts effecting in that person.Thus we can conclude that the CCRM has encouraged the use of charisms especially charism of healing and prophecy for the good of the community.

4.1.5 Intercessory Prayers

Jesus says, "For where two or three are gathered in my name, I am there among them" (Mt 18:20). Intercessory prayers are a common feature the CCRM prayer groups. During prayer meetings, conventions or retreats, members offer intercessory prayers for different intentions. The CCRM acknowledges the power in intercessory prayers. In some CCRM prayer groups, there are special intercessory prayer groups who meet on regular basis to pray for different needs of the Church and the society. Following are some of the testimonies about the power of intercessory prayers.

Aiko Hattori testified that she felt happy that her prayer group members are praying for her. She knew they would pray for her at all times. She feels it was because of the power of the intercessory prayer she had a profound experience of the Holy Spirit.[291] Fr. Francis Mathy, a Jesuit priest and one of the pioneers of the CCRM in Japan

---

290 Mayumi Tominaga, "*Reiteki Iyashi ni Kansha*" [Thanks for the Spiritual Healing], *Ikeru Mizu*, No. 94 (Fall Edition 2009): 2. Original in Japanese. [Translation mine].

291 Aiko Hattori, "*Seirei no Hi ha*" [The Fire of the Holy Spirit], *Ikeru Mizu,* No.46 (Special Edition 1998): 6. Original in Japanese. [Translation mine].

calls upon all those involved with the CCRM to spend more time in intercessory prayers. He feels that intercessory prayers are of a great help to bring back the youth and children to the Church. In Japan, usually the old people are attracted towards the Church and prayers. However, for a vibrant Church, all her members both young and old should gather to praise God. Fr. Francis Mathy believes intercessory prayers are very powerful and can help to illuminate the minds of the youth and children to come to the Lord.[292]

Hiromi Yamada received Baptism in the Holy Spirit when he was studying in the UK. After returning back, he could not experience the power of the Holy Spirit in the CCRM prayer meetings in Japan. He was confused because it is the same Holy Spirit, which worked so powerfully in the UK. It was in such a situation he realized that the prayer group in Japan had been praying for him even when he was in the UK. He realized that whether it is UK or Japan, it is the same Holy Spirit, which works. When people come together and pray, Jesus is present there.[293]

Momoko Kurozawa testified that she felt happy because she was a member of the intercessory prayer group. She notes that the intercessory prayers especially for healing of relationships between countries are very important. She shares her experience about a Korean prayer group. Generally, there is lot of hurt feelings in the hearts of the Korean people against the Japanese for the atrocities they did during the war. Korea had been a colony of Japan for some time and so there still exists rancor in the hearts of the Koreans against the Japanese. Momoko Kurozawa representing the Japanese asked for pardon from the Koreans for all the bad things that the Japanese did to the Koreans. The Koreans forgave her and all the Japanese. She feels intercessory prayers have great power and can be effective in bridging gap between nations and healing the broken relations.[294]

---

292 Francis Mathy, "*Utage no Ato ni*" [After the Wedding Banquet], *Ikeru Mizu,* No. 47 (Special Edition 1998): 1-2. Original in Japanese. [Translation mine].

293 Hiromi Yamada, "*Tokyo de no Zenkoku Taikai ni Sankashite*" [Participating in National CCRM Convention at Tokyo], *Ikeru Mizu,* No. 47 (Special Edition 1998): 7. Original in Japanese. [Translation mine].

294 Momoko Kurozawa, "*Torinashi no Houshi ni Manekarete*" [Called to the Ministry of Intercessory Prayers], *Ikeru Mizu,* No. 50 (Fall Edition 1998): 12-13. Original in Japanese. [Translation mine].

Masae Tsuchida participated in the 14th Hokkaido regional CCRM convention and prayed for his two friends who were critically ill. One of his friends had cancer operation, and the other suffered from progressive muscular dystrophy. God answered his prayers. God healed his friends miraculously and they regained good health. Because of this miracle, he is convinced of the power of the intercessory prayers.[295]

Intercessory prayers are very important to support spiritually the people who are in need of prayers. The CCRM prayer groups are places where intercessory prayers form a regular part of the prayer meeting. It has set up national network of intercessory prayers to pray for special intentions.

4.1.6 Fellowship

One of the features of the CCRM is fellowship. Prayer and love united the early Christian community. "Now the whole group of those who believed was of one heart and soul" (Acts 4:32). The CCRM insists on the importance of these characteristics of love, prayer, and fellowship found among the early Christians. The CCRM aims that every member of the Catholic Church establishes a fraternal relationship with others. In the CCRM groups, one can find the commitment of the members to form a community of like-minded Christians. Fellowship is very important to help a Christian live in a world, which, is far away from the Gospel values. The effects of secularization, materialism, utilitarianism, and individualism are threatening the faith life. In such a scenario, a community, solidly based on the values of Christ, becomes a place of refuge. It also replenishes one's energy to live according to the values of Christ. There may be arguments and discussions in a community. Not all members may agree on an issue. However, a community, which prays together, also has the courage to forgive and accept one another.[296] Pope John Paul II in his Apostolic Exhortation *Christifedeles Laici*

295 Shirou Ishii, "*Dai Juu Yon Kai Seirei ni Yoru Sasshin Hokkaido Taikai Hirakareru*" [14th Hokkaido Regional CCRM Convention Opens], *Ikeru Mizu*, No. 53 (Summer Edition 1999): 3. Original In Japanese. [Translation mine].

296 See Albert Marie DeMonléon, "The Movements as Places of a Transfigured Humanity," in *Movements in the Church*, 158.

notes that the new communities are a fruit of the divine intervention. He acknowledges their existence as useful for the life and the growth of the Church. He notes that:

> We can speak of a new era of group endeavours of the lay faithful. In fact, alongside the traditional forming of associations, and at times coming from their very roots, movements and new sodalities have sprouted, with a specific feature and purpose, so great is the richness and the versatility of resources that the Holy Spirit nourishes in the ecclesial community, and so great is the capacity of initiative and the generosity of our lay people.[297]

Following are some of the testimonies, which exhibit the importance of fellowship in the CCRM prayer groups.

Takaki Ishizaki notes that whenever he was in trouble or difficulty, he could always rely on the CCRM prayer group for spiritual support. He is grateful to the late Bishop Arikata Kobayashi, priests and religious who supported and loved him. He testifies that though he would be tired physically or mentally because of his problems at his work place, he could always find healing and relaxation when he would be with the prayer group. He first encountered the CCRM prayer group in 1980 and since then he has continued to take part regularly in the prayer meetings. He always found the presence of Christ in the community.[298]

Kayoko Yamaguchi was a nominal Christian. She did not know how to pray and deepen her relationship with God. She met the CCRM at the Okinawa regional CCRM convention held in 2000. Since then she has found spiritual support from the CCRM prayer group members. She thanks God for the group because it is through them she learnt how to have a deeper relationship with the person of the Holy Spirit. She started participating in the Holy Eucharist with great devotion and faith. She feels that, it is difficult to live in this world as a Christian because the values of the world are in conflict

---

297 Apostolic Exhortation *Christifideles Laici,* No. 29, *AAS* 88.1 (1989) 443-446.

298 Takaki Ishizaki, "*Touhoku Taikai ni Sankashite*" [Participating in the Northeast Regional CCRM Convention], *Ikeru Mizu,* No. 55 (Winter Edition 2000): 3. Original in Japanese. [Translation mine].

with the values of Christ. In such a situation, it is the support of the like-minded Christians, which is very important for growing stronger in faith and living the values of Christ in day-to-day life.[299]

Fr. Haku Sasaki notes that CCRM conventions and prayer meetings foster deeper communion among Christians. It is not merely a human endeavor but a deep spiritual communion. The basis for this fellowship is the Holy Trinity. St. John wrote in his letter, "We declare to you what we have seen and heard so that you also may have fellowship with us; and truly our fellowship is with the Father and with his Son Jesus Christ" (1 Jn 1.3). The fellowship of the Holy Trinity is base for the Christian life.

Fr. Sasaki notes that Christian fellowship exists not only during the conventions or during prayer meetings but also at all times. Even though when members are physically away from each other, there is spiritual fellowship among them.[300]

4.1.7 Serving Parishes

The main task of the CCRM is to serve the Church. It works for the renewal of the Church. The CCRM can contribute for the renewal of the parishes by promoting a better understanding of the role of the Holy Spirit in the life of a Christian. Doctrines and dissertations on the Holy Spirit will not suffice to make people aware of the dynamic presence of the Holy Spirit. The life of the Charismatics will influence people more than the doctrines. Those involved in the CCRM will have to bear witness to the activity of the Holy Spirit in their personal lives. Their lives must be renewed and transformed. All those who see them must see the change. If others can really see the role and the activities of the Holy Spirit in their lives, then surely they will accept the teachings of the CCRM. This can bring genuine renewal in the Church.[301]

---

299 Kayoko Yamaguchi, "*Seirei Sasshin Okinawa Taikai ni Sankashite*" [Participating in the Okinawa Regional CCRM Convention], *Ikeru Mizu*, No. 55 (Winter Edition 2000): 5. Original in Japanese. [Translation mine].

300 Haku Sasaki, "*Dai Sei Nen ni Ibuki wo Ukete*" [Receive the Breath During the Great Holy Year], *Ikeru Mizu*, No. 56 (Spring Edition 2000): 1. Original in Japanese. [Translation mine].

301 DeMontigny, "*Shoukyoku to Karisuma Sasshin*" [Parishes and CCRM], in *Shu no Ibuki: Bassui Ban* [Breath of the Lord: Excerpts], Vol. 4, 22-23. Original in

The CCRM could also contribute by promoting the necessity of the renewal in prayer life. The Holy Spirit deepens one's prayer life. St. Paul says, "Likewise the Spirit helps us in our weakness; for we do not know how to pray as we ought, but that very Spirit intercedes with sighs too deep for words" (Rom 8:26). The CCRM has the obligation to show to the Church that genuine apostolic work is not possible without a sustained prayer life. Lack of prayer can lead to a spiritual dryness. In spite of all the activism, a person may leave the Church, for he or she may find no meaning in his or her apostolic work. Modern science offers sophisticated gadgets as tools for apostolic work and evangelization. Even though, they are useful and important means for apostolic work, they would be ineffective for mission work if the person who uses them were not a person of prayer. In the Acts of the Apostles, we read that when the apostles had to deal with the problem of unequal distribution of goods among the early Christian community, they decided to set apart people to do this work. They chose other people because they did not want to neglect prayer and their missionary work. The twelve apostles called together the whole community of the disciples and said,

> It is not right that we should neglect the Sacred Scriptures in order to wait on tables. Therefore, friends, select from among yourselves seven men of good standing, full of the Spirit and of wisdom, whom we may appoint to this task, while we, for our part, will devote ourselves to prayer and to serving the word. (Acts 6:2-4)

The apostles chose prayer and the Word of God above all other activities. The same is true for the present day disciples of Christ. All the parish activities must flow from prayer of the parishioners and only then, they will bear an abundant fruit. Prayer and apostolic work goes hand in hand. Again, those who are involved in the CCRM must teach the importance of prayer through their own lives. They must be truly people of prayer, who participate in Holy Eucharist

---

Japanese. [Translation mine].

with ardent faith and devotion and bear fruits of prayer in their daily lives.[302]

No parish community is an ideal community. Each has its own merits and demerits. The CCRM can contribute greatly to the parishes by promoting true Christian fellowship. It emphasizes fellowship among its members. It can be a model for the parish community, if its members unite in love with one another. The base for a fruitful fellowship is sharing and caring. If others see these qualities in Charismatics, then it can give them a good example to follow.[303]

St. Paul says, "Our message of the Gospel came to you not in word only, but also in power and in the Holy Spirit and with full conviction" (1 Thes 1:5). St. Paul's message has link with the promise of Jesus. "But you will receive power when the Holy Spirit has come upon you; and you will be my witnesses in Jerusalem, in all Judea and Samaria, and to the ends of the earth" (Acts 1:8). Jesus promised His disciples power of the Holy Spirit to do the missionary work. Indeed the whole of the Acts of the Apostles clearly demonstrates this fact. The early Christians did the missionary work with the power of the Holy Spirit. The Acts of the Apostles reports that the apostles and disciples worked many miracles in the power of the Holy Spirit.

> Awe came upon everyone, because many wonders and signs were being done by the apostles. (Acts 2:43) Now many signs and wonders were done among the people through the apostles. And they were all together in Solomon's Portico. None of the rest dared to join them, but the people held them in high esteem. Yet more than ever believers were added to the Lord, great numbers of both men and women, so that they even carried out the sick into the streets, and laid them on cots and mats, in order that Peter's shadow might fall on some of them as he came by. (Acts 5:12-15)

302 DeMontigny, "*Shoukyoku to Karisuma Sasshin*" [Parishes and CCRM], in *Shu no Ibuki: Bassui Ban* [Breath of the Lord: Excerpts], Vol. 4, 22-23. Original in Japanese. [Translation mine].

303 Ibid., 24.

Another way, the CCRM can contribute to parish renewal is by promoting the use of spiritual charisms. The CCRM emphasizes the use of charisms. In its prayer meetings, people exercise their charism for the good of the community. However, it must take care to impart sound teaching on the discernment of charisms and the need to be submissive (of course not blindly) to Church authorities in matters pertaining to the use of charisms.[304]

The CCRM requests the following from the local parishes. The CCRM requests all the parishioners including the priest to make an objective judgment about the renewal movement. In the CCRM prayer meetings, people raise their hands, clap, sing spontaneously and praise God in loud voices. Some also use of gift of tongues. Some people may not like these features of the CCRM. They may think of the Charismatics as abnormal. However, the CCRM urges people not to judge it by these features alone. The Charismatic spirituality is much wider. These features are peripheral and not the core of the Charismatic spirituality.[305]

Successive Popes from Pope Paul VI to Pope Francis have highlighted the significance of the CCRM in the life of the Church. They agree that CCRM is a movement, which gives importance to prayer, Bible, Sacraments and service. Pope Paul VI defined the CCRM as follows:

> Certain common notes appear in this renewal: the taste for deep prayer, personal and in groups, a return to contemplation and an emphasis on praise of God, the desire to devote oneself completely to Christ, a great availability for the calls of the Holy Spirit, more assiduous reading of the Sacred Scriptures, generous brotherly devotion, the will to make a contribution to the service of the Church. In all that, we can recognize the mysterious and discreet work of the Spirit, who is the soul of the Church.[306]

---

304 DeMontigny, "*Shoukyoku to Karisuma Sasshin*" [Parishes and CCRM], in *Shu no Ibuki: Bassui Ban* [Breath of the Lord: Excerpts], vol. 4, 25. Original in Japanese. [Translation mine].

305 Ibid., 26.

306 Original Version in French is as follows, Certaines notes communes apparaissent dans ce renouveau: le goût d'une prière profonde, personnelle et

The CCRM prays for greater openness to the workings of the Holy Spirit in parishes. Some priests and parishioners can misjudge the relevance of the CCRM They may discard it as a cult. However, before making any judgment on the CCRM, they must read the advice of Gamaliel regarding judging spiritual movements.

> But a Pharisee in the council named Gamaliel, a teacher of the law, respected by all the people, stood up and ordered the men to be put outside for a short time. Then he said to them, 'Fellow Israelites, consider carefully what you propose to do to these men. For some time ago Theudas rose up, claiming to be somebody, and a number of men, about four hundred, joined him; but he was killed, and all who followed him were dispersed and disappeared. After him Judas the Galilean rose up at the time of the census and got people to follow him; he also perished, and all who followed him were scattered. So in the present case, I tell you, keep away from these men and let them alone; because if this plan or this undertaking is of human origin, it will fail; but if it is of God, you will not be able to overthrow them in that case you may even be found fighting against God.' (Acts 5:34-39)

If the CCRM is not a genuine movement of the Holy Spirit, it will die its natural death, but if it is genuine, then those who oppose it for any reasons, will be opposing the work of God. Pope Paul VI in his address of May 19, 1975 to the Participants of the Third Catholic Charismatic Renewal Congress noted that the CCRM is a *chance for the Church.* "How then could this 'spiritual renewal' not be 'a chance' for the Church and for the world? And how, in this case, could one

communautaire, un retour à la contemplation et un accent mis sur la louange de Dieu, le désir de se livrer totalement au Christ, une grande disponibilité aux appels de l'Esprit Saint, une fréquentation plus assidue de l'Ecriture, un large dévouement fraternel, la volonté d'apporter un concours aux services de l'Eglise. En tout cela, nous pouvons reconnaître l'oeuvre mystérieuse et discrète de l'Esprit, qui est l'âme de l'Eglise. "Address on the Occasion of First International Leaders' Conference, October 10, 1973," Insegnamenti di Paolo VI, 11(1973): 971-972.

not take all the means to ensure that it remains so?"[307] Pope John Paul in his private address of December 11, 1979 to ICCRO council members said that, "I am convinced that this movement is a sign of his [Lord's] action... I am convinced that this movement is a very important component in the total renewal of the Church, in this spiritual renewal of the Church."[308] These two Pontiffs acknowledged the CCRM as a genuine. Moreover, one must judge the CCRM by the fruits it bears.[309] (see Mt 7:16-18).

St. Paul writes to the Thessalonians, "Do not quench the Spirit. Do not despise the words of prophets, but test everything; hold fast to what is good" (1 Thes 5:19-21). It is important to both acknowledge and discern the works of the Holy Spirit. The CCRM is open to discernment and asks the ecclesial authorities to discern its activities. It urges them to weed out what is not from God.[310]

Some Charismatics may live a scandalous life. Their life can tarnish the image of the whole CCRM. However, it is important to note that the life of one Charismatic should not be standard to judge the entire movement. One can find scandalous people in any religion or movement. This does not mean that all the followers of that religion or movement are also bad. Judas was one of the apostles of Jesus. Jesus selected him. He saw the various miracles that Jesus performed and yet in the end, he became a traitor. One can apply this example in the case of Charismatics living a scandalous life. Like Judas, they too are witnesses to the mighty work of the Holy Spirit. However, they betray the Lord by choosing to live a life, against the values of the Gospel. We cannot judge Christ by the life of Judas. Similarly, we cannot judge the CCRM by the lives of some Charismatics. It is

---

307 "Address of Pope Paul VI to the Participants of the Third Catholic Charismatic Renewal Congress, May 19, 1975," *AAS 67* (1975): 364-368.

308 "Address to Members of ICCRO on December 11, 1979," in *Open the Windows: The Popes and Charismatic Renewal,* 26.

309 DeMontigny, "*Shoukyoku to Karisuma Sasshin*" [Parishes and CCRM], in *Shu no Ibuki: Bassui Ban* [Breath of the Lord: Excerpts], Vol. 4, 26. Original in Japanese. [Translation mine].

310 Ibid., 27.

important to make differences between individuals and the whole movement as such.[311]

The Leaders of the CCRM insist that all those who have received the baptism in the Holy Spirit must be active members of their local parishes. There may be opposition to the CCRM from many quarters in the parish but these people are supposed to be like flowers in the garden that diffuse their splendor come what may. If a person involved in the CCRM lives authentic Christian life then even those who are opposed to the CCRM will begin to acknowledge that it is indeed a movement from the Holy Spirit.[312] Therefore, the onus of bringing true renewal in the Church through the CCRM lies on individual Church members. It is their actual life witness, which would speak more powerfully than words.

4.1.8 Vocations to Priesthood and Religious Life

Vocation to priesthood and religious life is declining in Japan. Nevertheless, the CCRM has hope that the Lord will bless the Church with vocations. They offer petitions for vocations during the prayer meetings, conventions and retreats. Pope John Paul II in his General Audience of October 5, 1994, noted that the new movements are promoting vocations to priesthood and consecrated life. He emphasized that though these movements are lay in nature, they always orient their members towards priesthood and consecrated life.

> In recent times a number of 'movements' and 'ecclesial assemblies' have appeared. I spoke words of appreciation for them on the occasion of a conference, organized by Episcopal Conference of Italy, on the Christian community and the association of laity. Though these movements or assemblies are composed of lay people, they often orient their members or a part of their members to practice evangelical counsels.

---

311 DeMontigny, "*Shoukyoku to Karisuma Sasshin*" [Parishes and CCRM], in *Shu no Ibuki: Bassui Ban* [Breath of the Lord: Excerpts], Vol. 4, 26. Original in Japanese. [Translation mine

312 Ibid., 32.

> Consequently, though they are declared as lay group, among them groups or communities of consecrated life are born. And further, this form of consecrated life may be accompanied by an opening to the priestly ministry, if some of these Communities direct the young people to priestly ministry.[313]

Pope John Paul II in his address of February 25, 1995 to the Bishops of Japan on their '*Ad Limina*' visit called upon the bishops, priests, religious and all laity to pray for an increase in vocations in Japan because it is an important part in the life of the Japanese Church.

> I express my prayerful support of the men and women Religious who, through their witness and their various apostolates, play such an important part in the life of your particular Churches. I pray that the whole Japanese Catholic community will become more conscious of the need to pray for and to foster vocations to the priesthood and consecrated life. In all things 'be watchful, stand firm in your faith, be courageous, be strong. Let all that you do be done in love' (1 Cor. 16:13-14).[314]

Pope Benedict XVI in his message of May 22, 2006 to the participants of the Second World Congress of Ecclesial Movements and New Communities called on the CCRM to foster vocations to priesthood and consecrated life, to sustain and encourage the work of evangelization.

> Today, the Ecclesial Movements and New Communities are a luminous sign of the beauty of Christ and of the Church, his Bride. You belong to the living structure of the Church. She thanks you for your missionary commitment, for the formative action on behalf of Christian families that you are increasingly

313 "General Audience of October 5, 1994," *Insegnamenti di Giovanni Paolo II*, 17.2 (1994): 441-442. Original in Italian. [Translation mine].

314 "Address to the Bishops of Japan on their 'Ad Limina' Visit on February 25, 1995," *AAS* 88.2 (1996): 1030.

> developing and for the promotion of vocations to the ministerial priesthood and consecrated life, which you nurture among your members.[315]

Again, Pope Benedict XVI in his address of December 15, 2007 to the Bishops of Japan on their '*Ad Limina*' visit noted that the Church needs vocations.

> Young people especially are at risk of being deceived by the glamour of modern secular culture. Yet, like all the greater and lesser hopes that appear on first sight to promise so much, this turns out to be a false hope and tragically, disillusion not infrequently leads to depression and despair, even to suicide. If their youthful energy and enthusiasm can be directed towards the things of God, which alone are sufficient to satisfy their deepest longings, more young people will be inspired to commit their lives to Christ, and some will recognize a call to serve him in the priesthood or the religious life. Invite them to consider whether this may be their vocation. Never be afraid to do so. Encourage your priests and religious likewise to be active in promoting vocations, and lead your people in prayer, asking the Lord to 'send out labourers into his harvest' (*Mt* 9:38).[316]

The Church is in need of priests and religious to spread the Kingdom of God. In Japan, Christianity is a minority religion. Japanese youth are disinterested in Church activities. This attitude of the Japanese poses a serious challenge to the existence of the Church in Japan. Nevertheless, in spite of all these challenges there are signs of new life springing especially through movements like the CCRM. There are few youth after their encounter with the CCRM decided to dedicate their lives to the Lord as priests and religious. Following

---

315 "Message to the Participants of the Second World Congress of Ecclesial Movements and New Communities, May 22, 2006," in *Insegnamenti di Benedetto XVI*, 2.1 (2006): 662-665.

316 "Address to Bishops of Japan on their 'Ad Limina' Visit on December 15, 2007," *Insegnamenti di Benedetto XVI*, 3.2 (2007): 854-857.

are the cases of young men who joined priesthood because of their encounter with the CCRM.

Mutou attended the CCRM prayer meetings at Tokyo's Hatsudai Catholic Church. His involvement in the CCRM helped him to discover his vocation to the priesthood. He responded to the Lord's call. He later joined the Nagoya diocese and became the pioneer to start the CCRM prayer meeting at Nagoya.[317]

In 1998, on the 50th Anniversary of the beginning of the Society of St. Columban in Japan, Sr. Briege McKenna and Fr. Kevin Sallon organized a series of retreats. The book *Prayer: Springs of Grace* by Sr. Briege McKenna influenced a young Japanese man during the retreat. After reading the book, he felt the Lord is calling him to priesthood. At the end of the retreat, he decided to join the seminary to become a priest.[318]

Again, the CCRJ newsletter *Ikeru Mizu*, reports that one of the participants of the 17th Hokkaido regional CCRM convention held in May 2002, decided to join religious congregation. He received the grace to respond to the Lord's call during that convention.[319] Fr. Hata, a Passionist priest credits the CCRM for his vocation. He testifies the following:

> The CCRM began in Japan in 1972. I encountered the CCRM a few years later and had a life transforming experience. I decided to be a priest. I am convinced that these prayer meetings are the work of the Holy Spirit. In fact, love, peace and joy are the characteristic features of these prayer meetings. Even the Holy Father has encouraged the CCRM. He has asked all the faithful to

317 Keiko Fukuhara, "*Hitori no Shingakusei ni Yotte*" [Through One Seminarian], *Ikeru Mizu,* No. 46 (Special Edition 1997): 4-5. Original in Japanese. [Translation mine].

318 Editorial Board of *Ikeru Mizu*, "*Sei Coronban Kai Senkyo Gojuu Shunen wo Iwatte*" [Celebrating 50 Years of Mission of the Society of St. Columban Mission], *Ikeru Mizu*, No. 52 (Spring Edition 1999): 11. Original In Japanese. [Translation mine].

319 Ichigen Kimura, "*Watashitachi ha Heiwa to Yurushi wo Tsutaeru Messenja*" [We are the Messengers of Peace and Forgiveness], *Ikeru Mizu*, No. 65 (Summer Edition 2002): 2. Original in Japanese. [Translation mine].

> receive the power of the Holy Spirit to contribute to the mission of the Church. The power of the Holy Spirit is love and truth.[320]

Thus, we can conclude that the CCRM has been influential in attracting a few young people to join priesthood and religious life in Japan.

4.1.9 Integration with the Migrant Community

The statistics data of the *Catholic Commission of Japan for Migrants, Refugees and People on the Move* puts the number of Catholics, belonging to other nationalities (other than Japanese) at 563,698.[321] It is interesting to note that the population of Japanese Catholics was 444,441 according to the Statistics of the Catholic Church published by CBCJ.[322] This shows that around 56% of the total Catholic population in Japan consists of people belonging to different nationalities and only 44% of the total Catholic population is Japanese. In such a scenario, it is but natural that the Catholic Church must attend to the spiritual, pastoral and temporal needs of these people. Since 1960, The Catholic Church in Japan has been organizing various programs to cater to the needs of the migrant Catholics. In 2001 at the plenary meeting of the CBCJ, the bishops officially announced the *Catholic Commission of Japan for Migrants, Refugees and People on the Move* to work for the migrants. Since then this commission caters to the various needs of the migrant community. It organizes Holy Eucharist in foreign languages in different churches across Japan. It offers catechism courses for children and youth in various languages. It helps them to get just

---

320 Motoyuki Hata, "*Okinawa de Shinko Sasshin no Tameni no Mokusokai Hirakareru*" [Convention for Renewal of Faith at Okinawa], *Ikeru Mizu*, No. 65 (Summer Edition 2002): 3. Original in Japanese. [Translation mine].

321 Catholic Commission of Japan for Migrants, Refugees and People on the Move, *Survey of the Number of Faith* (Tokyo: Catholic Commission of Japan for Migrants, Refugees and People on the Move, 2005), 1-2. http://www.jcarm.com/eng/survey/survey05.pdf [accessed on September 14, 2014]

322 Catholic Bishops' Conference of Japan, *Statistics of* the Catholic Church in Japan 2014, 1-3.

wages. It also helps them to register in local ward offices. At times, it also offers food and temporary shelter. It also offers legal assistance especially if there is any violation of human rights at their work places. One of the problems, which the Catholic Church faces, is the integration of migrant community with the locals. Even though the *Catholic Commission of Japan for Migrants, Refugees and People on the Move* is organizing various programs to help the migrants, it has not succeeded in the task of total integration. It is both a challenge and the need of the Catholic Church. St. Paul writes to the Galatians, "There is no longer Jew or Greek, there is no longer slave or free... for all of you are one in Christ Jesus" (Gal 3:27-28). He emphasizes on Christian unity. Indeed, it is the mission of the Catholic Church to promote this universality of faith in Christ.

Pope John Paul II in his address of May 27, 1998 to the World Congress of Ecclesial Movements and New Communities notes that new ecclesial have played a great role in encouraging Catholics to live an authentic Christian life.

> Their presence is encouraging because it shows that this springtime is advancing and revealing the freshness of the Christian experience based on personal encounter with Christ. Even in the diversity of their forms, these movements are marked by a common awareness of the 'newness' which Baptismal grace brings to life, through a remarkable longing to reflect on the mystery of communion with Christ and with their brethren, through sound fidelity to the patrimony of the faith passed on by the living stream of Tradition. This gives rise to a renewed missionary zeal, which reaches out, to the men and women of our era in the concrete situations where they find themselves, and turns its loving attention to the dignity, needs, and destiny of each individual.[323]

Pope John Paul II in his address of February 25, 1995 to the Bishops of Japan on their '*Ad Limina*' visit noted about the increase

323 "Address to the World Congress of Ecclesial Movements and New Communities, May 27, 1998," *Insegnamenti di Giovanni Paolo II*, No. 2, 21.1 (1998): 1062.

in the number of migrant Catholics and the responsibility of the Catholic Church towards.

> The particular Churches over which you preside in love are undergoing a profound transformation, due to the arrival in your midst of large numbers of immigrant workers, many of whom are Catholics.... The presence among you of so many brothers and sisters from other cultural backgrounds should be seen by Japanese Catholics as an opportunity to give fuller expression to the universality and Catholicity of the Church. Paradoxically, while these immigrants face great difficulties and are sometimes subjected to unjust treatment, their situation is making many people more aware of the demands of justice and the implications of respect for universal human rights.[324]

Pope Benedict XVI in his address of December 15, 2007 to the Bishops of Japan on their '*Ad Limina*' visit noted that the migrant Catholic community must be integrated in the life of the Japanese Church and the Church must encourage them to use their diverse gifts for the growth of the Church.

> The Lord's harvest in Japan is increasingly made up of people of diverse nationalities, to the extent that over half of the Catholic population is formed of immigrants. This provides an opportunity to enrich the life of the Church in your country and to experience the true catholicity of God's people. By taking steps to ensure that all are made to feel welcome in the Church, you can draw on the many gifts that the immigrants bring.[325]

Late Stefen Fumio Cardinal Hamao, former President of the Pontifical Council for the Pastoral Care of Migrants and Itinerant People in his address to the participants of the *Fourth World Meeting*

---

324 "Address to the Bishops of Japan on their 'Ad Limina' Visit on February 25, 1995," *AAS* 88.2 (1996): 1028.

325 "Address to Bishops of Japan on their 'Ad Limina' Visit on December 15, 2007," *Insegnamenti di Benedetto XVI*, 3.2 (2007): 854-857.

of Families held in January 2003, underlined the role that the Renewal Movements can play in helping the immigrants to find comfort and solace in the foreign land. He noted in his address that people who move out to other countries no matter for what reason are vulnerable and in a weaker position in the society which is foreign to them. It is the duty of the Catholic Church and of the Renewal Movements to reach out to them. The Renewal Movements must practice the Gospel values, which they teach. They must work for the weak, the poor and the needy. The late Cardinal Hamao noted that the Holy Spirit has raised these movements to show to the world that Christians not merely talk about charity but also practice it.

> To this critical challenge, the Holy Spirit, who keeps watch over mankind's pilgrimage through history, responded also by giving rise to the movements and the new ecclesial communities. In the movements and new communities, it is especially taught that faith is not abstract talk, nor vague religious sentiment, but new life in Christ instilled by the Holy Spirit. These ecclesial movements, therefore, have a role to play also in evangelizing families, wherever they are in the world, even in diaspora.... But their evangelizing power goes even beyond the visible boundaries of the Church. This is a consequence of their missionary thrust and openness to all forms of dialogue which comes forth from the awareness that the Church is called to unity not only in itself but also in relation to the other Christian Churches or ecclesial communities, to the various religions and with every man of good will.[326]

In Japan, the CCRM has been helpful in welcoming the migrant Catholics to integrate with the Catholic Church. For instance, when the Brazilian Catholic Community had a CCRM convention,

326 Stefen Fumio Hamao, Address to the Participants of the Fourth World Meeting of Families: Renewal Movements and the Evangelization of the Families in Diaspora. This address was delivered in Manila, Philippines in January 2003. http://www.vatican.va/roman_curia/pontifical_councils/migrants/documents/rc_pc_migrants_doc_2003037_renewal_hamao_en.html#_ftnref28. [accessed on September 14, 2014]

members of CCRJ were also involved in it and took active part in the success of this convention. A week later, the members of the CCRJ invited the participants of this convention to join in their local prayer groups and gave them the opportunity to share their testimonies.[327] Thus such encounters and sharing of testimonies has helped both the migrant Catholic community as well as the Japanese community to discover the beauty of faith in Christ. It also showed them that the power of the Holy Spirit surpasses human made boundaries of nations, culture or language. The CCRM is of great help in bridging the cultural and linguistic differences between Catholics of various nationalities. The CCRM has presently no special program for the migrants. However, at individual level, Charismatics are working for integration of the migrant community with the locals. The Catholic Church has to put a lot of effort in reaching out to the migrant community; otherwise, it will be betraying Christ, who prayed for unity.

4.1.10 Promoting Ecumenical Dialogue

Pope John XXIII called the Second Vatican Ecumenical Council to renew the Catholic Church and build unity with Christians of other denominations. Renewal and unity are interconnected. True renewal means that there is unity among Catholics but also with all those who profess faith in the same Lord Jesus Christ. Thus, the very nature of the Second Vatican Council was to promote this spiritual unity with Christians belonging to other denominations. "The search for Christian Unity was one of the principal concerns of the Second Vatican Council."[328] St. Paul says, "[A]ll of you are one in Christ Jesus" (Gal 3:28). Jesus prayed to His Father for unity (see Jn 17:11) and sent His Spirit on His disciples who would unite them.

---

327 Atsu Kobayashi, "Zainichi Burajirujin ni Yori Seirei Sasshin Taikai ni Sankashite" [Participating in the CCRM Convention Organized by Brazilians Living in Japan], *Ikeru Mizu*, No. 61 (Summer Edition 2001): 1-2. Original in Japanese. [Translation mine].

328 The Pontifical Council for Promoting Christian Unity, Directory for the Application of Principles and Norms for Ecumenism, March 25, 1993, No. 1 *AAS* 85 (1993): 1039.

> It is the Holy Spirit, dwelling in those who believe and pervading and ruling over the Church as a whole, who brings about that wonderful communion of the faithful. He brings them into intimate union with Christ, so that He is the principle of the Church's unity. (*UR* 2)

The Protestant Pentecostal Movement influenced the beginning of the CCRM. Thus, the origin of the CCRM is ecumenical in nature. The aspect, which the CCRM emphasizes, is the spiritual ecumenism, which the Decree on Ecumenism described as the soul of ecumenism.

> This change of heart and holiness of life, along with public and private prayer for the unity of Christians, should be regarded as the soul of the whole ecumenical movement, and merits the name, *spiritual ecumenism.* (*UR* 8)

Spiritual ecumenism means conversion of mind and heart, holiness of life, spending qualitative time in public and private prayer and reading the Word of God. These qualities are also the teachings of all Christian denominations. The source of the spiritual ecumenism is the Holy Spirit who brings communion among the faithful.

> It is the Holy Spirit, dwelling in those who believe and pervading and ruling over the Church as a whole, who brings about that wonderful communion of the faithful. He brings them into intimate union with Christ, so that He is the principle of the Church's unity. (*UR* 2)

The emphasis on the role of the Holy Spirit as the principle of unity would greatly help the Catholic Church to have a meaningful ecumenical dialogue with various Protestant Pentecostal denominations and the Orthodox brethren.

> Catholics must gladly acknowledge and esteem the truly Christian endowments from our common heritage, which are to be found among our separated brethren.

> It is right and salutary to recognize the riches of Christ and virtuous works in the lives of others who are bearing witness to Christ, sometimes even to the shedding of their blood. For God is always wonderful in His works and worthy of all praise. Nor should we forget that anything wrought by the grace of the Holy Spirit in the hearts of our separated brethren can be a help to our own edification. Whatever is truly Christian is never contrary to what genuinely belongs to the faith; indeed, it can always bring a deeper realization of the mystery of Christ and the Church. (*UR* 4)

The Catholic Church recommends all Catholics to work for a fruitful ecumenical dialogue and to remove all the obstacles and prejudices in the way of true dialogue.

> It is the urgent wish of this Holy Council that the measures undertaken by the sons of the Catholic Church should develop in conjunction with those of our separated brethren so that no obstacle be put in the ways of divine Providence and no preconceived judgments impair the future inspirations of the Holy Spirit. (*UR* 24)

The Church cannot have a fruitful ecumenical dialogue with other Christian denominations because of the doctrinal differences. However, the Church can aim dialogue at spiritual level. The Holy Spirit can unite people in spite of doctrinal differences. Pope Paul VI in his address of April 28, 1967 to the members of the Secretariat for Christian Unity noted that:

> If there is a case where our human effectiveness is powerless to achieve a good result and shows itself mainly dependent on the mysterious and powerful Holy Spirit, then that is surely that of ecumenism.[329]

329 "Address of Pope Paul VI to the Members of the Secretariat for Christian Unity, April 28, 1967," *Insegnamenti di Paolo VI*, 5(1967): 193. Original text in French is as follows: S'il y a une cause où notre efficacité humaine s'avère impuissante à atteindre quelque bon résultat et se révèle essentiellement dépendante de

Pope John Paul II in his address to the Leaders of the CCRM on May 7, 1981 asked them to work for ecumenical unity in the Church. He noted that:

> [B]y your experience of many gifts of the Holy Spirit which are shared also with our separated brothers and sisters, yours is the special joy of growing in a desire for the unity to which the Spirit guides us and in a commitment to the serious task of ecumenism.[330]

The prayer meetings of the CCRM can be helpful to organize and promote ecumenical meetings.[331] An ecumenical prayer meeting can help the participants irrespective of the denominations to be one at heart in prayer. The CCRM can contribute to ecumenism by emphasizing on the unity in the Holy Spirit, prayer, Word of God and conversion of heart. The Holy Spirit is the principal agent of unity. The CCRM emphasizes on the phenomenon of baptism in Holy Spirit and the charisms of the Holy Spirit. Pentecostals too emphasize on baptism in the Holy Spirit and the use of the charisms. Even though there are theological differences in defining the concept of the baptism in the Holy Spirit in various denominations, the effects are the same. The effects of the baptism in the Holy Spirit like desire for deeper prayer life, more interest in the Sacred Scriptures, fellowship and love of neighbor can help Christians of various denominations to come together in love. Pope John Paul too emphasized on the role of the Holy Spirit in ecumenism. He noted that the Church should invoke the Holy Spirit to foster Christian unity.[332] The Decree on Ecumenism noted that:

> In recent times more than ever before, He [Holy Spirit] has been rousing divided Christians to remorse

---

l'action mystérieuse et puissante du Saint-Esprit, c'est bien celle-là, celle de l'œcuménisme. [Translation mine].

330 "Address to the Fourth International Leaders' Conference," *Insegnamenti di Giovanni Paolo II*, 4.1 (1981): 1126.

331 See Reginald Alva, "The Ecumenical Calling of the Catholic Charismatic Renewal Movement," *Academia*, 5 (January 2013): 268-269.

332 See "Apostolic Letter *Tertio Millennio Adveniente*" *AAS* 87 (1995): 26.

> over their divisions and to a longing for unity. Everywhere large numbers have felt the impulse of this grace and among our separated brethren also there increases from day to day the movement, fostered by the grace of the Holy Spirit, for the restoration of unity among all Christians. (*UR* 1)

The Holy Spirit empowers Christians to work for genuine ecumenical dialogue. Pope John Paul II noted in his encyclical *Ut Unum Sint* that:

> The power of God's Spirit gives growth and builds up the Church down the centuries. As the Church turns her gaze to the new millennium, she asks the Spirit for the grace to strengthen her own unity and to make it grow towards full communion with other Christians... The Spirit is able to grant us clear-sightedness, strength and courage to take whatever steps are necessary, that our commitment may be ever more authentic.[333]

In his message of November 30, 1997 to the youth on the XIII World Youth Day in 1998, Pope John Paul II asked them to pray to the Holy Spirit for true unity among all Christians.

> It is the Spirit who brings human beings to understand and accept one another, to recognize that they are children of God and brothers and sisters on their way towards the same goal, eternal life, and to speak the same language over and above divisions of culture or race.[334]

Pope John Paul II in his encyclical, *Ut Unum Sint* noted that prayer as the key for fostering real unity among Christians of various denominations.

> When Christians pray together, the goal of unity seems closer.... Along the ecumenical path to unity,

333 "Encyclical *Ut Unum Sint.*" *AAS* 87 (1995): 981.

334 "Message of the Holy Father on Occasion of the XIII World Youth Day, November 30, 1997," *Insegnamenti di Giovanni Paolo II,* 20.2 (1997): 886.

> pride of place certainly belongs to common prayer, the prayerful union of those who gather together around Christ himself. If Christians, despite their divisions, can grow ever more united in common prayer around Christ, they will grow in the awareness of how little divides them in comparison to what unites them. If they meet more often and more regularly before Christ in prayer, they will be able to gain the courage to face all the painful human reality of their divisions, and they will find themselves together once more in that community of the Church which Christ constantly builds up in the Holy Spirit, in spite of all weaknesses and human limitations.[335]

Again, Pope John Paul II noted in the Encyclical *Ut Unum Sint* noted that when Christians pray together it has a great impact on the people. Prayer has a great witness value. When people pray together they clearly exhibit the fraternal love and fellowship they share, which are the hallmarks of Christianity.

> [F]ellowship in prayer leads people to look at the Church and Christianity in a new way. It must not be forgotten in fact that the Lord prayed to the Father that his disciples might be one, so that their unity might bear witness to his mission and the world would believe that the Father had sent him (see Jn 17:21). Ecumenical prayer discloses this fundamental dimension of brotherhood in Christ, who died to gather together the children of God who were scattered, so that in becoming 'sons and daughters in the Son' (cf. Eph 1:5) we might show forth more fully both the mysterious reality of God's fatherhood and the truth about the human nature shared by each and every individual. Pope John Paul II sees prayer as an effective means to achieve authentic unity. He calls on the Church to be in prayer to realize this goal of unity with all the Christians of various denominations. How is the Church to obtain this grace? In the first place,

335 "Encyclical *Ut Unum Sint*" *AAS* 87 (1995): 934.

> through prayer. Prayer should always concern itself with the longing for unity, and as such is one of the basic forms of our love for Christ and for the Father who is rich in mercy. In this journey which we are undertaking with other Christians towards the new millennium prayer must occupy the first place.[336]

Pope John Paul II asked all Catholics to pray for unity not only in community prayers but also in their personal prayers.

> In the deep personal dialogue which each of us must carry on with the Lord in prayer, concern for unity cannot be absent. Only in this way, in fact, will that concern fully become part of the reality of our life and of the commitments we have taken on in the Church.[337]

Prayer is an effective means for fostering ecumenical dialogue and unity among Christians of other denominations. However, Catholics are obliged to follow certain guidelines laid down by the Church while conducting ecumenical prayer meetings. The CCRM through its emphasis on personal prayer and community praise can be a suitable forum to bring together Christians of various denominations to pray together for unity which Jesus prayed to His Father before His death (Jn 17:21). "Shared prayer is in itself a way to spiritual reconciliation."[338] The *Directory for the Application of Principles and Norms for Ecumenism* recommends all Catholics to discover the rich spiritual heritage in other Christian denominations and create occasions like common prayer meetings to share the spiritual treasures found in Catholic Church and the other Christian denominations.

> Catholics should also give value to certain elements and goods, sources of spiritual life, which are found in other Churches and ecclesial Communities, and which

336 "Encyclical *Ut Unum Sint*" AAS 87 (1995), 981.

337 Ibid., No. 27, 938.

338 The Pontifical Council for Promoting Christian Unity, Directory for the Application of Principles and Norms for Ecumenism, March 25, 1993, *AAS* 85 (1993): 1083.

> belong to the one Church of Christ: Holy Scripture, the Sacraments and other sacred actions, faith, hope, charity and other gifts of the Spirit. These goods have borne fruit for example in the mystical tradition of the Christian East and the spiritual treasures of the monastic life, in the worship and piety of Anglicans, in the evangelical prayer and the diverse forms of Protestant spirituality. This appreciation should not remain merely theoretical; in suitable particular conditions, it should be completed by the practical knowledge of other traditions of spirituality. Therefore, sharing prayer and participating in some form of public worship or in devotional acts of other Christians can have a formative value when in accord with existing directives.[339]

Praying and meditating on the Word of God can unite people of various denominations. The Bible can be an effective means to hold an ecumenical dialogue. Christians, irrespective of their denominations, can use it to learn from one another.[340] Further, the Bible calls us to live a life of holiness. It asks us to open ourselves to the Holy Spirit. It challenges our selfishness and stubbornness. Our contemplation of the life, death and resurrection of Jesus through the Sacred Scriptures helps us to realize that Christ intended unity among His followers. We can witness Christ through unity among Christians.

> A love and reverence of Sacred Scripture which might be described as devotion, leads our brethren to a constant meditative study of the sacred text. For the Gospel is the power of God for salvation to everyone who has faith, to the Jew first and then to the Greek. (*UR* 21)

---

339 The Pontifical Council for Promoting Christian Unity, Directory for the Application of Principles and Norms for Ecumenism, March 25, 1993, *AAS* 85 (1993), No. 63, 1065.

340 See Simon Oxley, *Creative Ecumenical Education: Learning From One Another* (Geneva: WCC Publications, 2002), 54-56.

The Catholics and the Christians of other denominations interpret the Bible differently. Unlike the other Christian denominations, the Catholics have clear guidelines regarding the interpretation of the Bible laid down by the Magisterium.

> [S]ince God speaks in Sacred Scripture through men in human fashion, the interpreter of Sacred Scripture, in order to see clearly what God wanted to communicate to us, should carefully investigate what meaning the sacred writers really intended, and what God wanted to manifest by means of their words. To search out the intention of the sacred writers, attention should be given, among other things, to literary forms. For truth is set forth and expressed differently in texts, which are variously historical, prophetic, poetic, or of other forms of discourse... Since Holy Scripture must be read and interpreted in the sacred spirit in which it was written, no less serious attention must be given to the content and unity of the whole of Scripture if the meaning of the sacred texts is to be correctly worked out. The living tradition of the whole Church must be taken into account along with the harmony which exists between elements of the faith. It is the task of exegetes to work according to these rules toward a better understanding and explanation of the meaning of Sacred Scripture, so that through preparatory study the judgment of the Church may mature. For all of what has been said about the way of interpreting Scripture is subject finally to the judgment of the Church, which carries out the divine commission and ministry of guarding and interpreting the word of God. (*DV* 12)

The Decree on Ecumenism (*Unitatis Redintegratio*) notes that Catholics must interpret the Bible in the light of the teaching of the Church. The Bible is an important source for organizing ecumenical dialogue. However, Catholics must be aware of the differences that exist between the Protestants and them regarding the interpretation of the Bible.

> While invoking the Holy Spirit, they seek in these very Scriptures God as it were speaking to them in Christ, Whom the prophets foretold, Who is the Word of God made flesh for us. They contemplate in the Sacred Scriptures the life of Christ and what the Divine Master taught and did for our salvation, especially the mysteries of His death and resurrection. But while the Christians who are separated from us hold the divine authority of the Sacred Books, they differ from ours-some in one way, some in another-regarding the relationship between Scripture and the Church. For, according to Catholic belief, the authentic teaching authority of the Church has a special place in the interpretation and preaching of the written Word of God. But Sacred Scriptures provide for the work of dialogue an instrument of the highest value in the mighty hand of God for the attainment of that unity which the Saviour holds out to all. (*UR* 21)

In his address to the Members of the Catholic Fraternity of Charismatic Covenant Communities in Rome on November 14, 1994, Pope John Paul II asked all those involved in the CCRM to foster ecumenical dialogue by effectively using the Word of God, which is also one of the characteristic features of the CCRM. He noted that:

> Likewise, your emphasis on the centrality of Scripture for the Christian life can greatly help ecumenical understanding and co-operation, as all believers seek to hear the voice of the Spirit which continues to speak to the Churches.[341]

Pope John Paul II emphasizes in the Encyclical *Ut Unum Sint* that the Church has done significant ecumenical progress in the area of the Sacred Scriptures by publishing ecumenical translations of

341 "Address to the Members of the Catholic Fraternity of Charismatic Covenant Communities, November 14, 1994," *Insegnamenti di Giovanni Paolo II*, 17.2 (1994) 775-777.

the Bible in different languages.[342] However, he cautions Catholics regarding the interpretation of the Bible. He emphasizes on the deeper study of the Word of God in the light of the teachings of the Church. He notes that,

> The relationship between Sacred Scripture, as the highest authority in matters of faith, and Sacred Tradition, as indispensable to the interpretation of the Sacred Scriptures.[343]

The *Directory for the Application of Principles and Norms for Ecumenism* too notes that the importance of using the Bible during ecumenical encounters. It further notes that:

> The Catholic Church has always considered Sacred Scriptures, together with Tradition, as the supreme rule of faith; they are for its children the food of the soul, the pure and perennial source of spiritual life. Our brothers and sisters of other Churches and ecclesial Communities have a deep love and reverence for the Holy Sacred Scriptures. This occasions their constant and deep study of the sacred books. The Sacred Scriptures, then, being one and the same for all Christians, will progressively strengthen the path towards unity insofar as it is approached with religious attention and loving study.[344]

The CCRM, which aims at the renewal of the Church, can contribute greatly to promote true ecumenical dialogue. The characteristic features of the CCRM such as desire for deep personal prayer, love for the Sacred Scriptures, emphasis on conversion of heart, renewal of mind and the great reliance on the power of the Holy Spirit who is the principle of unity, are also basic elements of faith found in various Christian denominations. Even though, there may be theological and doctrinal differences regarding the

---

342 "Encyclical *Ut Unum Sint*," No. 44 *AAS* 87(1995) 947.

343 Ibid., No. 79, 968-969.

344 The Pontifical Council for Promoting Christian Unity, Directory for the Application of Principles and Norms for Ecumenism, March 25, 1993, No. 59 *AAS* 85 (1993) 1063.

interpretation of the Bible, all those who are truly open to the Holy Spirit sincerely long for an interior renewal of heart and mind. In addition, true renewal always promotes the call for unity.

Christianity is a minority religion in Japan. The official statistical data puts their number at 19,08,479 (1%).[345] This includes Protestants, Roman Catholics, Anglicans, Orthodox and unaffiliated Christians. Christianity entered Japan in 1549 with the coming of St. Francis Xavier and other missionaries. Initially Christianity had a rapid growth but the road was not always smooth as there were some *Samurais* (Warlords) who were ill disposed towards Christianity. Christianity flourished in areas where the local rulers supported it, while it suffered in those areas where the local rulers were against it. Persecutions and welcome were part of the history of the Church in Japan.

Protestant missionaries started pouring in Japan only as late as 1873 after the Japanese government rescinded the edict, which banned Christianity. The Meiji government of that time was neither pro nor against Christianity. It took a neutral position to promote Nationalism on one hand and on the other, improve trade relations with the Western countries. The Meiji government tried to identify nationalism with Shinto. Therefore, Japanese especially Christians who were not part of Shinto religion, suffered the blemish of not being true Japanese.[346] The cold shoulder treatment meted to Christianity diminished considerably in the early 20th century, as Japan concentrated on industrialization and the Western influence grew stronger. Both the Protestant and Roman Catholic Churches marked a growth in these years.[347]

After World War II Christianity was seen as the religion of hope, as it offered spiritual and moral support to the Japanese who were demoralized because of the humiliating defeat in the war. The Catholic Church increased its members from 108,324 in 1946 to

---

345 Ministry of Education, Culture, Sport, Science and Technology, Japan, "*Zenkoku Jinja Kyokai Nado Shukyo Dantai, Kyoshi, Shinjasu*" [National Statistics of Shrines, Churches etc, Religious Organizations, Adherents]. http://www.e-stat.go.jp/SG1/estat/List.do?bid=000001052797&cycode=0 [accessed on September 14, 2014]

346 Mullins, Christianity Made in Japan: A Study of Indigenous Movements, 19.

347 See Ibid., 18.

357,478 in 1971 an average increase of 5%.[348] However, the growth rate decreased in the following years. From 1971 to 1990, the total Catholic population was 438,834, an average annual increase of only 1%. According to *Statistics of the Catholic Church in Japan*, the Catholic population in 2014 was 444,441 i.e., 0.35% of the total population of Japan. It indicates that the average annual increase is less than 1% from 1990 to 2014. On the other hand, the Protestant Churches, which began much later than the Catholics, had 436,059 members in 1970 increased to 570,881 in mid-2000.[349] All other denominations too have a very low growth rate.

The pains and persecutions suffered during the World War II made the Japanese Christians realize that with their miniscule presence in Japan, they would be totally isolated if they do not come together as brothers and sisters professing faith in the same Lord Jesus Christ. However, the indigenous Christian movements always kept a distance from the mainline Christian denominational Churches. They usually do not like to be associated with ecumenical movements.[350] However, most of the mainline Protestant Churches and Roman Catholic Church have taken a lead in establishing ecumenical contact with each other.

> Having experienced the oppression of the Church during the war, Japanese Christians have learned that the individual Christian has need of other Christians, and that he can have fellowship with other Christians through the mediation of Jesus Christ. The wartime experience fostered the realization that the consciousness of unity in Christ is stronger than that of denomination. The conscious and unconscious recollection of the wartime experience constitutes an important contributing factor to the ecumenical movement in Japan.[351]

348 See Barrett, *World Christian Encyclopedia: A Comparative Survey of Churches and Religions in the Modern World*, 2nd ed. Vol. 1, 415.

349 See Ibid.

350 Mullins, Christianity Made in Japan: A Study of Indigenous Movements, 29.

351 Kishi Chitose, "The State of the Ecumenical Movement in Japan," in *The Japan Christian Yearbook 1969-1970* , eds. Ryokzo Hara, James Colligan, Lan Macleod, (Tokyo: Kyo Bun Kwan, 1970), 177.

Even though, major Protestant Churches and Roman Catholic Church are trying ways to dialogue, ecumenical dialogue is still weak in Japan. Japanese Christians need the support of each other to survive in a society, which has little interest in religious affairs. They have limited personnel and resources to carry out the mission work. Hence, the Church recognizes the need for ecumenism in Japan. Moreover, the Second Vatican Council also encouraged ecumenical dialogue.

The Catholic Church has an Episcopal Commission for Ecumenism. The Oriens Institute for Religious Research in Tokyo promotes ecumenical cooperation in Bible translation. Besides it, there are other institutes, which promote ecumenical dialogue in Japan.[352] Sophia University run by the Jesuits in Tokyo and Nanzan University run by the Divine Word Missionaries (SVD) have specialized institutions to do research and studies on ecumenism and Japanese religions.

Japanese Christians have realized that divisions among them are creating an obstacle for the vast majority of Japanese to accept Christianity. Even though, the indigenous Christian movements do not take much interest in ecumenical activities, the mainline Protestant Churches and Roman Catholic Church are actively involved in promoting ecumenical dialogue. Kishi Chitose summarizes the need for the ecumenical movement in Japan as follows:

> The ecumenical movement is not just another movement. It is a movement, which aims fundamentally at the restoration of all men before God through the living and working Gospel of Christ. Countless matters relevant to the movement receive attention. However, to facilitate discussing them, they are categorized and seriously studied by men who are specialists in their respective fields. Here, again, appear both the unity of the members, as united with the body of Christ, and their diversity. Within the fellowship of this warm community, work is divided but frequent contact kept with one another. 'That there

352 See John England et al., eds. Asian Christian Theologies: A Research Guide to Authors, Movements, Sources, Vol. 3 (Delhi: ISPCK, 2004), 457-458.

> may be no discord in the body, but that the members may have the same care for one another. If one member suffers, all suffer together, if one member is honoured, all rejoice together' (I Cor.12:25-27). When these words are realized within us, the ecumenical movement fulfills its role of healing our disunity.[353]

The Church looks with hope towards the CCRM to promote ecumenical dialogue. The Pontifical Council for promoting Christian Unity notes that ecclesial movements have a great potential to further the cause of ecumenism. It notes that:

Christian life, notably the life of particular Churches has been enriched throughout history by a variety of expressions, enterprises and spiritualities, according to the charisms given by the Spirit for the building up of the Church, revealing a clear distinction of tasks in the service of the community.Those involved in such groups, movements and associations should be imbued with a solid ecumenical spirit, in living out their Baptismal commitment in the world, whether by seeking Catholic unity through dialogue and communion with similar movements and associations or the wider communion with other Churches and ecclesial Communities and with the movements and groups inspired by them. These efforts should be carried out on the basis of a sound formation and in the light of Christian wisdom and prudence.[354]

The CCRM prayer meetings organized by Mother John Marie Stewart and Sr. Stephanie at the Franciscan Chapel Center were ecumenical in nature.[355] The Assembly of God pastor, Hiroshi Yoshiyama and other Pentecostal ministers supported the CCRM.[356] In 1974, the CCRM organized many ecumenical meetings at Hatsudai Catholic Church in Tokyo. It invited prominent speakers

---

353 Kishi Chitose, "The State of the Ecumenical Movement in Japan," in *The Japan Christian Yearbook 1969-1970*, 179-180.

354 The Pontifical Council for Promoting Christian Unity, Directory for the Application of Principles and Norms for Ecumenism, March 25, 1993, No. 69 *AAS* 85 (1993) 1068.

355 Stewart, *Laying the Foundation: A History of the Disciples of the Lord Jesus Christ*, 44.

356 Mathy, "What in the World is going on? Japan," 4.

like David Du Plessis (1905-1987) and other Protestant Pentecostal leaders to lead the prayer meetings.[357]

As the CCRM spread to different parts of Japan like Nagoya, Osaka, it organized ecumenical prayer meetings in these regions too. Protestant Pentecostals generously supported the Catholics to begin the CCRM prayer groups. In spite of all the theological and doctrinal differences, the Protestants and Catholics could come together and pray. Pope John Paul II emphasized in his General Audience of December 5, 1990 that, "This sincere inclination towards unity in the Body of Christ comes from the Holy Spirit, and it is only through His action that the ideal of unity can be fully realized."[358] Following are excerpts from the testimonies and articles of people who took part in ecumenical prayer meetings.

Keiko Fukuhara wrote an article about the beginning of the CCRM prayer meeting in Nagoya. She notes that:

> Missionaries like Professor Fast and other Protestant Christians also joined us in the prayer meeting and it was an ideal ecumenical type meeting. The melody of praise and worship was extremely soothing. It was indeed a meeting, which relaxed our souls.[359]

Mikiko Hayashi wrote about the beginning of the CCRM prayer meeting in Osaka. She notes that:

> The prayer meeting at Sakai Church started with only four people. I came to know about the CCRM for

357 David Johannes Du Plessis was an international Pentecostal and ecumenical spokesperson. He was instrumental in setting the stage of Roman Catholic – Pentecostal Ecumenical Dialogue. He effectively linked the three movements, namely Ecumenical, Pentecostal and Charismatic movements of the 20th century together. He strongly recommended the new comers to Charismatic-Pentecostal movement to remain in their respective Church and continue to follow their newfound conviction of the Christian life in their respective Churches.

358 "General Audience of December 5," *Insegnamenti di Giovanni Paolo II*, 13.2 (1990): 1381. Original in Italian. [Translation mine].

359 Keiko Fukuhara, "*Hitori no Shingakusei ni Yotte*" [Through One Seminarian], *Ikeru Mizu,* No. 46 (Special Edition 1997): 5. Original in Japanese. [Translation mine].

> the first time during this meeting. In the beginning Sr. Glenten, Mr. & Ms. Tetsuno, Yasunaga and Protestants shared their testimonies, which were very interesting.[360]

Fr. Bernadine Schneider, a Catholic priest was closely associated with the CCRM from its beginning in Japan shared his experience about the ecumenical meetings in *Ikeru Mizu.* The bishops of the Catholic Church and Protestant pastors organized a joint committee for translating the Bible. He says that during these meetings, whenever there were differences of opinions among the Catholics and the Protestants regarding the translation of any particular biblical text, he as the chairperson of the meeting would not side with any group but pray in silence to the Holy Spirit to enlighten them all. Moreover, to his surprise within the next 5 minutes, the members of the committees would come to an agreement to adopt not their respective translations but a different translation.[361]

Noriko Masuda noted her experience about the CCRM prayer meetings, which were truly ecumenical in nature.

> I encountered the CCRM in Kumamoto. When I look back, I can say that the CCRM has brought abundant fruits in our lives.... The CCRM has helped us to read, meditate and live the Word of God together as a group. We are aspiring to live our daily life according to the Word of God. During Easter celebrations around 100 youth both Protestants and Catholics come together for exchange .Thanks and praise to God.[362]

Yuko Sugiura a Protestant Christian noted her experiences of the CCRM seminar, as follows:

---

360 Mikiko Hayashi, "*Osaka ni Seirei no Hi ga*" [The Fire of the Holy Spirit in Osaka], *Ikeru Mizu,* No. 46 (Special Edition 1997): 7. Original in Japanese. [Translation mine].

361 Bernadine Schneider, "*Seirei Kitekudasai*" [Come Holy Spirit], *Ikeru Mizu,* No. 50 (Fall Edition 1998): 11. Original in Japanese. [Translation mine].

362 Noriko Masuda, "*Inori no Tsudoi wa Ikiteiru*" [The Prayer Meeting is Living], *Ikeru Mizu,* No. 52 (Spring Edition 1999): 3. Original in Japanese. [Translation mine].

> Since many years, I had a weak faith life. It had reached rock bottom. One of the Church members suggested me to join the Alpha Course at Yukinoshita Catholic Church at Kamakura, Kanagawa prefecture. When I went there, the Charismatics recommended me to attend the Life in the Spirit seminar. I decided to participate in it. I forgot that I am a Protestant and was totally engrossed in the seminar organized by the Catholic Church to seek the Living Water….I will carry to my Church the joy of the Holy Spirit which I received in this seminar. I will share my faith experience with my Church members and work for evangelization. I thank God for His love, which I experienced through the Holy Spirit. I also thank the members of the CCRM Seminar and Kanagawa Prayer Meeting who happily accepted me though I am a Protestant.[363]

Joshua, a priest belonging to Daikan Anglican Church shares his experience of the 24th Hokkaido regional CCRM convention.

> I was very much impressed and strengthened to see the Catholic brothers and sisters united in the Holy Spirit. Differences in nationalities or denominations cannot restrict the wonderful work of the Holy Spirit. It is truly wonderful that you (Catholics) are continuing this grace-filled work for more than 20 years.[364]

Kunio Muroi a protestant attended the National CCRM convention in 2000. Previously he had strong anti-Catholic feelings in him. He shares in the following testimony how the experience of the CCRM convention helped him to realize his mistakes especially about his ill feelings toward the Catholic Church and her teachings. He also found great joy and peace through this convention. He

363 Yuko Sugiura, "Kakuchi no Inori no Tsudoi no Hataraki Kara" [The Happenings in Each Region], *Ikeru Mizu,* No. 78 (Fall Edition): 12. Original in Japanese. [Translation mine].

364 Joshua, "*Hajimete no Sankasha no Koe*" [From First Time Participants], *Ikeru Mizu,* No. 93 (Summer Edition): 7. Original in Japanese. [Translation mine].

committed himself to follow Jesus and overcome the barriers of denomination, which separated him from the Catholics.

> This is the first time I participated in the National CCRM convention. I received countless graces from God. Even now, that experience resounds in my heart. I always had an ill feeling towards Catholics. I am very grateful to God for the wonderful National CCRM convention and through it; I had a new experience about Catholics. I always considered the Catholic Church as rigidly structured and not a friendly institution. I thought the Catholic Church preached about love but always maintained its cold attitude. I considered the Catholic Church as a world devoid of joy and Catholics as people without heart. I thank God because I realized I was wrong. On the contrary, through my experience of the convention I now feel that Catholics are a group of joyful people who praise God. It may have been also the atmosphere of the convention, which helped the faithful to relax joyfully in the Lord. The passion with which the faithful were praising God through hymns impressed me. I too joyfully joined them in the singing. I was also very much impressed by the talks given by the priest who came from the USA. I was overwhelmed to see that the priest's faith and his attitude of surrender to Jesus were just like a child. I felt very much at home by listening to the humorous talks given by that priest. I attend the services in the Protestant Church but we have no pastor like that priest. On the contrary, now I feel that the sermons of the pastors are rigid and structured. When I would see the Holy Father on television, I used to think that the Holy Father is merely the symbolic head of the Catholic hierarchy who has nothing to do with the mission of the Church. However, this time when I heard the talks given by the priest I changed my opinion. I experienced it is an exceptional thing to have faith. I realized that I could not understand faith through my

> reason alone. I needed the Holy Spirit. I want to pass over the denominational differences and experience the true joy in the Holy Spirit.... I want to experience Jesus in my everyday life.[365]

Through the above real life experiences of various people we can conclude that the CCRM has promoted ecumenical dialogue.

4.1.11 Evangelization

Evangelization is at the heart of the Church. The Church is obliged to spread the good news of salvation in Jesus Christ. Pope Paul VI in the Apostolic Exhortation *Evangelii Nuntiandi* noted that evangelization is an important part of the Church's mission.

> Evangelizing is in fact the grace and vocation proper to the Church, her deepest identity. She exists in order to evangelize, that is to say, in order to preach and teach, to be the channel of the gift of grace, to reconcile sinners with God, and to perpetuate Christ's sacrifice in the Mass, which is the memorial of His death and glorious resurrection.[366]

The CCRM emphasizes on the dynamic role of the Holy Spirit in the Church's mission of evangelization. Pope Paul VI noted that the Holy Spirit is the principal agent of evangelization.

> It is in the 'consolation of the Holy Spirit' that the Church increases. The Holy Spirit is the soul of the Church. It is He who explains to the faithful the deep meaning of the teaching of Jesus and of His mystery. It is the Holy Spirit who, today just as at the beginning of the Church, acts in every evangelizer who allows himself to be possessed and led by Him. The Holy Spirit places

365 Kunio Muroi, "*Kami Chushin de Ikiteikitai*" [I Want to Live A God-Centered Life] in *Jesus 2000: Shu no Eiko he no Maneki* [Jesus 2000: Invited to Partake in the Glory of the Lord] (Tokyo: Catholic Charismatic Renewal of Japan, National Service Committee, 2000), 53. Original in Japanese. [Translation mine].

366 "Apostolic Exhortation *Evangelii Nuntiandi*," *AAS* 68 (1976): 13.

on his lips the words which he could not find by himself, and at the same time the Holy Spirit predisposes the soul of the hearer to be open and receptive to the Good News and to the kingdom being proclaimed.Techniques of evangelization are good, but even the most advanced ones could not replace the gentle action of the Spirit. The most perfect preparation of the evangelizer has no effect without the Holy Spirit. Without the Holy Spirit the most convincing dialectic has no power over the heart of man. Without Him the most highly developed schemas resting on a sociological or psychological basis are quickly seen to be quite valueless.We live in the Church at a privileged moment of the Spirit. Everywhere people are trying to know Him better, as the Scripture reveals Him. They are happy to place themselves under His inspiration. They are gathering about Him; they want to let themselves be led by Him. Now if the Spirit of God has a preeminent place in the whole life of the Church, it is in her evangelizing mission that He is most active. It is not by chance that the great inauguration of evangelization took place on the morning of Pentecost, under the inspiration of the Spirit.It must be said that the Holy Spirit is the principal agent of evangelization: it is He who impels each individual to proclaim the Gospel, and it is He who in the depths of consciences causes the word of salvation to be accepted and understood. But it can equally be said that He is the goal of evangelization: He alone stirs up the new creation, the new humanity of which evangelization is to be the result, with that unity in variety which evangelization wishes to achieve within the Christian community. Through the Holy Spirit the Gospel penetrates to the heart of the world, for it is He who causes people to discern the signs of the times signs willed by God-which evangelization reveals and puts to use within history.[367]

367 "Apostolic Exhortation *Evangelii Nuntiandi,*", No. 75, *AAS* 68 (1976): 64.

Pope Paul VI exhorts all Catholics to pray to the Holy Spirit to do the work of evangelization. He noted that:

> [W]e exhort all evangelizers, whoever they may be, to pray without ceasing to the Holy Spirit with faith and fervor and to let themselves prudently be guided by Him as the decisive inspirer of their plans, their initiatives and their evangelizing activity.[368]

Pope John Paul II too noted in his Encyclical *Redemptoris Missio*, "The Holy Spirit is indeed the principal agent of the whole of the Church's mission" (*RM* 21). The Holy Spirit continues to guide the Church in her mission of evangelization. The CCRM has taken active part in evangelization. Pope John Paul II appreciated the work of the CCRM to promote evangelization. He noted that:

> The Catholic Charismatic Renewal has helped many Christians to rediscover the presence and power of the Holy Spirit in their lives, in the life of the Church and in the world; and this rediscovery has awakened in them a faith in Christ filled with joy, a great love of the Church and a generous dedication to her evangelizing mission.[369]

Religious pluralism is a reality in Japan. Besides, Shinto the traditional religion of Japan, there are other religions like Buddhism and Chinese traditional religions. The CCRM has to respect the other religions in order to spread the Kingdom of God. In the following sections, we shall examine the evangalization work done by the CCRM in Japan.

4.1.11.1 National Incentive for Catholic Evangelization

Shinto, Buddhism and New Religious Movements form the major religions in Japan. According to the survey of Ministry of Education, Culture, Sport, Science and Technology the Christian population was

---

368 Ibid.

369 "Address to the Participants in the International Conference for Catholic Charismatic Leaders," *Insegnamenti di Giovanni Paolo II*, 21.2 (1998): 886-887.

around 1% in 2014.[370] However, David Barrett in *World Encyclopedia of Religion* puts the figure as high as 3.6% in mid-2000.[371] This may be due to the difference in the methodology of the surveys. Nevertheless, both the surveys point that Christianity is a minority religion.

In the light of the teachings of Second Vatican Council and the visit of Pope John Paul II to Japan in 1980, the CBCJ announced the "Basic Orientations and Priorities of the Church in Japan" in 1984. In response to the "Basic Orientations and Priorities of the Church in Japan," the CBCJ invited all priests, religious and laity to prepare a program for evangelization. The CBCJ announced the first NICE I (National Incentive for Catholic Evangelization) Conference in 1987. The theme of the NICE I conference was "Building an Open Church." NICE I conference took place in Kyoto, with 275 representatives (17 bishops, 112 priests, 53 religious, 93 laity). Besides the official representatives, 127 secretaries and 150 members of the Kyoto preparatory committee also took part in the NICE conference. After the closure of the NICE I conference the CBCJ had an extraordinary session. It published a document "Let us Live Together in Joy."[372]

The CBCJ had pointed to two specific problems regarding evangelization in Japan. The first was the gap between the lifestyle and the faith of Catholics. They pointed out that Catholics were practicing their faith only in the Church. They were not witnessing to Christ through their life. The second problem was the gap between the Catholic Church and the Japanese society. People saw the Catholic Church as an institution obsessed with dogmas, doctrines and structures. They felt the Church had lost contact with

---

370 Ministry of Education, Culture, Sport, Science and Technology, Japan, "*Zenkoku Jinja Kyokai Nado Shukyo Dantai, Kyoshi, Shinjasu*" [National Statistics of Shrines, Churches etc, Religious Organizations, Adherents]. http://www.e-stat.go.jp/SG1/estat/List.do?bid=000001052797&cycode=0 [accessed on September 18, 2014].

371 Barrett, *World Christian Encyclopedia: A Comparative Survey of Churches and Religions in the Modern World*, 2nd ed. Vol.1, 412.

372 Catholic Bishops' Conference of Japan, *An Overview of the History of the Catholic Church in Japan*. http://www.cbcj.catholic.jp/eng/ehistory/table02.htm. [accessed on September 18, 2014].

the society. The CBCJ urged all Catholics to examine their lifestyles. Further, they requested all the priests and laity to work with them for reducing the gap between the Church and the society. They requested suggestions to reach out to the society.[373]

Six years later after NICE I conference, CBCJ organized the NICE II conference in 1993 at Nagasaki. The theme was "The Family." Bishops decided that the ideal of evangelization and the reality of family life should be the objective of NICE II conference. Two hundred and twenty nine delegates participated in the NICE II conference. They published a report entitled '*Outlook: Toward a Renewal of the Church of Japan in the Work of Evangelization*'. Following are the some of the important observations made in this report.[374] It emphasized on the work of the Holy Spirit without which no mission would be possible. It noted the problems facing the Japanese society, especially the problems of materialism, rigid structures, over-emphasis on intelligence in addition, egoism are distorting the basic structure of the Japanese society i.e., the family. On the other hand, the report praises those who work for the sick, the aged, the weak and the poor. The report noted the danger of secularization and its influence on Japanese families. The report stressed the importance of respecting life, dialogue within the family members and sharing.

In order to realize the goal of evangelization the report noted the importance of renewal of the Church community. Renewal of the Church will make it a place where all feel at home. The report proposed five concrete areas where the Church community is in need of renewal. First, the report encouraged sharing of material things, time and one's own life. For this, the report recommended the community to prepare a manual or program to encourage sharing. It also suggested

---

373 Catholic Bishops' Conference of Japan, *Dai Ikkai Fukuin Senkyo Suishin Zenkoku Kaigi (NICE I) Kadai* [First National Incentive for Catholic Evangelization Conference (NICE I)] (Tokyo: Catholic Bishops' Conference of Japan, 1986), 1.

374 Participants Report of the Second National Incentive for Catholic Evangelization Conference, "Tenbo: Fukuin Senkyosuru Nihon no Kyoukai no Sasshin no Tameni" [Outlook: Toward a Renewal of the Church of Japan in the Work of Evangelization], Nagasaki, October 24, 1993. Original in Japanese. [Translation mine].

that all Church members including priests and religious must take this aspect of sharing seriously. The second area, which the report pointed out, was to build community, which was sympathetic and had joint ownership. The Church community must be sympathetic towards the weak in the society especially the immigrants, refugees, lower class tribes, handicaps, sick, aged and children. The Church administration must focus not on implementation of programs and schedules but evangelization. The third area, which the report suggested, was the formation of faithful who would discern the signs of the time. They suggested having workshops to train the faithful to grow in faith, without which the task of evangelization is impossible. Further, they suggested the faithful to train themselves to be more attentive to the needy and the suffering. The fourth area, which the report suggested was regarding the liturgy. It strongly recommended the renewal and reformation of liturgy especially the Sunday liturgy. It suggested that the Sunday liturgy must be lively and an ideal place for growing in faith. The fifth area, which the report noted, was that of faith formation programs for the youth. In order to train and teach the youth about the Christian faith it is important to train teachers and prepare material for training. The report strongly recommended the renewal of the Church as an important factor in the work of evangelization.

The bishops Takeo Okada, Jun Ikenaga, and Mitsuaki Takami issued a document on June 3, 2008 entitled "Twenty years after NICE I: Approaching the Pauline Year and Beatification Ceremony". This report was in response to the survey sent out to dioceses, monasteries and convents, concerning National Incentive for Catholic Evangelization in Japan. The report noted that in general the NICE conferences influenced the Church, dioceses, religious, Catholic schools and institutions.[375] However, the report also noted the drawbacks of the two conferences. It noted the lack of connection between the themes and areas of focus of the two NICE conferences.

375 Takeo Okada, Jun Ikenaga and Mitsuaki Takami, "*NICE I Kara 20 Shunen: Pauro Toshi to Reppukushiki wo Mukaete*" [Twenty Years After NICEI: Approaching the Pauline Year and Beatification Ceremony], (Tokyo: Catholic Bishops' Conference of Japan, 2008), 1-2. Original in Japanese. [Translation mine].

However, the bishops expressed satisfaction over the response of the two documents, 'Living Together with Joy' and 'Sharing.'[376] The bishops urged all the Catholics to open up themselves to build a community of hope and joy.[377]

4.1.11.2 Alpha Course

In 1977, Charles Marnham, a curate belonging to Holy Trinity Brompton in London, England prepared a course for faith formation, and named it *Alpha Course.*[378] In 1990s, Nicky Gumbel, a curate of Holy Trinity Brompton took charge of directing the Alpha course. He reorganized the course to make it attractive. Alpha Course consists of basic Christian teachings on faith. It also deals with questions about the meaning of life. The course runs for a period of 10 weeks and has a weekend outing. The course usually has short talks, video presentations and discussions. The leaders and participants discuss the various topics about faith in a relaxed atmosphere. They also share a light meal or refreshment with each other.

Some Charismatics in Japan use this course as a means of evangelization. They welcome all faith seekers, especially the youth and the students. Ichiro Sanda organized this course for University students. He shares his experience as follows:

> I was extremely disheartened to see that the youth of our country (Japan) go through an education system where it is a taboo to speak about God. They do not find meaning in their lives. 5 years ago I read the following verse in the Bible, "ministry, in ministering; the teacher, in teaching" (Rom 12:7). After reading this verse, I decided to start the Alpha Course for the university students. Presently there are 32 of us including leaders, helpers, kitchen staff and anchorpersons. We gather every Thursday from 18-21 at Logos Center of Nanzan University. The Course runs for 12 weeks and includes an alpha weekend outing at the SVD Monastery in Tajimi. The participants of this

376 Ibid.

377 Ibid.

378 Peter Hocken, "Alpha Course," in The New International Dictionary of Pentecostal and Charismatic Movements, 312.

> course say that they have encountered God. For them it was a heavenly atmosphere, singing joyful songs and learning the doctrines of faith... Most of the participants are non-Christian university students who have little or no knowledge about Christianity. Therefore, we avoid using bombastic terminology and sophisticated doctrinal level teachings. Instead, we use teachings of the Church, Bible, video presentations or simple 20-minute talks. The content of the talk is very simple. We take examples from day to day life so that the students may understand them well. I was personally impressed when a student told me that she accidentally dashed her umbrella across a poster of Alpha Course and came to know about it. She decided to join this course. Another student who could not come for the alpha weekend saw the glittering faces of those who had attended and said that he would certainly like to join the next time. I thank God for His continual support.[379]

Thus, we see that people involved with the CCRM are also involved in various other evangelization programs like Alpha Course, to do the work of evangelization in Japan.

4.1.11.3 CCRM's Zeal for Evangelization

Pope Paul VI noted evangelization does not mean mere religious conversion. It also means to reach out to others with God's love. He noted that:

> Evangelization, as we have said, is a complex process made up of varied elements: the renewal of humanity, witness, explicit proclamation, inner adherence, entry into the community, acceptance of signs, apostolic initiative. These elements may appear to be contradictory, indeed mutually exclusive. In fact, they are complementary and mutually enriching. Evangelization therefore also includes

379 Ichiro Sanda posted an article on the web of Alpha Japan, about his experience of conducting the Alpha Course for university students in Nagoya, Japan. Original in Japanese. [Translation mine].

> the preaching of hope in the promises made by God in the new Covenant in Jesus Christ; the preaching of God's love for us and of our love for God; the preaching of brotherly love for all men the capacity of giving and forgiving, of self-denial, of helping one's brother and sister which, springing from the love of God, is the kernel of the Gospel; the preaching of the mystery of evil and of the active search for good.[380]

Pope John Paul II in the General Audience of September 16, 1998 noted that the Catholic Church has profound respect for the spiritual and moral values found in other religions. However, God's love impels us to share the Good News of Jesus Christ to all. He noted that:

> [T]he attitude of the Church and of individual Christians towards other religions is marked by sincere respect, profound sympathy and, when possible and appropriate, cordial collaboration. This does not mean forgetting that Jesus Christ is the one Mediator and Saviour of the human race. Nor does it mean lessening our missionary efforts, to which we are bound in obedience to the risen Lord's command: 'Go therefore and make disciples of all nations, baptizing them in the name of the Father and of the Son and of the Holy Spirit' (Mt 28:19). The attitude of respect and dialogue is instead the proper recognition of the 'seeds of the Word' and the 'groaning of the Spirit'. In this sense, far from opposing the proclamation of the Gospel, our attitude prepares it, as we await the times appointed by the Lord's mercy. 'By dialogue we let God be present in our midst; for as we open ourselves in dialogue to one another, we also open ourselves to God'[381]

---

380 "Apostolic Exhortation *Evangelii Nuntiandi*," *AAS* 68 (1976): 21-24.

381 "General Audience of September 16, 1998," *Insegnamenti di Giovanni Paolo II*, 21.2 (1998): 470. See also "Address to Members of Others Religions, Madras February 5, 1986," No. 4; *L'Osservatore Romano* English edition, February 19, 1986: 14.

Pope John Paul II in his address of May 30, 1998 to the members of the Ecclesial Movements and New Communities prayed that all those associated with the Ecclesial Movements and New Communities may be powerful witnesses and messengers of the Gospel.

> Today, from this upper room in St Peter's Square, a great prayer rises: Come, Holy Spirit, come and renew the face of the earth. Come with your seven gifts. Come, Spirit of Life, Spirit of Communion and Love. The Church and the world need you. Come, Holy Spirit, and make ever more fruitful the charisms you have bestowed on us. Give new strength and missionary zeal to these sons and of daughters of yours who have gathered here. Open their hearts; renew their Christian commitment in the world. Make them courageous messengers of the Gospel, witnesses to the risen Jesus Christ, the Redeemer and Saviour of man. Strengthen their love and their fidelity to the Church.[382]

Pope Benedict XVI in his homily on April 24, 2005 during the Holy Mass on the *Occasion of the Imposition of the Pallium and Conferral of the Fisherman's Ring for the Beginning of the Petrine Ministry of the Bishop of Rome* noted that evangelization means to speak about the friendship and the personal encounter that one has with Jesus.

> There is nothing more beautiful than to be surprised by the Gospel, by the encounter with Christ. There is nothing more beautiful than to know Him and to speak to others of our friendship with Him."[383]

---

382 "Address to Ecclesial Movements and New Communities," *Insegnamenti di Giovanni Paolo II*, 21.1 (1998): 1119-1125.

383 "Homily on the Occasion of the Imposition of the Pallium and Conferral of the Fisherman's Ring for the Beginning of the Petrine Ministry of the Bishop of Rome, April 24, 2005," *Insegnamenti di Benedetto XVI*, 1.1 (2005): 25.

Again, Pope Benedict XVI in his message of June 3, 2006 to the participants of the Second World Congress of Ecclesial Movements and New Communities noted that:

> The Holy Spirit desires unity, he desires totality. Therefore, his presence is finally shown above all in missionary zeal. Anyone who has come across something true, beautiful and good in his life - the one true treasure, the precious pearl - hastens to share it everywhere, in the family and at work, in all the contexts of his life. He does so without any fear, because he knows he has received adoption as a son; without any presumption, for it is all a gift; without discouragement, for God's Spirit precedes his action in people's 'hearts' and as a seed in the most diverse cultures and religions. He does so without restraint, for he bears a piece of good news which is for all people and for all the peoples.[384]

The three Popes, Paul VI, John Paul II and Benedict XVI noted that the work of evangelization is very important part of the Church's mission. However, they clarified that evangelization does not mean the conquest of other religions by forcefully converting others. It rather means to share the good news of Jesus Christ. It means to spread the love of Christ in this world.

The CCRM is playing a vital role in the work of evangelization in Japan. Charismatics are actively involved with the various programs of the Catholic Church of Japan for evangelization. The CBCJ organized a conference, National Incentive for Catholic Evangelization (NICE II & I) with the aim of reforming the Church and promoting the work of evangelization. Many Charismatics participated in the NICE II conferences and I. The final report of NICE II noted the need of renewal of the Catholic Church in Japan.[385] The CCRM too seeks the renewal of the Church in the

---

384 "Message to the Second World Congress of Ecclesial Movements and New Communities, June 3, 2006," *Insegnamenti di Benedetto XVI*, 2.1 (2006) 757-765.

385 Participants Report of the Second National Incentive for Catholic Evangelization Conference, "*Tenbo: Fukuin Senkyosuru Nihon no Kyoukai no*

Holy Spirit. The CCRM actively support bishops, priests and the religious in the work of evangelization. Even though, most of the Charismatics are lay people they make an effort to engage in the work of evangelization through the means of sharing, witness and dialogue.

Pope John Paul II in his Encyclical *Redemptoris Missio* welcomed the new ecclesial movements within the Church as a true gift of God for carrying out the work of evangelization. He wished that these movements spread and flourish, to promote the missionary work of the Church. He noted that:

> Within the Church, there are various types of services, functions, ministries and ways of promoting the Christian life. I call to mind, as a new development occurring in many Churches in recent times, the rapid growth of 'ecclesial movements' filled with missionary dynamism. When these movements humbly seek to become part of the life of local Churches and are welcomed by bishops and priests within diocesan and parish structures, they represent a true gift of God both for new evangelization and for missionary activity properly so-called. I therefore recommend that they be spread, and that they be used to give fresh energy, especially among young people, to the Christian life and to evangelization, within a pluralistic view of the ways in which Christians can associate and express themselves.[386]

In his address to the Members of the Catholic Fraternity of Charismatic Covenant Communities in Rome on November 14, 1994, Pope John Paul II urged all those involved in the CCRM to proclaim boldly the Gospel of Christ. He also suggested them to study the *Catechism of the Catholic Church*, which would be their right guide in their missionary work. He noted that:

Sasshin no Tameni" [Outlook: Toward a Renewal of the Church of Japan in the Work of Evangelization], Nagasaki, October 24, 1993. Original in Japanese. [Translation mine].

386 "Encyclical *Redemptoris Missio*," *AAS* 83.1 (1991): 320.

> As the Church prepares to celebrate the Third Christian Millennium by committing all her resources to a new proclamation of the Gospel, the members of your Communities are being challenged to bear ever more convincing witness to the truths of the Gospel as taught by the Church. For this, I am certain that you will encourage your fellow-members to make a careful reading and attentive study of the 'Catechism of the Catholic Church'.[387]

Fr. Francis Mathy noted about the involvement of the CCRM in the evangelization of the Japan. In his article published in *Pentecost Today* he noted that:

> At a time when converts are becoming fewer and fewer, a great number of Japanese have had their first encounter with Christ in our prayer groups, especially the small home groups, and have gone on to Baptism and a full Church life. The theme of our upcoming Tokyo conference is *Duc in altum* (put out into the deep), one of the principal themes of Pope John Paul's apostolic letter, *Novo Millennio Ineunte*. This is the very direction in which the Holy Spirit seems to be leading us. Our experiences until now, to paraphrase the Holy Father, 'inspire in us new energy and impel us' to draw up an effective pastoral plan for the new millennium according to the lines he proposes in his letter.[388]

Motoyuki Hata, a Catholic priest belonging to the Congregation of Passion noted in an article published in *Ikeru Mizu*, newsletter of CCRJ that his association with the CCRM gave him the zeal to do the work of evangelization.

> The Acts of the Apostles mentions that Peter realized at Cornelius' house that God pours His Holy Spirit on

387 "Address to the Members of the Catholic Fraternity of Charismatic Covenant Communities, November 14, 1994," *Insegnamenti di Giovanni Paolo II*, 17.2 (1994): 775-777.

388 Mathy, "What in the World is going on? - Japan,": 15.

> all, even the unbelievers and this event enlarged his vision about the Gospel (Acts 10). I realized the real meaning of this text this year. The work of the Holy Spirit is creation and salvation. However, these two activities are same. This faith, which the Holy Spirit enkindled in me, encourages me to proclaim the power of the Gospel. The new vision, which I got, is that the CCRM can contribute towards the work of evangelization by the evangelization of the culture (inculturation). Research study on inculturation is increasingly becoming important for doing evangelization in Japan. Nevertheless, the Gospel message is the faith experience of the apostles and the early Christian community about the resurrection of Jesus Christ. We, who are involved in the CCRM, have received the grace to experience the resurrection of Jesus. The Holy Spirit calls us to live this experience in our lives, share it with others and above all, bear witness to it.[389]

On the 50th Anniversary of the beginning of the Society of St. Columban in Japan in 1998, Sr. Briege McKenna and Fr. Kevin Sallon organized a series of retreats for the members of the Columban Congregation. The CCRJ reported that some non-Christians who attended this retreat had decided to become Catholics.[390]

A non-Christian, Mitsuo Iwamoto who attended the 14th Hokkaido regional CCRM convention held from May 2-4, 1999, received the grace to be an evangelizer himself. He also noted in his testimony that he received the grace to surrender his children's problem to the Lord.[391] Naomi Yamada, an ardent Buddhist also

389 Motoyuki Hata, "*Atarashi Uta wo Utaou*" [Let Us Sing a New Song], *Ikeru Mizu,* No. 50 (Fall Edition 1998): 4-5. Original in Japanese. [Translation mine].

390 Editorial Board of *Ikeru Mizu*, "*Sei Coronban Kai Senkyo Gojuu Shunen wo Iwatte*" [Celebrating 50 Years of Mission of the Society of St. Columban Mission], *Ikeru Mizu*, No. 52 (Spring Edition 1999): 11. Original in Japanese. [Translation mine].

391 Shirou Ishii, "*Dai Juu Yon Kai Seirei ni Yoru Sasshin Hokkaido Taikai Hirakareru*" [14th Hokkaido Regional CCRM Convention Opens], *Ikeru Mizu*, No. 53 (Summer Edition 1999): 2. Original in Japanese. [Translation mine].

attended this convention. During the convention, she declared Jesus as the lord of her life. She noted in her testimony that:

> I am not a Christian yet. However, I received many graces. I cannot comprehend how a non-baptized person like me can receive such graces. I was an ardent believer of Buddha (Amida). I was worried because one of my intimate friends was having cancer. It was at that time I met Jesus. My younger brother who is a monk questioned me about my encounter with Christianity. I was feeling that I am doing something wrong and in such a situation, I participated in the convention. In the convention, I shared my thoughts with a priest. The priest quoted the following words from the Bible, 'I am the way, the truth and the life.' He told me that there are many religions but all pass through Jesus to the Father. Listening to these words of the priest all my doubts disappeared. During the convention, I was praying for the cure of my friend who was suffering from cancer, but I realized that Jesus does more than curing He heals.[392]

Keizi Sakakura, the liaison between the Tokyo Archdiocese and the CCRJ noted in an article in *Ikeru Mizu* that the CCRM has contributed to the growth of the Catholic Church of Japan. However, he noted that the CCRM must share the graces it enjoys with all. In other words, he emphasized the need of witnessing and proclamation. He pointed some practical difficulties, which a person not associated with the CCRM, or Christianity may encounter with the CCRM prayer meetings. He cautioned about the use of difficult vocabulary in the CCRM prayer meetings. He suggested simplifying the prayer meetings and clarifying the doubts of the people.[393]

---

392 Shirou Ishii, "*Dai Juu Yon Kai Seirei ni Yoru Sasshin Hokkaido Taikai Hirakareru*" [14th Hokkaido Regional CCRM Convention Opens], *Ikeru Mizu,* no. 53 (Summer Edition 1999): 4. Original in Japanese. [Translation mine].

393 Keizi Sakakura, "*Seirei Sasshin Madoguchi Shisai Toshite: Herumenein*" [As a Liaison Priest of CCRM: Hermeneutics], *Ikeru Mizu,* No. 68 (Spring Edition 2003): 1-2. Original in Japanese. [Translation mine].

The CCRM reported that the CCRM praise and worship meeting organized at Nanzan Catholic Church on June 8, 2003 was a great success. The preaching was inspiring and the whole prayer session helped many to have a deeper experience of God. Especially the Catholics who attended the CCRM prayer meeting for the first time were able to praise and thank God without any inhibitions. This prayer meeting also served as a powerful means of evangelization. The non-Christians who attended this prayer meeting had a healing experience and expressed their desire to come to the Church again.[394]

Moto Yamaura, a protestant frequently attended the CCRM prayer meetings at Tokyo. He got the grace to receive Baptism in the Catholic Church. Moto Yamaura became Catholic in his eighties. He wrote in his testimony published in *Ikeru Mizu* that he had a deep experience of God, which led him to the grace of Baptism in the Catholic Church at an advanced age.[395]

Masaaki Terada who is actively involved in the CCRM influenced his friend in New Zealand to go to the CCRM meetings. He mentioned that his friend received baptism in the Holy Spirit and he in turn influenced his son who was then 22 years old. His son was not a Christian but expressed his desire to receive Baptism that year.[396]

A sister who attended the 23rd Hokkaido regional CCRM convention testified that she was convinced of spreading the good news of Jesus Christ to her parish in spite of all the problems of daily life as she became aware of the presence of Jesus within her.[397]

---

394 Editorial Board of *Ikeru Mizu*, "*Nagoya de Seirei Korin no Tsudoi Hirakareru*" [Pentecost Meet at Nagoya], *Ikeru Mizu*, No. 68 (Summer Edition 2003): 5-6. Original in Japanese. [Translation mine].

395 Editorial Board of *Ikeru Mizu*, "*Yamaura Moto Sama no Shinko no Akashi*" [The Testimony of Faith of Mr. Moto Yamaura], *Ikeru Mizu*, No. 73 (Summer Edition 2004): 3-4. Original in Japanese. [Translation mine].

396 Masaaki Terada, "*Shu ga Hataraiteorareru Koto wo Chokkan*" [I Perceived that the Lord is Indeed Working], *Ikeru Mizu*, No. 74 (Fall Edition 2004): 5-6. Original in Japanese. [Translation mine].

397 Editorial Board of *Ikeru Mizu*, "*Dai 23 Kai Seirei ni Yoru Sasshin Hokkaido Tai Kai no Hokoku: Anatagata ha Yo no Hikari Desu*" [Report of the 23rd Hokkaido

A catechumen who was attending the Alpha Course noted that after attending the 24th Hokkaido regional CCRM convention she realized the importance of prayer, faith and worship in her life.[398] It gave her a deep conviction to receive Baptism and be a powerful witness of Christ.

In March 2001, the bishops of Japan met the Holy Father, Pope John Paul II in Vatican City for '*Ad Limina*' visit. Chikara Hashimoto, a Catholic priest of Sapporo diocese analyzed the Pope's message to the Bishops of Japan and suggested the CCRM to support actively the bishops to implement the directives of the Holy Father.[399] The Holy Father emphasized that the call to holiness and the vocation to evangelize is for all Catholics. The call to live a holy life, in other words means to have a deeper relationship with the Holy Trinity, to experience the love of the Holy Trinity, to serve the community, to witness to the love of God and to spread the Gospel. The Holy Father's message was entirely in harmony with the goals of the CCRM. Fr. Hashimoto noted that,

> Most of those who have been involved with the CCRM have been transformed by the grace of the Holy Spirit, deepened their prayer lives, serve the community with greater zeal and witness faith through their lives.[400]

Pope John Paul II suggested that the bishops should consider the following directives in their pastoral plan for the work of evangelization.

> One of the principal objectives of your pastoral planning in union with your collaborators will be to help

---

Regional CCRM Convention: You are the Light of the World], *Ikeru Mizu,* No. 90 (Fall Edition 2008): 5. Original in Japanese. [Translation mine].

398 Editorial Board of *Ikeru Mizu*, "*Dai 24 Kai Seirei ni Yoru Sasshin Hokkaido Tai Kai no Hokoku*" [Report of the 24th Hokkaido Regional CCRM Convention], *Ikeru Mizu,* No. 93 (Fall Edition 2008): 7. Original in Japanese. [Translation mine].

399 Chikara Hashimoto, "*Kyouko no Nihon No Kyokai he no Messegi*" [Holy Father's Message to the Church of Japan], *Ikeru Mizu*, No. 61 (Summer Edition 2001): 1-2. Original in Japanese. [Translation mine].

400 Ibid.

> Christian communities in Japan to become more than ever 'genuine schools of prayer', 'where the meeting with Christ is expressed not just in imploring help but also in thanksgiving, praise, adoration, contemplation, listening and ardent devotion, until the heart truly falls in love'. Such prayer is more than comfort and strength in the disciple's life: *it is also the well-spring of evangelization.* It is from a new depth of prayer and contemplation that a 'new evangelization' will come. A 'new evangelization' in Japan will also mean *a discerning but generous openness to the communities and movements* which the Holy Spirit is raising up in the Church as *a special fruit of the Second Vatican Council.* It is often in such groups that people, especially the young, find the spiritual fervor and experience of community which leads them to a personal encounter with Christ and makes them in turn missionaries of the new millennium. Clearly these communities and movements have to work in union with the Bishops and priests, and in full harmony with the pastoral life of the local Churches. It is the Bishops' task to 'test everything and hold fast what is good' (1 Thes 5:21).[401] [Italics in original]

The Holy Father urged the bishops of Japan to give prime importance to build communities of prayer where people can have a real encounter with the person of Christ. It is only when people have this experience of Christ then they can be true evangelizers. In this context, the Pope urges the Bishops of Japan to be *discerning but generously open* to the various ecclesial movements, which have sprung up in the Church as the fruit of the Second Vatican Council. The Holy Father strongly believes that these movements can attract many people especially the youth. The bishops of Japan have a tremendous task of discerning and encouraging what is genuinely coming from the Holy Spirit to boost the work of evangelization in Japan. The CCRM on its part has contributed in the work of evangelization.

401 "Address to the Bishops of Japan on their '*Ad Limina*' Visit on March 31, 2001," *AAS* 93.2 (2001): 531.

Catholics involved with the CCRM share the joy of their Christian life with others. On the other hand, there are non-Christians who have become Catholics because of their encounter with the CCRM. Thus, we can conclude that the CCRM has been instrumental in spreading the good news of Jesus Christ.

4.1.12 Social Commitment

The CCRM emphasizes spiritual renewal. However, the CCRM must also involve itself in social reformation. Jesus preached salvation from all oppressions. Jesus spoke about His mission quoting the words of Is 61.

> The Spirit of the Lord is upon me, because he has anointed me to bring good news to the poor. He has sent me to proclaim release to the captives and recovery of sight to the blind, to let the oppressed go free, to proclaim the year of the Lord's favor. (Lk 4:18-19)

St. James wrote in his letter that there is relation between spirituality and social commitment.

> Religion that is pure and undefiled before God, the Father, is this: to care for orphans and widows in their distress and to keep oneself unstained by the world" (Jas 1:27). What good is it, my brothers and sisters, if you say you have faith but do not have works? Can faith save you? If a brother or sister is naked and lacks daily food, and one of you says to them, 'Go in peace; keep warm and eat your fill,' and yet you do not supply their bodily needs, what is the good of that? So faith by itself, if it has no works, is dead. But someone will say, 'You have faith and I have works.' Show me your faith apart from your works, and I by my works will show you my faith. (Jas 2:14-18)

During the FABC assembly at Thailand, Antonio De Los Reyes criticized the CCRM for its lack of intereste in social work.[402]

402 See Antonio B. De Los Reyes, *The Charismatic Movements and Small Christian Communities*. FABC Paper: 92h, Seventh Plenary Assembly: Workshop

The CCRM aims the spiritual renewal of a person. However, it cannot neglect its commitment to social issues. It must work for the dignity of every person, because God created every human person in His image.[403] The Church makes it her mission to work for the promotion and protection of the dignity of the human person.

> The Church can anchor the dignity of human nature against all tides of opinion, for example those which undervalue the human body or idolize it. By no human law can the personal dignity and liberty of man be so aptly safeguarded as by the Gospel of Christ which has been entrusted to the Church. For this Gospel announces and proclaims the freedom of the sons of God, and repudiates all the bondage which ultimately results from sin. (cf. Rom. 8:14-17); it has a sacred reverence for the dignity of conscience and its freedom of choice, constantly advises that all human talents be employed in God's service and men's, and, finally, commends all to the charity of all (cf. Matt. 22:39). (*GS* 41)

Pope Benedict XVI in his message of May 22, 2006 to the participants of the Second World Congress of Ecclesial Movements and New Communities noted that it is important to spread Christ's reign in all activities. He noted that the true love of Christ has the power to construct a just social order.

> The extraordinary fusion between love of God and love of neighbour makes life beautiful and causes the desert in which we often find ourselves living to blossom anew. Where love is expressed as a passion for the life and destiny of others, where love shines forth in affection and in work and becomes a force for the construction of a

---

Discussion Guide. Antonio De Los Reyes prepared this discussion guide for the workshop of the Seventh Plenary Assembly of the Federation of Asian Bishops' Conferences. FABC organized this assembly in January 2000, at "Baan Phu Waan," the pastoral formation center of the Archdiocese of Bangkok, Samphran, Thailand. The theme of the Plenary was "A Renewed Church in Asia: A Mission of Love and Service."

403 Ibid.

> more just social order, there the civilization is built that can withstand the advance of barbarity.[404]

Pope Benedict XVI in his message of June 3, 2006 to the participants of the Second World Congress of Ecclesial Movements and New Communities noted that the Holy Spirit guides a person to respond to the call of God to work for the good of the whole humanity. He noted that:

> The Holy Spirit, on the other hand, makes us sons and daughters of God. He involves us in the same responsibility that God has for his world, for the whole of humanity. He teaches us to look at the world, others and ourselves with God's eyes. We do not do good as slaves who are not free to act otherwise, but we do it because we are personally responsible for the world; because we love truth and goodness, because we love God himself and therefore, also his creatures. This is the true freedom to which the Holy Spirit wants to lead us.[405]

In Japan, the CCRM has motivated all those who attending prayer meetings, retreats and conventions to be active members not only of their local parish but also in the society where they live. A number of social problems are present in Japan. Increase in graying population, falling birth rate, economic recession, unhealthy competitiveness, loneliness, high rate of divorce, high rate of suicide, homelessness, gender discrimination and shortage of labor are some of the social problems prevalent in Japan.[406] The gap between the rich and the poor is widening. Depression is one of the main causes of suicide. Japan has a very high rate of suicide. According to World Health Organization report in the year 2009, 30,707 people

---

404 "Message to the Participants of the Second World Congress of Ecclesial Movements and New Communities, May 22, 2006," *Insegnamenti di Benedetto XVI*, 2.1 (2006): 662-665.

405 "Message to the Second World Congress of Ecclesial Movements and New Communities, June 3, 2006," *Insegnamenti di Benedetto XVI*, 2.1 (2006): 757-765.

406 Pradyumna P. Karan, *Japan in the Twenty-First Century: Environment, Economy and Society* (Lexington: University Press of Kentucky, 2005), 164-171.

committed suicide.[407] These figures show that a big number of people in Japan are depressed. In such a scenario, people involved in the CCRM can add their mite to help the needy in the society. They have a responsibility to share the message of God's infinitive love to all humankind. The spiritual experience, which the people involved in the CCRM have, must move them to reach out to those who are depressed. Following are the testimonies of Charismatics who taken the task of social commitment.

A woman wrote in an article published in *Ikeru Mizu*, the newsletter of CCRJ that her association with the CCRM gave her the realization that the graces she has received from the Lord are not for her alone but also for others. Keeping this in mind, she ventured out to reach out to the Human Immunodeficiency Virus (HIV) patients in the society. She noted the following about her experience with the HIV patients:

> I heard the panel discussion in an International Acquired Immune Deficiency Syndrome (AIDS) Conference on March 25, 1993. The panel discussions by Magic Jones and other AIDS patients impressed me. It was because of this panel discussion I decided to volunteer at the 'HIV and Human Rights Information Center' (*HIV to Jinken Jouhou Centa*). Previously I used to think, I neither had prejudices nor any discrimination against the HIV patients but I realized that unknowingly I had these negative feeling towards them. I believe the Lord transformed me. I begin my day by participating in the Holy Eucharist. I offer all the people and myself to the Lord. I consider my offering like the drop of water, which the priest pours in the wine during the preparation of the offertory gifts in the mass. The tiny drop of water, which is not important, becomes the Blood of Christ by the power of the Holy Spirit... Jesus says 'those who

407 World Health Organization, *Statistics of Suicide Rates in Japan* posted on their web page. http://www.who.int/mental_health/media/japa.pdf. [accessed on September 20, 2014].

> are well have no need of a physician, but those who are sick; I have come to call not the righteous but sinners to repentance' (Lk 5:31-32). I believe that Jesus loves even the HIV patients unconditionally. I reach out to the HIV patients with the love of Jesus, especially the youth who have no courage even to tell their parents about their disease. When I reach out to them in love, I realize that I get more than what I give. I am receiving many graces, new convictions and a deeper experience of the love of the Lord. On my own, I could have never changed my old self. The Holy Spirit has made me His instrument… For me the weekly prayer meeting is the time for relaxation, healing and drawing energy to begin my volunteer work the next week.[408]

The parish priest asked Aiko Okuyama to take charge of the social welfare committee of the parish. The social welfare committee was practically non-functional and its existence was a mere formality. Even Aiko Okuyama had no regard for this committee because she thought that the religious are doing an excellent work in this field. She thought that this committee is not doing any significant work like the religious. In such a situation, she headed the committee. She decided to leave the things as they are. However, the parish priest announced a meeting for planning some activities for the social welfare committee. Initially some 7 to 8 people gathered for this meeting. Even though, they did not discuss anything special, she decided to put an article in the parish newsletter about the proposed plans of the social welfare committee. Quoting 1 Jn 3:17, "How does God's love abide in anyone who has the world's goods and sees a brother or sister in need and yet refuses help?" she wrote that as a community, all the parishioners must work together to bring Christ's love to others. Meanwhile she received a phone call from a friend to teach some yoga classes for a day care center of a hospital. This particular day care center was for patients suffering from mental illness. She started teaching some yoga classes for these patients and later joined

408 Shigi, "*Seirei no Michibiki no Naka de*" [Led by the Holy Spirit], *Ikeru Mizu* No. 48 (Spring Edition 1998): 4-5. Original in Japanese. [Translation mine].

them for a meal. After some time she decided to start cooking classes for the patients. She asked for volunteers from her parish and the CCRM prayer group. To her surprise as many as 40 people, both men and women volunteered to take cooking classes for the patients. These activities led to the expansion of the social work done by the parishioners. The youth and the elders also started helping in various programs for the weak and the sick in the hospital center or in the parish itself. Okuyama wonders the powerful work of God through them. The social welfare committee, which she initially thought was irrelevant became an opportunity for the parish community to come together, pray together and serve others imitating Christ.[409]

In Japan sometimes there is a possibility of mistaking the CCRM as a cult. This is because there are cults in Japan, which stress healings and prophecies. The CCRM too emphasizes the importance of healing and prophecy. In the past some fanatics and cults created havoc among the people.[410] For instance, the *Aum Shinrikyo* was responsible for the lethal sarin gas tragedy in 1995. When a movement loses its link with the society it can easily lose its direction. For this reason, it is very important that along with the spiritual activities, the CCRM must have touch with the people and their problems. Firstly, all the social welfare activities of the CCRM must be in harmony with the local parishes to which they belong. When the CCRM has the backing of the parish community then it can be a powerful witness to Christ's love. True humanism and faith in God never contradict each other. The love of Christ is the base for all social welfare works of the CCRM. Charismatics must not hesitate to reach out to the poor and the needy in the society with the power of the Holy Spirit. True prayer helps humanity to restore its relationship with God. True social welfare activities bring healing to the wounded and the needy.

---

409 Aiko Okuyama, "*Seito no Majiwari no Naka de*" [Among the Communion of Saints], No. 49 (Summer Edition 1998): 6-8. Original in Japanese. [Translation mine].

410 Motoyuki Hata, "*Shu no Fukkatsu Omedetou Gozaimasu*" [Happy Easter], *Ikeru Mizu* No. 64 (Spring Edition 2002): 1-2. Original in Japanese. [Translation mine].

4.1.13 Promoting Interreligious Dialogue

Japan is land of religious pluralism. Even though, Shinto is the traditional religion, there are other religions, which co-exist along with it. In general, Japanese are not much interested in religion. Moreover, the spread of secularization is further reducing the space of religion in the society. In such a situation, religious leaders belonging to different faiths must come together to promote the richness in different religions. They must work together to serve the people and spread peace in the world. In the following sections, we shall study the major religions in Japan.

4.1.13.1 Major Religions in Japan

4.1.13.1.1 Shinto

The word Shinto means the way of God. *Shin* means God (*kami*) and *To* means path (*michi*). Japanese used the word Shinto, to distinguish it from Buddhism (*Butsudo* that means the path of Buddha).[411] Hirai Naofusa defines Shinto "as the traditional indigenous religious practices of the Japanese people as well as their worldview, based on their concept of *kami*."[412] There is no founder of the religion Shinto. It evolved in the Japanese society. The concept of *kami* (god) is polytheistic. It refers to gods (*kamigami*). The word *kami* (god) means something mysterious, supernatural, or sacred. *Kami is* a Japanese term "having general meaning of 'above', 'superior' is the most common and comprehensive word for deity in Japanese language."[413]

---

411 Hirai Naofusa, "Shinto," in *The Encyclopedia of Religion*, Vol. 13, ed. Mircea Eliade (New York: Macmillan Publishing Company, 1987), 280.

412 Ibid. The Japanese term *kami* is a very complicated term. Even though, the English translation of *kami* is god, it does not mean God, in the Christian sense. However, because of the insufficient translation skills the earlier Christian missionaries employed the same term *kami* to refer to God. Christians continue to use the word *kami* for God. The usage of this term has created confusion among Japanese who have a different image of the term *kami*, very much different from the Christian image of God.

413 Howard Smith, "Kami," in *A Dictionary of Comparative Religion,* ed. S.G.F. Brandon (New York: Charles Scribners's Sons, 1970), 389-390.

> A *kami* is a being that is capable of inspiring awe in humankind and is mysterious and supernatural. The simple objects of the folk cult, as well as the deities of the imperial house and those revered by the great clans, are all considered *kami*.[414]

The concept of *kami* includes all the natural deities, anthropomorphic deities and conceptual deities. "Since ancient times, phenomena that possess some awe-inspiring, extraordinary quality have been designated *kami*: thunder, lightning, rocks, mountains, plants, trees, fish, animals, as well as such human beings as a family ancestor, a great warrior, or an emperor."[415] The Japanese believe that their ancestors after a certain period of purification would return once in a year to their homes bestowing happiness and good fortune. Japanese refer the souls of their ancestors also as *kami*.[416]

Shinto had originally no shrines. Shinto priests performed all rituals and worship near sites of volcanic eruption, hot springs, rivers, mountaintops or forests. They considered these sites as sacred. Later as people gathered to take part in the rituals, they built huts to protect themselves and the altar from wind and rain. Eventually these huts became shrines. They believed that god (*kami*) permanently dwelt in these shrines. This belief was different from the original thinking that god (*kami*) would visit the sacred place during the rituals.[417] The major rituals of Shinto revolve around agricultural activities as Japan used to be an agricultural country. During these rituals, the priests serve food and alcohol to the god (*kami*). They do so to appease the god and seek favors like blessing of an abundant harvest, good weather, fertility of the livestock and prosperity.

Shinto has two cosmologies, which exist simultaneously. One is the vertical pattern and the other is the horizontal pattern. In the vertical pattern, there are three planes, namely *takamanohara* (the world of gods), *nakatsukuni* (the world of humankind) and *yomi* (world of dead). In the horizontal pattern there are two sections,

---

414 Naofusa, "Shinto," in *The Encyclopedia of Religion*, Vol. 13, 280.

415 Minor Rogers, "Kami," in *Abingdon Dictionary of Living Religions,* eds. Keith Crim, Roger A. Bullard, Larry D. Shinn (Nashville: Abingdon, 1981), 399.

416 Naofusa, "Shinto," in *The Encyclopedia of Religion*, Vol. 13, 282.

417 Ibid.

the first the phenomenal world and the second the utopian land far beyond the sea. Cosmologies of the Southeast and North Asian origin religions influenced the cosmology of Shinto. Shinto does not consider the world of humankind to be of a lower value than the world of gods. This explains the strong focus on this world and its things among Japanese who follow Shinto.[418]

Shinto's beliefs and teachings center on the festivals, myths and the societal norms. The core of the Shinto consists of the belief in the profound and mysterious power of the way of the god (*kami*). In other words, it means to follow the natural course of things in the world. The way of the *kami* is the harmony and balance in the creation. For Japanese *kami* is not an abstract being but a proximate being who bestows blessings and good fortune. Therefore, Shinto strongly advocates prayers and rituals to these gods.[419] Shinto considers human beings as children of *kami*. In other words, life is sacred and life comes from *kami*. All human life is sacred and it is the duty of each person to respect the other. Human beings continually need to besiege *kami* for blessings to carry out their daily tasks. This respect for human life forms the theoretical basis for the peace movement in Shinto. Human beings have the divine within them but pollution in the heart (untruthfulness) blurs their awareness of the presence of the god within. Therefore, Shinto advocates purification. A person needs to do purification in order to let the divine essence shine in his or her life.[420]

Shinto strongly advocates the concept of *makoto no kokoro* (truthfulness) or *magokokoro* (sincerity of heart). Shinto believes god has these qualities. Therefore, all must strive to have a pure and sincere heart. Every person must live these qualities in their everyday life. They must be conscious of their divine origin. Sincerity of heart forms the base of Shinto ethics.[421]

Shinto has no fixed canon or dogmas. It advocates societal ethics. As Shinto evolved, Japanese created myths, rituals and feasts. They started including prayers addressed to the various mythological

418 Naofusa, "Shinto," in *The Encyclopedia of Religion*, Vol. 13, 282.

419 Ibid., 288.

420 Ibid.

421 Naofusa, "Shinto," in *The Encyclopedia of Religion*, Vol. 13, 288.

gods (*kamigami*). Presently Shinto is a part of the Japanese culture. Even though the Japanese may not be conscious of the influences of Shinto, it does influence their lifestyle, thinking and living.[422] It is a part of the Japanese society.

Shinto is very flexible. It changed to adapt to the needs of the time. Shinto had no classification initially. However, over the passage of time, the Japanese classified it into three major categories namely, Shrine Shinto, Sect Shinto and Folk Shinto.[423] Shrine Shinto (*Jinja Shinto)* means worship in Shinto shrines. It is the traditional form of Shinto worship. Even though, Shinto has no founder, over the years the Shinto priests created rituals and precepts. Each shrine has a particular feast day and festival. The locals flock to the shrines in great numbers on the feast days and celebrate the festivals with great pomp. The Meiji government identified the Shrine Shinto with national pride and used it as an instrument for the unification of the nation.[424] Sect Shinto in Japanese is *Kyoha Shinto* or *Shuha Shinto*. It refers to the thirteen groups of Shinto formed during the 19th century. Each group has a founder. The founders formed sects based on their religious experience. Sect Shinto includes all the new Japanese religions since the end of the World War II. Generally, the followers of various sects do not use the term shrines (*ginja*) for their places of worship. They use the term church (*kyokai*). However, their church has no relation with the Christian Churches.[425]Folk Shinto (*Minzoku Shinto*) consists of beliefs and traditions. It uses elements like magic, divination, rituals and myths as a part of worship. It also advocates abstinence, purification and mortification to please the deities. It has also inserted some features from foreign religions like Buddhism and Catholicism.[426]

Shinto had a prominent role in Japanese society until the end of the reign of the Meiji emperor. The Meiji government considered it as the national religion. It identified Shinto with national pride. The

422 Naofusa, "Shinto," in *The Encyclopedia of Religion*, Vol. 13, 288.

423 Ibid.

424 Ibid. See also Joseph J. Spae, *Shinto Man* (Tokyo: Oriens Institute for Religious Research, 1972), 41-50.

425 Ibid., 280-281.

426 Ibid. See also Joseph J. Spae, *Shinto Man* (Tokyo: Oriens Institute for Religious Research, 1972), 280-281.

Meiji government forced the Japanese to support the Shinto shrines. It also declared most of the Shinto festivals as national holidays. The Meiji government also paid for the maintenance and the up keeping of the Shinto shrines. After the World War II, things changed dramatically in Japan with the occupational authorities ordering the Japanese government to stop all patronages to Shinto Shrines and to separate the activities of state and religion. Presently the government cannot support any of the Shrines officially but under the pretext of aiding national mausoleum of fallen soldiers of the war some governments did try unsuccessfully to pay for the maintenance of the Shinto Shrines. The Catholic Church has staunchly opposed patronages to Shinto Shrines. In the past the Meiji government supported Shinto shrines and in the process persecuted all other religions especially Christianity. The Catholic Church does not want the same to happen.[427]

According to the statistics of the Ministry of Education, Culture, Sports, Science and Technology there are 81,121 Shinto shrines in the year 2014 in Japan. It also puts the number of the adherents of Shinto as 100,939,613, which includes the various sects, and sub-sects of Shinto.[428]

Shinto is part of Japanese people's life. No matter which religion they belong to they like to celebrate the traditional festivals. Even though, the number of people professing Shinto religion decreased over the years, it forms an important part of the cultural and social life of the Japanese.[429] Shinto promotes peace and harmony among all. It also advocates peace with other religions.

---

427 Naofusa, "Shinto," in *The Encyclopedia of Religion*, Vol. 13, 292-293.

428 Ministry of Education, Culture, Sport, Science and Technology, Japan, "*Zenkoku Jinja Kyokai Nado Shukyo Dantai, Kyoshi, Shinjasu*" [National Statistics of Shrines, Churches etc, Religious Organizations, Adherents]. http://www.e-stat.go.jp/SG1/estat/List.do?bid=000001052797&cycode=0 [accessed on September 18, 2014].

429 Ministry of Education, Culture, Sport, Science and Technology, Japan, "*Zenkoku Jinja Kyokai Nado Shukyo Dantai, Kyoshi, Shinjasu*" [National Statistics of Shrines, Churches etc, Religious Organizations, Adherents]. http://www.e-stat.go.jp/SG1/estat/List.do?bid=000001052797&cycode=0 [accessed on September 18, 2014].

4.1.13.1.2 Buddhism

India is the birthplace of Buddhism. However, it spread to Japan in the middle of the sixth century. The Japanese have accepted Buddhism as a part of their culture. However, Buddhism in Japan always co-existed with other religions like Shinto, Confucianism and later Christianity. It never became the state religion of Japan. However, it influences Japanese society. Interestingly, Japanese culture and Shinto has also influenced Buddhism. Thus, Buddhism in Japan is very different from the original Buddhism, originated in India.[430]

China had developed a highly refined culture and the neighboring countries like Japan looked upon China for imparting skills and techniques to enhance their culture. Japan had borrowed its writing system and political system from China. Chinese culture greatly influenced Japan. The Japanese considered Buddhism as a part of the superior Chinese culture, though it originated in India.[431] Therefore, the new religion initially influenced the imperial family and the members of the imperial court. Chinese officials and missionary monks preached Mahayana Buddhism in Japan.[432]

Buddhism was the religion of the upper class until the beginning of the Nara period (710-784). During the Nara period, it started influencing the commoners and many people of the lower class of the society accepted Buddhism as their religion. Gradually the influence of Buddhism grew during the Kamakura period (1185-1333) and the Muromachi period (1338-1573).[433]

The acceptance of a foreign religion namely Buddhism was not without problems. Initially the imperial family who were followers of Shinto resisted it. Shinto religion attested the emperor as the son of the sun god. It was obligatory for all to obey his laws as these laws had divine origin. Buddhism entered Japan with an all together new

430 Tamaru Noriyoshi, "Buddhism in Japan," in *The Encyclopedia of Religion*, Vol. 2, 426.

431 Ibid., 427.

432 There are two major schools of Buddhism, namely Mahayana Buddhism and Theravada Buddhism. People of Southeast Asia mainly practice Theravada Buddhism.

433 Noriyoshi, "Buddhism in Japan," in *The Encyclopedia of Religion*, Vol. 2, 427.

form of teachings and beliefs. However, the imperial family favored Shinto because it accorded them high status. Moreover, they used Shinto religion to unite the warring warlords. However, a small group of Japanese favored Buddhism. It is rather interesting to note that both the groups, those favoring it and those opposing had no proper knowledge of the real teachings of Buddhism. Therefore, they debated about the peripheral (external) issues of Buddhism.

Buddhism had a dramatic transformation in Japan. The statues of Buddha fascinated the Japanese more than his teachings. Moreover, there was also the language barrier. Average Japanese could not read the Chinese Buddhist texts. Only scholars and learned people could read the Chinese characters and translate them in Japanese. Even though Buddhism faced resistance initially, the Soga clan granted the Japanese people permission to practice Buddhism.[434]

The appearance of Kamakura *shogunate* marked the beginning of a new era in Japanese history. The power slipped out of the hand of the imperial family and passed on to a number of warlords thereby creating feudal states within Japan. This period is also prominent for Buddhism as three schools of Buddhism namely Pure Land Buddhism, Zen Buddhism and Nichiren Buddhism began in this period. Even though these schools differed in their characteristic features, they had some common elements. For instance, the *Tendai* tradition formed the base of all these schools. They focused on the same teaching as the most important element for salvation. The Pure Land Buddhism focused on the way of salvation through faith in *Amida* Buddha. Zen Buddhism focused on the way of meditation as the path to enlightenment. In addition, Nichiren Buddhism advocated the path of devotion to the truth as revealed in the Lotus *sutra*. Indian and Chinese philosophies influenced the Pure Land. The Chinese way of meditation *chan* influenced Zen Buddhism. Nichiren Buddhism is a typical from of Japanese Buddhism as no foreign philosophy influenced it.[435]

Honen (1133-1212) propagated Pure Land Buddhism known as *Jodo* or *Sukhavati* (Land of Bliss). Honen was upset with the Buddhist followers of his time. He felt the deteriorating political and

---

434 Noriyoshi, "Buddhism in Japan," in *The Encyclopedia of Religion*, Vol. 2, 428.
435 Noriyoshi, "Buddhism in Japan," in *The Encyclopedia of Religion*, Vol. 2, 431.

social system could no longer offer any insight to the people. He left the monastery and after a long period of spiritual quest, he found a new way of Buddhism, namely the Buddhism of Pure Land. He preached that repeating the name of Buddha incessantly (*Nembutsu*) is sufficient for salvation. He preached salvation as rebirth in the Pure Land or the Place where Buddha lives. In his treatise *Senchaku Hongan Nembutsu Shu,* he divides Buddhism into two types: one in which a person seeks salvation through self-discipline and perseverance and the other is to rely on the mercy of Buddha. Honen strongly favored the way of relying on mercy as the sure way to salvation. In addition, the simplest way to plead mercy was by repeating the name of Buddha. In this way, Honen introduced a simple form of Buddhism, which was strikingly different from other forms of Buddhism as it gave more importance to rituals and external practices. Honen was deeply convinced that a person could not obtain enlightenment by his or her own power (*jiriki*) but instead had to rely on the power of the other (*tariki*). This allowed the common people to understand Buddhism as a very personal religion. Honen preached that they should not worry about the costly ceremonies to obtain salvation. The mercy of Buddha would save them.[436]

Honen had many faithful disciples and the most prominent among them is Shinran (1173-1262). Shinran radically transformed the face of Buddhism by refining his master's teachings and giving it his own interpretation. Shinran was convinced about the mercy of Buddha, which was instrumental in salvation, but he believed that the salvific work of Buddha is already completed and the recitation of the name of Buddha (*Nembutsu*) was an act of gratitude. He concluded that Buddha saved each person irrespective of his or her societal status or stature. Out of this conviction, he dared to call himself *hizo hizoku* (neither monk nor lay). He ignored rules of monastic life by marrying and raising children. By this act, he wanted to reduce the gap between the secular and monastic life. He wanted to join secular life with monastic life. He considered both the life of the commoners as well as the monks, sacred. Thus, Shinran's school known as *Jodo Shinshu* (the True Pure Land School) differs from his master Honen's

436 Noriyoshi, "Buddhism in Japan," in The Encyclopedia of Religion, Vol. 2, 431.

Jodoshu, Pure Land School. Shinran's school grew and spread rapidly. It continues to exercise influence on many in Japan.[437]

Zen Buddhism developed the concept of *Kyoge Betsuden*, which means that written words (referring to Buddhist texts) or talks do not enlighten a person. Experience alone enlightens a person. Zen Buddhism uses the catchword *Furyumonji* that means that the master's heart transmits enlightenment to the disciples' heart. Zen Buddhism made a major departure from the traditional Buddhism as it did away with abstract metaphysical philosophical thinking, complicated rules and rituals. It gave more importance to one's personal experience. In this sense, Zen Buddhism's understanding of salvation resembled the Pure Land Schools. However, unlike Pure Land Schools, which considered mercy alone as essential for salvation, Zen's proponents considered works of righteousness essential for salvation.[438]

Zen Buddhism (*Chan*, in Chinese) came from China. There are two major schools of Zen Buddhism, namely *Rinzai* and *Soto*. Eisai founded the *Rinzai* School. Dogen founded the *Soto* School. These two Schools differed in their understanding about enlightenment. The *Rinzai* School proposed the question-answer model between the master and the disciple to discuss salvation. It uses Indian and Chinese folk stories and anecdote to discuss salvation. The Soto School stressed that meditation is essential to achieve salvation. Dogen equated the practice of meditation to enlightenment. He wanted a radical separation from the world and so he chose to withdraw himself from all worldly affairs. He went to a remote province to lead a peaceful life, dedicating all his time and energy for meditation and training a few selected disciples.[439]

The *Rinzai* School started by Eisai enjoyed patronage from high-ranking *samurai* (warlords). He built *Gozan* (Five Temples). These five temples were the centers of teaching Zen Buddhism to the common people. On the other hand, Soto Buddhism remained aloof from worldly affairs. It did not find much support from the people and had to resort to other means to attract attention. They did this by creating rituals and ceremonies for the dead. The funeral and

---

437 Noriyoshi, "Buddhism in Japan," in *The Encyclopedia of Religion*, Vol. 2, 432.

438 See Ibid.

439 See Ibid.

memorial services have made a great impact on the Japanese. They continue to remain important in the life of the Japanese people. Even though, the Japanese prefer to marry in Churches, they prefer the Buddhist funeral and memorial services as they like ceremonies.[440]

Nichiren (1222-1282) proposed a new form of Buddhism. Nichiren was dissatisfied with the state of affairs of the nation. He was also not happy with the practices of Buddhism of his time. However, he loved his country as well as Buddhism. After being troubled for a long time over the state of affairs in Japan, he came to a conclusion that the Buddhism, which was preached and practiced in Japan, was not true and only true teachings of Buddhism can bring a true material as well as spiritual development of Japan. He developed his thesis in the book *Rissho Ankoku* that means that only right teaching can lead to a safe and secure nation. According to him, the Lotus *Sutra* in the *Tendai* tradition was the right teaching. He criticized and condemned all other forms and teachings of Buddhism particularly Zen and Pure Land Buddhism. He was very vocal about his teachings and had conflicts with the warlords of Kamakura. The *shogunate* of Kamakura exiled him to a northern island of Sado. He did not attract many followers during his lifetime, but later his teaching attracted the merchant class of Kyoto. They also started an armed uprising known as *Hokke Ikki* against the warlords to restore the right teaching thereby establishing peace in Japan. The teachings of Nichiren influenced many later schools, which emerged in Japan. The contemporary new religions movements of Buddhist origin contain his teachings on political and social involvement. Prominent among them are *Reiyukai*, *Rissho Koseikai* and *Soka Gakkai*.[441]

Buddhism enjoyed a privileged position in the Japanese society until the beginning of the Meiji period. Even though there were many Buddhists, Shinto became important religion during the Meiji period. Buddhism lost its privileged status in the society. In Japan, Shinto and Buddhist, practices are mixed. There is a syncretism of Shinto-Buddhist traditions and many Japanese follow these mixed traditions even though they may not know understand these traditions.

---

440 Noriyoshi, "Buddhism in Japan," in *The Encyclopedia of Religion*, Vol. 2, 432.
441 See Ibid.

On the organizational level, Buddhist temples and monasteries, which were centers of study and social welfare, started establishing schools, universities and other social welfare institutions to serve humanity. Buddhism has stressed the need of scientific studies of all the religions. It believes in humanism. It strongly advocates peace and harmony. It promotes dialogue, exchange of ideas and thoughts with other faiths. According to the statistics conducted by the Ministry of Education, Culture, Sports, Science and Technology in 2014 there were 75,911 Buddhist shrines in Japan. It also puts the total figure of the adherents of Buddhism as 85,138,694, which also includes the various sects, and sub-sects of Buddhism.[442]

Presently Buddhism has very little influence on the Japanese people. Even though around 85 million claim to be, Buddhist there may be very few who actually know the basic tenets and teachings of Buddhism. Japanese prefer the Buddhist funeral and memorial services because of their traditional ceremonies. Buddhism has undergone a metamorphosis in Japan. An adherent of Buddhism from India or any other South Asian country may even find it difficult to recognize it as Buddhism.

4.1.13.1.3 New Religious Movements

New religious movements have mushroomed all over Japan. The *Encyclopedia of Religion* describes the following attributes that a new religious movement has:

> 1. Establishment within the last two centuries, usually characterized by features that suggests a religious response to the crises of modernity. 2. A definite moment of establishment and usually a founder possessing special charisma. 3. An important new, distinctive revelation or realization, expressed through some novel doctrine and

442 Ministry of Education, Culture, Sport, Science and Technology, Japan, "*Zenkoku Jinja Kyokai Nado Shukyo Dantai, Kyoshi, Shinjasu*" [National Statistics of Shrines, Churches etc, Religious Organizations, Adherents]. http://www.e-stat.go.jp/SG1/estat/List.do?bid=000001052797&cycode=0 [accessed on September 18, 2014].

usually attributed to supernatural sources. 4. A separate institutional structure. 5. Distinctive rites or practices.[443]

Scholars categorize the leading new religious movements in Japan in three groups. The first group appeared and developed towards the end of the Tokugawa *shogunate* period i.e. from the beginning to the middle of the 19th century. Tokugawa *shogunate* had prohibited the establishment of new religious movements beyond the 13th sect of Buddhism.[444] The second group appeared from the end of the World War I to 1931, a period that was marked by a devastating economic depression and the rise of militaristic totalitarianism. Most of the religious movement formed during these times suffered severe setbacks as the government was ill disposed towards them. The third group of religious movements appeared immediately after World War II. It was a time of chaos and utter despair. People had lost hope and were looking on to religion as a means to support their crisis. Most of the religious movements formed during these times thrived, as there were no obstacles from the government as the occupying forces had compelled the government of Japan to pass the law granting freedom of religion and there was a clear-cut division between state and religion.[445]

Scholars of religion summarize the general tendencies of the Japanese new religious movements as follows. The founding figure is a charismatic figure. He or she claims god asked him or her to create a religious movement. He or she is generally critical about the organized religion but never condemns it. The new movement formed rejects the doctrines and dogmas of the parent religion but does not offer any new insight itself. They generally focus on one dogma or deity and try to propagate devotion to that teaching or figure. A lot of syncretism exists in these religious movements. They are an amalgamation of the Buddhist schools of thought and the traditions of Shinto. They also liberally add features from Western religions

443 Robert Ellwood, "New Religions in Japan," in *Encyclopedia of Religion*, Vol. 10, 410.

444 Ibid. See also Ichiro Hori, *Folk Religion in Japan: Continuity and Change*, eds. Joseph Kitagawa and Alan L. Miller (Chicago: University of Chicago Press, 1968), 224-225.

445 See Ichiro Hori, Folk Religion in Japan: Continuity and Change, 225-227.

and some of them add notions of healing and psychology in order to make them more appealing among the people. They employ the traditional morality of Confucianism. They also emphasize on mental meditations. These religious movements have their headquarters in particular places or cities, which become pilgrim centers and places of gathering for all the adherents. Generally, the adherents have close bonds among themselves.[446]

Kurozumi Munetada (1780-1850) founded the Kurozumikyo in 1814. He claimed to have received a revelation and in response to it, he started this movement. He claimed the Shinto sun goddess Amaterasu possessed him. The main teachings of this movement are the worship of the indwelling divine spirit and healing.[447]

Nakayama Miki (1798-1887) a farmer's wife is the founder of Tenrikyo. She claimed that a deity possessed her. Tenrikyo stressed on the healing gifts imparted to Miki. Tenrikyo also narrates the beginning of the creation and stresses dance rituals.[448] Kawate Bunjiro (1868-1912) claimed to have divine calling to start Konkokyo, which means religion of golden light. He claimed that *Tenchi Kane no Kami*, the high god directed him to do so. He preached the mercy of god and *toritsugi* (intercessory prayers of a Konkokyo priest).[449]

In 1892, Deguchi Nao (1837-1918) a peasant woman experienced divine calling to deliver oracles. She was a member of the Konkokyo sect but she gave up her faith and met a mystic spiritualist Ueda Kisaburo (1871-1948). She adopted Ueda as her son-in-law and gave him the name Deguchi Onisaburo. It was under him, Omoto sect became well organized. The voluminous oracular scriptures, the *Ofudesaki* and *Reikai Monogatari* contain the main teachings of Omoto. Omoto emphasizes on the oneness of god, the existence of a spiritual world, the land of souls and spirits. It also stresses on healing like the Konkokyo.[450]

---

446 Ellwood, "New Religions in Japan," in *Encyclopedia of Religion*, Vol. 10, 411. See also Ichiro Hori, *Folk Religion in Japan: Continuity and Change*, 220-223.

447 Ibid., 412.

448 Ibid.

449 Ibid.

450 Ellwood, "New Religions in Japan," in *Encyclopedia of Religion*, Vol. 10, 411. See also Ichiro Hori, *Folk Religion in Japan: Continuity and Change*, 220-223.

Seicho no Ie means house of growth in Japanese. It is a product of cross-fertilization between the Japanese spiritual tradition and American New Thought. Taniguchi Masaharu (1893-1985) is the founder of this religious movement. He was a voracious reader of both Western and Eastern philosophy from his youth. He founded Seicho no Ie based on the ideas he received by reading a book by Fenwicke Holmes, an American New Thought teacher. Seicho no Ie's main philosophy is to accept the spiritual and discard the material. They consider all material things as illusion and deny the reality of matter, suffering or evil. One can escape illusion by the affirmative power of the mind. Taniguchi Masahura supported the government policies during the war. Presently this religious movement has relationship with right wing political parties.[451]

Sekai Kyuseikyo means "World Messianity." It is a development of the eschatological wing of Omoto religious movement. Okada Mokichi (1882-1955) founded it in 1934. The main belief of this religious movement is that human beings must seek the infilling of the divine light in order to prepare the earth for the coming of the paradise. They emphasize a practice called *jorei*, which means channeling divine light through a cupped upraised hand to a body or other object to cleanse it of evil.[452]

Miki Tokuchika (1900-1983) founded Perfect Liberty or PL *Kyodan* (PL Group) in 1946. He emphasized the role of art and beauty in prayer. All their prayers and rituals have a great sense of aesthetics. They are monotheistic in belief and consider evil on earth as warnings from god. PL or Perfect Liberty teachers are available to interpret the warnings and messages from god.[453]

Soka Gakkai means value creation society. It is an offshoot of Nichiren Buddhism. Makiguchi Tsunesaburo (1871-1944) established it in 1937. Soka Gakkai holds that matters, which benefit humans is of greater importance than truth or other philosophical abstracts. The leadership of Soka Gakkai passed on to Toda Josei (1900-1958) who had a mass appeal and boasted having many followers. Later the leadership passed on to Ikeda Daisaku who

451 Ellwood, "New Religions in Japan," in *Encyclopedia of Religion*, Vol. 10, 411.

452 Ibid., 412-413.

453 Ibid.

founded a political party called *Komeito* (clean government party), a political offshoot of Soka Gakkai.[454]

Kubo Kakautaro (1892-1944) and his sister-in-law Kotani Kimi (1901-1971) founded Reiyukai in 1925. It is a lay organization, which depends on informal groups and volunteers. The regular practices of Nichiren Buddhism forms its basic teaching. In addition, it holds healing rituals, ancestor worship and counseling called *hoza*. It inculcates conservative social values in Japan.[455]

Rissho Koseikai (society to establish righteousness and harmony) is an offshoot of Nichiren Buddhism. Niwano Nikkyo (1906-1999) and Nagauma Myoko (1889-1957), who were former members of Reiyukai, founded it in 1938. Rissho Koseikai includes all elements found in Reiyukai like healing, group counseling and divination. One of the main features of this movement is its work for peace especially through interreligious dialogue.[456]

4.1.13.2 The Reality of the Interreligious Dialogue in Japan

There is a great need for interreligious dialogue in Japan. All the Popes after the Second Vatican Council have consistently stressed on the importance of inter-religious dialogue. The Popes have suggested to the bishops of Japan to promote dialogue between Catholics and the adherents of other faiths in their dioceses. Pope Paul VI in his address of September 5, 1974 to a group of Japanese belonging to different religions noted that there is a need of fostering peace not only among their adherents but also among all people.

> Now that we have this most welcome opportunity of speaking with you, the representatives of our own religion, as well as of Shintoism and Buddhism in Japan, we would like to develop this call for the adequate preparation of the individual adherents of our religions to play their part in the search for peace. Peace must depend not only on

454 Ellwood, "New Religions in Japan," in *Encyclopedia of Religion*, Vol. 10, 411. See also Ichiro Hori, *Folk Religion in Japan: Continuity and Change*, 412-413.

455 Ibid.

456 Ibid.

> the good will of religious and national leaders, but be anchored firmly and securely in the hearts of all men.[457]

In his address of February 26, 1975 to representatives of Shintoism, Pope Paul VI appreciated the good values in Shinto and expressed his desire for a fruitful dialogue with them to further spiritual and moral values in Japan.

> We recognize and appreciate the religious and moral values that your religion in the course of the history of Japanese culture and civilization....The meeting is an expression of the commitment of the Catholic Church to promote relations and dialogue with religions for a better mutual understanding and friendly collaboration in view of peace and the development of spiritual and moral values among them.[458]

Pope John Paul II in his address of February 28, 1979 to representatives of the Shinto Religion urged them to dialogue with Catholics, in order to serve humanity, which is also one of the aims of both Christianity and Shinto. "The many things that we hold in common impel us to unite ever more closely in friendship and brotherhood in the service of all humanity."[459]

Pope John Paul II in his address of February 20, 1980 to representatives of Buddhism and Shinto in Japan appreciated the high spiritual values found in Shinto and Buddhism. He prayed for a meaningful dialogue with them because interreligious dialogue is essential for the future of the world.

> The Catholic Church expresses her esteem for your religions and for your high spiritual values, such as purity, detachment of heart, love for the beauty of nature, and benevolence and compassion for everything that lives. It

---

457 "Address to a Group of Japanese, September 5, 1974," *Insegnamenti di Paolo VI*, 12 (1974): 789-790.

458 "Address to the Representatives of Shinto, February 26, 1975," *Insegnamenti di Paolo VI*, 13 (1975): 184-185.

459 "Address to Representatives of the Shinto Religion, February 28, 1979," *Insegnamenti di Giovanni Paolo II*, 2.1(1979): 478-479.

> gives me great joy to know that you have come here to carry forward your dialogue and collaboration with the Holy See's Secretariat for Non-Christians. The themes you are discussing together, each from the standpoint of his own religion, are the relationship between man and nature and the relationship between religion and culture. I am deeply convinced that these are themes of great importance for the future of our world. Indeed, this conviction of mine is reflected in my first Encyclical Letter '*Redemptor Hominis*'. Be assured, then, that I shall follow this dialogue and subsequent ones with interest and appreciation.[460]

Pope John Paul II during his visit to Japan met a group of representatives of other religions on February 24, 1981. He noted in his address the need for greater dialogue among all religions to promote the dignity and sacredness of life. In a highly developed country like Japan, materialism and utilitarianism are a great threat to humanity as they corrode the country's spiritual and moral values. In this scenario, all religions must be active agents to bring meaning in the life of people. He noted that:

> In our commitment to man, we Christians are willing and ready to collaborate with you on behalf of man's dignity, his innate rights, the sacredness of his life even in his mother's womb, his freedom and self-determination on the individual level and on the level of society, his moral upbringing and the primacy of his spiritual dimension. As religious people we must devote particular attention to fostering cordial social relations and adopting a lifestyle marked by personal sobriety and sincere respect for the beauty of the world in which we live. This is more than ever our duty today, when humanity faces increasing threats from materialistic ideologies and from forms of industrialism that could strip man of his dignity. I know that a start has been made in dialogue

460 "Address to Some Representatives of Buddhism and Shinto in Japan, February 20, 1980," *Insegnamenti di Giovanni Paolo II*, 3.1 (1980): 438-439.

> and collaboration for this purpose, both in Japan and in Rome, between the Catholic Church and the religious organizations that you represent.[461]

In his address of October 7, 1991 to a group of religious representatives from Japan participating in the 5th International Meeting for Peace, Pope John Paul II noted that interreligious dialogue not only promotes peace but also removes the misunderstandings and obstacles among various religions.

> Your desire to meet believers of all traditions in order to pray for peace in the world illustrates the conviction which we share that religion has a vital part to play in the building of more just and harmonious relations between individuals and peoples. I therefore wish to assure you of my interest in your work for peace and I am happy that we have this occasion to meet.... Peace, the desire of every human heart, is essential to the well-being of the human family and indeed to its very survival.... We are aware that, in a sense, peace is beyond us. It is a gift to be implored. It is heartening that so many people around the world pray, individually and collectively, for this divine gift, for the success of efforts to promote true peace. The gathering of people from different religious backgrounds to pray in this manner takes on the added significance of a sign to the world that even profound differences of outlook and conviction need not be obstacles to mutual understanding, esteem and cooperation, which are the path to peace.[462]

In his address of February 25, 1995 to the Bishops of Japan on their '*Ad Limina*' visit Pope John Paul II noted that the bishops must promote interreligious dialogue in Japan because all people are

461 "Address to Representatives of Non Christian Religions of Japan, February 24, 1981," *Insegnamenti di Giovanni Paolo II*, 4.1 (1981): 508. Original in Italian. English version from *L'Osservatore Romano* English Edition of March 9, 1981.

462 "Address to a Group of Religious Representatives from Japan Participating in the 5th International Meeting of Peace, October 7, 1991", *Insegnamenti di Giovanni Paolo II*, 14.2 (1991): 770-771.

children of the same God and have a common destiny in His eternal love. The Pope asked the bishops to focus on education, social action and communications to build a civilization of love. He noted that:

> On a different plane, modern Japan offers many opportunities for a serious and fruitful interreligious dialogue with the followers of other religions, especially Shintoism and Buddhism. Catholics must be concerned to promote this dialogue, both because we all have a common origin as God's chosen creatures and a common destiny in his eternal love, and because the Church's mission in the world is one of solicitude for the whole human family, especially in its search for truth, happiness and solidarity with all who suffer or are in want. Of vital importance is the dialogue of life between Catholics and the followers of other religious traditions, a dialogue which springs naturally from the presence of the Church's members in the social sphere, primarily in education, social works and communications. The laity in particular should be conscious of the importance of their witness and example in fostering understanding and cooperation among all people of good will.... Perhaps interreligious dialogue is the proper context in which the Church in Japan can give attention to the widespread 'crisis of civilization' which, as I wrote in the Apostolic Letter 'Tertio Millennio Adveniente', is becoming more and more apparent in societies which are highly developed technologically but which are interiorly impoverished by the tendency to forget God or to keep him at a distance. Many people are beginning to reconsider their single–minded devotion to economic success at all costs, realizing its price in human and spiritual terms. In your quinquennial reports you have referred to the spiritual emptiness which prompts people to seek new religious experiences, sometimes in groups which do not have a solid basis in Christianity. Herein lies a twofold challenge for the Catholic community: to be easily accessible and

> available to those who show a sincere interest in the Church's message, and to co–operate with other believers in building the civilization of love, founded on the universal values of peace, solidarity, justice and liberty, which find their full realization in Christ.[463]

Pope Benedict XVI in his address of November 13, 2006 to His Excellency Mr. Kagefumi Ueno, Ambassador of Japan to the Holy See noted that the importance of interreligious dialogue in Japan. He noted that:

> Society's recognition of the spiritual dimension, which is giving rise to an authentic dialogue between religions and cultures, cannot but encourage a common journey in brotherhood and solidarity; this alone will make possible the integral development of the human being. In fact, many possible fields of action are open to these interreligious and intercultural forms of cooperation, especially in the areas of commitment to a just society, to world peace and to the fight against poverty in growing solidarity.[464]

Pope Benedict XVI in his address of December 15, 2007 to the Bishops of Japan on their '*Ad Limina*' visit asked them to engage in fruitful dialogue with other religions in order to tell them about Jesus Christ. He noted that:

> Indeed the world is hungry for the message of hope that the Gospel brings. Even in countries as highly developed as yours, many are discovering that economic success and advanced technology are not sufficient in themselves to bring fulfillment to the human heart. Anyone who does not know God 'is ultimately without

463 "Address to Bishops of Japan on their 'Ad Limina' Visit on February 25, 1995," *AAS* 88.1 (1996): 1026, 1028-1029.

464 "Address to His Excellency Mr. Kagefumi Ueno, Ambassador of Japan to the Holy See, November 13, 2006," *Insegnamenti di Benedetto XVI*, 2.2 (2006): 615-617.

> hope, without the great hope that sustains the whole of life.' Remind people that there is more to life than professional success and profit. Through, the practice of charity, in the family and in the community, they can be led towards 'that encounter with God in Christ which awakens their love and opens their spirits to other.' This is the great hope that Christians in Japan can offer their compatriots; it is not foreign to Japanese culture, but rather it reinforces and gives new impetus to all that is good and noble in the heritage of your beloved nation. The well-merited respect which the citizens of your country show towards the Church, on account of her fine contribution in education, health care and many other fields, gives you an opportunity to engage with them in dialogue and to speak joyfully to them of Christ, the 'light that enlightens every man' (Jn 1:9).[465]

Pope Benedict XVI in his letter dated June 23, 2007 to Venerable Kahjun Handa on the 20th anniversary of the Religious Summit Meeting on Mount Hiei, Kyoto noted that interreligious prayer summit is very important to pray for peace in the world.

> From the supernatural perspective we come to understand that peace is both a gift from God and an obligation for every individual. Indeed the world's cry for peace, echoed by families and communities throughout the globe, is at once both a prayer to God and an appeal to every brother and sister of our human family. As you assemble on the sacred Mount Hiei, representing different religions, I assure you of my spiritual closeness.[466]

Pope Francis has stressed on the friendship between Christians and followers of other religions. He noted that inter-religious

465 "Address to Bishops of Japan on their '*Ad Limina*' Visit on December 15, 2007," *Insegnamenti di Benedetto XVI,* 3.2 (2007): 854-857.

466 "Letter to Venerable Kahjun Handa on the occasion of the 20th Anniversary of the Religious Summit Meeting on Mount Hiei," *Insegnamenti di Benedetto XVI,* 3.1 (2007): 1176-1177.

dialogue has become important because of large-scale migrations in the world. Further, he noted that inter-religious dialogue could help to combat the negative influences of secularization in the society. He noted that:

> He noted that due to increasing movement of peoples because of phenomena such as migration, Christians are being challenged to be more open to different cultures, religions and traditions... Constructive dialogue between people of different religious traditions, Pope Francis continued, also serves to overcome another fear, which, unfortunately we find on the increase in a more heavily secularized society.[467]

Thus, it is evident from the above quotes of the successive Popes after the Second Vatican Council that they encourage inter-religious dialogue. They have always spoken in favor of a meaningful dialogue with the other religions in Japan. Japan being a country where religious pluralism is a reality, Catholics following the directives of the Magisterium and the teachings of the Catholic Church must make efforts to seek every possible occasion for a meaningful dialogue with people of other religions. This dialogue is important, as Popes have noted in their various addresses to the people and bishops of Japan. Materialism and secularization are threatening the dignity of human life. Unborn children, the terminally sick, the weak, the poor, the disabled and the environment are at a greater risk in societies where materialism is rampant. In such a scenario, it is the obligation of all religions to fight for the cause of justice and dignity of every human person. When different religions have a meaningful dialogue among themselves, then they can promote the spiritual and moral values, which are common among them and thus bring peace and sustainable development in the society.

467 "Address to the Participants in the Plenary Assembly of the Pontifical Council for Inter-religious Dialogue, November 28, 2013." http://w2.vatican.va/content/francesco/en/speeches/2013/november/documents/papa-francesco_20131128_pc-dialogo-interreligioso.html [accessed on September 22, 2014].

In the spirit of the teachings of the Second Vatican Council, there were many efforts from the side of the Catholic Church to engage seriously in interreligious dialogue with other religions. As Japan has two main traditional religions, namely Shinto and Buddhism it is but natural that these two major religions form the partners in interreligious dialogue. There are also a large number of new religious movements in Japan. They are either splinter groups of the two traditional religions of Japan or an amalgamation of various religious. Thus, it is rather difficult to enter into dialogue with this group. Some of these groups are fundamentalists. They refuse to accept other religions as partners in dialogue. In spite of all the difficulties, the Catholic Church has made tremendous progress in the field of interreligious dialogue. The Church has done interreligious dialogue on two levels in Japan, one at individual level and other at communitarian level.

4.1.13.2.1 Individual Level

Buddhism and Shinto have fascinated many Catholic theologians. A lot of academic and practical work in the field of interreligious studies has been taking place in Japan. One of the pioneers in Zen–Christian dialogue is a Jesuit priest from Germany, Hugo Makibi Enomiya-Lassalle (1898-1990). He came to Japan with a burning zeal to spread the gospel of Christ. However, he discovered the richness of the religions existing in Japan. He took special interest in Zen Buddhism. Three Zen masters Sogaku *Daiun* Harada, Haku *un* Yasutani and Ko *un* Yamada trained him. It was under the Zen master, Ko *un* Yamada, he got the title *Roshi* (Zen Master). The title *Roshi* (Zen Master) means qualification to teach Zen. Hugo Makibi Enomiya-Lassalle opened a retreat center in Hiroshima, *Shinmeikutsu* (Cave of Divine Darkness) to train others in Christian-Zen meditation. He contributed significantly for promoting the interreligious dialogue between Buddhism and Christianity by transmitting the richness found in both the religions.[468] Another person who has made significant contribution to promote interreligious dialogue is a Jesuit priest, Heinrich Dumoulin (1905-1995) who was a professor at

468 See James Ishmael Ford, *Zen Master Who?: A Guide to the People and Stories of Zen* (Somerville: Wiston Publications, 2006), 184-185.

Sophia University, Tokyo. He dedicated his whole life in publishing scientific research papers on Zen Buddhism. He founded an Institute for Oriental Religions at Sophia University and helped Nanzan University in founding Nanzan Institute of Religion and Culture. He was the first director of Nanzan Institute for Religion and Culture (1975-1976).[469] Some of his famous books on Zen Buddhism are as follows: *The Development of Chinese Zen After the Sixth Patriarch in the Light of the Mumonkan* (1953, First Zen Institute of America), *A History of Zen Buddhism* (1963, Pantheon Books), *Christianity Meets Buddhism* (1974, Open Court Publishing), *Buddhism in the Modern World* (1976, Macmillan Publishing), *Zen Enlightenment: Origins and Meaning* (1979, Weatherhill), *Zen Buddhism in the Twentieth Century* (1992), *Zen Buddhism: A History; Volume 1 India and China,* (2005, World Wisdom), *Zen Buddhism: A History; Volume 2 Japan,* (2005, World Wisdom).

Other prominent leaders include Joseph Spae (1913-1989) who founded the Oriens Institute of Religious Research in Tokyo in 1959. He is the author of many books and articles on Christianity and Japanese culture and religions. Some of the prominent books are: *Christian Corridors to Japan* (1965), *Christianity Encounters Japan* (1968) and *Japanese Religiosity* (1971). He regular published articles about Japanese religions and Christianity in a journal called *Japanese Missionary Bulletin.* He worked as the editor of this bulletin for a few years.[470]

Some other great theologians and thinkers who contributed for a meaningful dialogue between the Catholic Church and the other major religions of Japan are Onodera Isao (b.1922), Oshida Shigeto (1922-2003), Okumura Ichiro (1923-2014), William Johnston (1925-2010), Kadowaki Kakichi (1926-) and Jan Van Bragt (1928-2007).

A number of Catholic missionaries and theologians, a great number of them foreign missionaries, took keen interest in the traditional religions of Japan and added their mite for the fruitful inter-religious dialogue.

---

469 See England, *Asian Christian Theologies: A Research Guide to Authors, Movements, Sources*, Vol. 3, 379.

470 See Ibid., 393.

4.1.13.2.2 Communitarian Level

In Japan, academicians have attempted to promote inter-religious dialogue at a communitarian level. Joseph Spae founded the Oriens Institute for Religious Research in 1959 to promote interreligious studies, pastoral research and publishing of scientific papers on religious studies. The Institute publishes the quarterly *Japan Mission Journal* (formerly known as the *Japan Missionary Bulletin*) which exclusively deals with evangelization and inculturation of Christianity in Japan. It approaches Christian mission from an Asian perspective. Some of the scholars associated with this institute are, Jan Swyngedouw, Fujiwara Takanori, Thomas Imoos, Ernest D. Piryns and John A. Raymaker. This institute is also publishing many books on religious studies and research.[471]

Nanzan University started an Institute for Religion and Culture in 1976. This institute conducts regular symposia, colloquia and research projects to promote dialogue among religions, philosophies, and cultures. It also has a wide array of publications, which include a semiannual journal *Japanese Journal of Religious Studies* dedicated to the academic studies of Japanese religions, a semiannual journal *Asian Ethnology* dedicated to promote the scholarly research on peoples and cultures of Asia. In addition, annually in the spring the Institute publishes the English language *Bulletin* and the Japanese language *Kenshusho,* which serve as the annual report of the Nanzan Institute for Religion and Culture. It lists the events, reports of the members' activities, academic contributions and summaries of conferences. It also contains short articles of general interest. Besides these journals and reports, this institute has published a large number of books authored by well-known scholars. These include the 18 volumes of *Nanzan Studies in Religion and Culture* with contributions from Heinrich Dumoulin, Frederick Franck, Paul Mommaers, Jan Van Bragt, Nishitani Keiji, Tekeuchi Yoshinori, Tanabe Hajime and Taitetsu Unno.[472] The Nanzan Institute for Religion and Culture organized the tenth symposium on "*What does Christianity have to learn from Buddhism?*" in March 1997. The Institute invited many

471 See England, *Asian Christian Theologies: A Research Guide to Authors, Movements, Sources,* Vol. 3, 379.

472 See Ibid., 379-380.

Buddhist and Christian thinkers to take part in this symposium. The purpose of this symposium was to promote interreligious dialogue. It also aimed to promote respect for other religions among Catholic scholars. It holds in high esteem the great spiritual values found in other religions.[473]

Prof. Douglas Van Steere (1901-1995), an American Quaker served as a professor of philosophy at Haverford College from 1928 to 1964. He was the visiting professor of theology at Union Theological Seminary from 1961 to 1962. The Church invited Steere to participate as an ecumenical observer in the Second Vatican Council. He also co-founded the Ecumenical Institute of Spirituality. He sought a personal audience with Pope Paul VI to propose his plans about a Zen-Christian Colloquium. He organized the first Zen-Christian Colloquium from March 3 to April 1, 1967 at Ooiso, Kanagawa prefecture at a Protestant Training Center. It was the first Zen-Christian interreligious colloquium held in the world. He did not call this meeting dialogue but Zen-Christian Colloquium.[474]

The organizers of the *World Conference of Religions for Peace* organized the first conference in October 1970 at Kyoto's International Conference Center. They organize this conference once in 4 years in different places around the world. It serves as forum for leaders of various religions to gather together to discuss not only about religious matters but also matters like nuclear disarmament, plight of the refugees, hunger, political system, and economics, environment.[475]

In June 1981, the organizers of *World Conference of Religions on Ethics* organized a conference in Tokyo. Unlike *World Conference of Religions for Peace,* it does not include leaders of all the religions but only six major world religions, namely Judaism, Christianity, Islam,

---

473 Ichiro Okumura, "*Kirisutokyo to Bukkyo to no Taiwa no Ayumi*" [The History of Dialogue Between Christianity and Buddhism] in *Shoshukyo Taiwa* [Interreligious Dialogue] ed. Catholic Bishops' Conference of Japan, Department of Interreligious Dialogue (Tokyo: Catholic Bishops' Conference of Japan, 2006), 166. Original in Japanese. [Translation mine].

474 Ibid., 167-168. See also Ichiro Okumura, *Tabunka ni Ikiru Shukyou* [Religions Living in Cultural Pluralism], Vol. 2 (Tokyo: Oriens Institute for Religious Research, 2009), 32.

475 Ibid., Vol. 2, 33.

Hinduism, Buddhism and Shinto. They discussed about Religion, Culture and Ecology.[476]

Cardinal Jean-Louis Pierre Tauran head of the Vatican's Pontifical Council for Interreligious Dialogue visited Japan from August 2-10, 2009. He noted in an interview to Radio Vatican that he was impressed with the interreligious dialogue carried out by the Catholic Church. The Cardinal applauded the Catholic Church in Japan, though a minority, for contributing tremendously to the Japanese society especially in areas of education, health and care for the aged. He also met representatives of the major religions in Japan and was very much struck to see that religion is everywhere in Japan.[477]

4.1.13.3 Charismatic Renewal Movement and Interreligious Dialogue in Japan

The Catholic Church encourages interreligious dialogue to promote peace and harmony in the society.[478] However, the CCRM in Japan has not organized yet any program to foster interreligious dialogue. The CCRM welcomes people of other faith to prayer meetings. Leaders of the CCRM make effort to reach out to people belonging to other religions. They also welcome people with no religious affiliations. Apart from this, the CCRM has not focused on organizing prayer meetings to bring people belonging to different religions together. We examined in the above sections, the reality of religious pluralism in Japan. The CCRM as an ecclesial movement has great potential to

476 Ibid.

477 Gerald O'Connell, *Vatican Cardinal Applauds Japan for Interreligious Dialogue.* August 14, 2009. This article is about the interview of Cardinal Jean-Louis Pierre Tauran to Radio Vatican on August 12, 2009 following his return from a trip to Japan. UCAN (Union of Catholic Asian News) published excerpts of this interview in their website. http://www.ucanews.com/story-archive/?post_name=/2009/08/14/cardinal-applauds-japan-church-for-interreligious-dialogue&post_id=50794 [accessed on September 23, 2014].

478 See Conciliar Documents *Lumen Gentium* No. 8, 16; *Gaudium et Spes* No.22; *Nostra Aetate* No.1, 2, 3, 4, 5 and *Ad Gentes* No. 3, 11 for reflections on the attitude of Catholic Church about other religions. All these quotes point the necessity to acknowledge the genuine goodness found in other religions and promote harmony and dialogue among religions.

discern the working of the Holy Spirit in other faiths. The CCRM needs to develop forums to bring people of different faiths together. Thus, it can take part in the Church's mission of interreligious dialogue.

4.2 The Challenges of the Charismatic Renewal Movement in Japan

The CCRM faces challenges from within the group (*ad intra*) as well as from outside (*ad extra*). It also has some weaknesses. The purpose to point out the drawbacks is not to judge or condemn the CCRM. We intend the CCRM realizes its weaknesses and make every effort to imporve. Some of the challenges, which the CCRM in Japan faces, are unique.

4.2.1 Ad Intra

Akabae Kenichi, a priest and leader of CCRM noted the following weaknesses, which exist within the CCRM prayer groups in Japan.[479] The CCRM has to accept its drawbacks and reform itself to be vibrant force in the Church.

4.2.1.1 Lack of Proper Formation Programs for Leaders

The Holy Spirit is principal animator and guide of the CCRM prayer group. However, the CCRM does have human leaders to animate the groups. Leaders have an important role to play in the smooth functioning of a prayer group, which is heart of the CCRM. The CCRM had a good growth rate in Japan. It has prayer groups all over Japan, from Hokkaido in the far north to Okinawa in the far south. However, one of the major problems, which the CCRM faces, is lack of young leaders. Most of the leaders are elderly. There is an urgent need to train young people to become future leaders and animators.[480]

---

479 Akabae Kenichi, "*Pentecoste 2006: Kokusai Taikai Tokushu, ICCRS Shusai Kokusai Lida Kenshukai ni Sankashite*" [Pentecost 2006: Special International Convention, Sponsored by ICCRS, Some Thoughts About the Leaders' Workshop], *Ikeru Mizu,* No.81 (Summer Edition 2006): 1-2.

480 Ibid.

Since 1973, the CCRJ send its representatives to International Leaders' Conferences held in different countries. However, there is no particular center to train leaders and animators in Japan. For the smooth functioning of the CCRM prayer meetings and conventions, the CCRJ must make itself attractive to the youth. They must organize programs to reach out to the young.

4.2.1.2 Divisions within Prayer Groups

Divisions in prayer group are scandalous. Animosity among leaders defeats the very purpose of the existence of the prayer groups. Charismatics believe that the Holy Spirit is the true animator. If it is so, then there must no divisions in the group. The Holy Spirit does not divide but unite people in love. St. Paul wrote to the Church of Corinth, "Now I appeal to you, brothers and sisters, by the name of our Lord Jesus Christ, that all of you be in agreement and that there be no divisions among you, but that you be united in the same mind and the same purpose" (1 Cor 1:10). "For we are God's servants, working together; you are God's field, God's building" (1 Cor 3:9). Again St. Paul noted in his letter to the Galatians that "jealousy, anger, quarrels, dissensions, factions" (Gal 5:20) are all works of flesh.

One of the problems plaguing the CCRM in Japan is division within prayer groups. Sometimes there is a spirit of unhealthy competitiveness.[481] Divisions cause great harm. It becomes an obstacle for all. Some people may also discontinue attedning the prayer meetings. St. Paul prayed for unity of Christians in Jesus. He noted "[Jesus] is our peace; in his flesh he has made both groups into one and has broken down the dividing wall, that is, the hostility between us" (Eph 2:14).

4.2.1.3 Excessive Emotionalism

Emotions play an important in the spirituality of a person. However, if a person craves only for emotional gratification then there is a possibility of having a distorted spirituality. Singing, clapping, dancing

481 Akabae Kenichi, "*Pentecoste 2006: Kokusai Taikai Tokushu, ICCRS Shusai Kokusai Lida Kenshukai ni Sankashite*" [Pentecost 2006: Special International Convention, Sponsored by ICCRS, Some Thoughts About the Leaders' Workshop], *Ikeru Mizu*, No.81 (Summer Edition 2006): 1-2.

and praising God in loud voices form a part of the Charismatic spirituality. The CCRM also encourages people to use charisms of the Holy Spirit during prayer meetings. These features make the CCRM prayer meetings lively. However, excessive attachment to emotional gratification has the danger of drifting away a person from true spiritual experience. In addition, some wrongly think that loud praises is the norm for prayer meetings. They force people to raise their voices. This can make some people very uncomfortable. Thus, Charismatics must not impose their way of worship on others.

Some Charismatics also emphasize on the use of charisms. They think charisms display the spiritual strength of a person. However, charisms are not a measure of personal holiness. The Holy Spirit gives them for the good of the community. There must be a balance in all the things, which one does.[482]

There are some people in CCRM who take a great pride in falling down while praying for the infilling of the Holy Spirit. They feel by falling down they can impress others. They think that falling down means to have a great faith. They think God has specially chosen them.[483] These thoughts do not come from the God. Excessive focus on use of charisms and emotional gratification can discourage people from participating in the prayer meetings. Therefore, it is very essential to strike a balance in the prayer meetings. Use of charisms and loud praises are good. However, over-attachment is dangerous. The Holy Spirit gives true freedom to everyone, and no one in the prayer meeting has the moral right to force anyone to adapt to a particular form of praise and worship. The purpose of the CCRM is to witness Christ. Charisms and lively prayer meetings are features of the charismatic spirituality. However, these features are not the only way to worship God.

---

482 Editorial Board of *Ikeru Mizu*, "Seirei Sasshin wo Meguru Q & A" [Questions and Answers Regarding Catholic Charismatic Renewal], *Ikeru Mizu*, No. 72 (Spring Edition 2004): 9. Original in Japanese. [Translation mine].

483 Kenichi, "*Pentecoste 2006: Kokusai Taikai Tokushu, ICCRS Shusai Kokusai Lida Kenshukai ni Sankashite*" [Pentecost 2006: Special International Convention, Sponsored by ICCRS, Some Thoughts About the Leaders' Workshop], 1-2.

4.2.1.4 Faulty or Inadequate Leadership Skills

God has indeed blessed the CCRJ with able leaders. However, some leaders act like dictators. One of the essential qualities of the leader is openness to the Holy Spirit. The CCRM needs leaders who take inspiration of the Holy Spirit to do their work. Leaders not only have the task of organizing the prayer meeting but also creating an atmosphere of fellowship among the participants. A leader must be not biased or prejudiced against anyone. He or she must be a person of prayer.[484] All the decisions that he or she makes must flow from a deep prayer and reliance on the Holy Spirit. The participants of the prayer group must feel that God is truly present among them when they gather to praise and worship Him. The Holy Spirit must be the main animator.

4.2.1.5 Spiritual Pride

Spiritual pride is very dangerous. "Pride goes before destruction, and a haughty spirit before a fall" (Prv 16:18). Charismatics sometimes consider themselves as super-spiritual. They act as if they do not live in this world anymore. They judge others harshly and are intolerant. They criticize others. They take pride in their spiritual growth. They think God has told them to reprimand others. However, they forget that they are also human and thus vulnerable. They too can make mistakes. They too are in need of ongoing renewal and transformation.

4.2.1.6 Gap between Practice and Preaching

The gap between practice and preaching is one of the weaknesses of the CCRM.[485] One must practice what one preaches. St. Paul wrote in his letter to Galatians, "Are you so foolish? Having started with the Spirit, are you now ending with the flesh?" (Gal 3:3-4). If there is dichotomy in the lives of the Charismatics then they can become obstacles for others, especially the newcomers. The CCRM has the potential to contribute towards the spiritual renewal of the Church.

484 Kenichi, "*Pentecoste 2006: Kokusai Taikai Tokushu, ICCRS Shusai Kokusai Lida Kenshukai ni Sankashite*" [Pentecost 2006: Special International Convention, Sponsored by ICCRS, Some Thoughts About the Leaders' Workshop], 2.

485 Ibid.

However, Charismatics must bear witness to their faith through their lives. Their exemplary life-style must convince people to seek spiritual renewal.

4.2.2 Ad Extra

The CCRM enjoys freedom in Japan. It faces opposition neither from the civil authorities nor from the ecclesial authorities. However, the CCRM has some external challenges (*ad extra*). These challenges can stifle the growth of the CCRM. Thus, the CCRM must know these problems and tackle them. Some of these problems are as follows:

4.2.2.1 Lack of Encouragement from Ecclesial Authorities

The ecclesial authorities do not oppose the CCRM activities. However, they also do not sufficiently encourage them. Francis Mathy, a CCRM leader noted that,

> The obstacles to the movement's growth have been formidable. The resistance of the average Japanese Catholic to charismatic renewal is probably greater than anywhere else in the world. Because of the natural reluctance of Japanese to display their emotions and the formalism of a Catholic Church life that is cold, duty-oriented, and lacking in true community, charismatic renewal has tough going. Most of the Japanese bishops and clergy seldom have a good word to say for it and keep it well at a distance. (The priests involved in the Renewal are mostly foreign missionaries.)[486]

The CBCJ has not issued any official document on the CCRM. As the Holy See has given official approval to the CCRM, the bishops in Japan maintain that there is no need for any formal approval from them. However, the bishops' councils of other countries have issued guidelines to the CCRM in their dioceses. They encourage and guide the CCRM. However, the bishops in Japan have failed to do so.

Some Cardinals, archbishops, bishops and priests are personally involved with the CCRM activities in Japan. Late bishop Sato Keiichi

---

486 Mathy, "What in the World is going on?- Japan", 4.

of Niigata Diocese attended the National CCRM convention held in 2000. Late Peter Seiichi Cardinal Shirayanagi celebrated the closing Holy Eucharist of the convention. Besides that archbishop of Nagasaki Diocese, Late archbishop Francis Xavier Kaname Shimamoto and The Holy See Ambassador to Japan, Late archbishop Ambrose de Paoli sent their written messages to the organizers and participants of the convention.[487] Late bishop Peter Arikata Kobayashi was personally involved with the activities of the CCRM. The CCRJ sent him as its official representative to attend International Leaders' Conference in 1978 and again in 1981.[488] Therefore, it would be not justified to say that the lack of support from ecclesial authorities is a block for the growth of the CCRM in Japan. The ecclesial authorities have been sympathetic to the cause of the CCRM in Japan. Pope John Paul II urged the bishops and priests to guide the renewal movement groups. He asked them to animate the groups according to the teachings of the Catholic Church.[489] The bishops need to take the late pontiffs suggestion seriously.

4.2.2.2 Drifting Towards Protestant Pentecostalism

The Catholic Church teaches and promotes ecumenism. The Second Vatican Council document *Unitatis Redintegratio* emphasizes on the role of ecumenical dialogue between Catholics and the Christians belonging to other denominations. When the CCRM began in Japan, initially some Protestant Pentecostal Pastors helped the Catholics in organizing the prayer meetings. These meetings were truly ecumenical in nature. However, Catholics taking part in such meetings must know their faith well, or else there is a strong possibility of drifting towards Protestant Pentecostalism. As Protestant Pentecostal churches are independent of any central authority, they decide their policies without any consultation with other churches. However, the Catholic Church has ecclesial

---

487 Caspian Raly, "*Dai Juu Gokai Seirei ni Yoru Sasshin Zenkoku Taikai wo kaerimite*" [Evaluation of 15th National Catholic Charismatic Renewal Convention], *Ikeru Mizu*, No. 56 (Spring Edition 2000): 3.

488 Nakamura, "*Nihon ni Okeru Katorikku Seirei ni Yoru Sasshinn no Ayumi*," [The History of the Catholic Charismatic Renewal of Japan], 1-2.

489 See John Paul II, "Audience with the Bishops of Southern France," *Insegnamenti di Giovanni Paolo II*, 5.3 (1982): 1611-1617.

authorities. The CCRM must take care to follow the Church teachings and obey the ecclesial authorities.

4.2.2.3 Secularization and its Effects

Japan is developed nation. Religion has lost its relevance. Consumerism, materialism, greed and selfishness are influencing the society. The effects of secularization do not spare Catholics too. Faith and spirituality have no space in the secular world. Christian values are no longer attractive. The CCRM has the difficult task to guard the Church from the onslaughts of the secularization and make Christianity relevant.

4.2.2.4 The Dangers of Overstressing Healings

The Catholic Church encourages people to pray for healing. Prayers for healing are a part of the Church's tradition. However, Japanese can misunderstand prayers for healing as magic. There are many cults in Japan, which advertise healing. They do so to cheat people. Therefore, the CCRM must not overstress healings. They must encourage people to pray for healing but not think of it as magic. They must educate people about the charisms of healing. The members of the Kansai regional CCRM committee reported in their evaluation that during the convention some people were more interested in seeking healing rather than faith in Jesus. They were looking for priests with charisms of healings. Some people approached a priest and asked him to pray for healing. He could not refuse the people out of respect and courtesy. Immediately there was a long queue of people requesting prayers. All this happened during the praise and worship session. People skipped the prayer session in order to seek healing prayers. Again, the evaluation report noted that, after the celebration of Healing Mass, some people demanded that a priest must pray over them individually.[490] Even though, the priest was extremely tired he agreed to their demand. However, later he commented, "Truly there is no one here who thinks of me."[491]

490 Catholic Charismatic Renewal, Kansai Regional, "*Dai Juu San Kai Kansai Taikai no Hansei*" [Evaluation of the 13th Kansai Regional Convention], *Ikeru Mizu*, No. 90 (Fall Edition 2008):11. Original in Japanese. [Translation mine].

491 Ibid.

This shows that the people came to convention with the intention of seeking healing. They did not understand the real power of the Holy Eucharist. The Holy Eucharist is the greatest form of thanksgiving to God the Father, through Jesus in the Holy Spirit. It is the source of all healing and goodness.

In addition, sufferings are a part of anyone's life. Jesus too suffered even though he had done no wrong. He saved us through His sufferings. The Catholic Church recognizes the importance of redemptive suffering. Therefore, the CCRM must focus on Jesus and not on healings alone. Faith in Jesus is greater than seeking healings.

Thus the CCRM has to deal with the weaknesses, both *ad intra* and *ad extra*, to effectively do the work of renewal in the Church.

4.3 Need of an Unique Approach in Japan

The Catholic Church and the CCRM have a difficult mission in Japan. The uniqueness of Japanese culture and secularization has made the Church's mission of evangelization more difficult. Therefore, the Popes have suggested that the Church respect the culture differences. Pope John Paul II in his address of September 2, 1985 to the Bishops of Japan on their '*Ad* Limina' visit noted that evangelization is the grace and vocation of the Catholic Church and "it is her deepest identity in Japan and everywhere throughout the world."[492] Pope Benedict XVI in his address of December 15, 2007 to the Bishop's of Japan on their '*Ad Limina*' visit pointed out that the Church has the duty to proclaim Christ and it is her priority. However, the Church must consider the cultural setting of the modern Japan in their work of evangelization.

> The need to proclaim Christ boldly and courageously is a continuing priority for the Church; indeed it is a solemn duty laid upon her by Christ who enjoined the Apostles to 'go out to the whole world, proclaim the Good News to all creation' (*Mk* 16:16). Your task today is to seek new ways of bringing alive the message

492 "Address to the Bishops of Japan on their '*Ad Limina*' Visit, September 2, 1985," *Insegnamenti di Giovanni Paolo II*, 8.2 (1985): 555.

> of Christ in the cultural setting of modern Japan. Even though Christians form only a small percentage of the population, the faith is a treasure that needs to be shared with the whole of Japanese society.[493]

Taking a cue from Pope Benedict XVI's reference to the cultural setting of modern Japan in the work of evangelization all missionaries must know the mindset of the Japanese people. Pope John Paul II in his address of September 2, 1980 to the Bishop's of Japan on their '*Ad Limina*' visit noted that it not an easy task to understand the culture of Japan and introduce Christ to them. Pope John Paul II noted that the need of Christ becoming Japanese in His Church. He implied that the people of Japan must not see Christ as a foreign entity imposed on them by missionaries but the God who is among them even before the arrival of the missionaries.

> The theme of evangelization immediately introduces you to the great challenge of inculturation, for which the grace of God is abundantly supplied to you....The power of God's word is so great that a truly evangelized Church immediately realizes its call to evangelize. And this in turn involves the question of method and the incarnation of the Christian message in the lives of each people and each community. We know the esteem that the Church has for proper inculturation linked to fidelity to the ageless and universal faith. And we know how much Christ himself truly desires, in the members of his body, to become fully one with them. And this is truly what happens as Christ becomes Japanese in his Church.[494]

One of the primary tasks of all missionaries, especially the Charismatics is to rely on the power of the Holy Spirit who is the 'principal agent of evangelization'.[495] Pope John Paul II noted that,

---

493 "Address to Bishops of Japan on their 'Ad Limina' Visit on December 15, 2007," *Insegnamenti di Benedetto XVI*, 3.2 (2007): 854-857.

494 "Address to the Bishops of Japan on their 'Ad Limina' Visit, September 2, 1985, No. 2," *Insegnamenti di Giovanni Paolo II*, 8.2 (1985): 556-557.

495 "Apostolic Exhortation *Evangelii Nuntiandi*," *AAS* 68 (1976): 64.

> As in any immense project.... it is altogether fitting that we should turn our thoughts to the Holy Spirit. All evangelization depends on him; the success of every endeavor is linked to his grace.[496]

The Holy Spirit can open the minds of the Charismatics to understand the mindset of the Japanese people. In the past the Japanese misunderstood Christianity as a foreign religion which tried to uproot the traditional religions of Japan and force upon them Western culture. This sort of thinking still exists tacitly in the minds of the people. It seems in the past the missionaries had misconceptions about the Japanese.[497] The CCRM must not imitate the Western style of prayer meetings in Japan. They must organize prayer meetings, keeping in mind the features of the Japanese culture. However, it is not an easy task. In order to attract the Japanese to the CCRM prayer meetings, the Charismatics must be aware of the mindset of the Japanese people.[498] Following are some of the major characteristics of Japanese people, which differ largely from the cultures of the people in the West.

4.3.1 Japanese, a People with Striking Contrasts

Japan is a modern society. They Japanese society invests a lot of time, energy and resources in developing technology. It worships technological progress. However, in spite of all the sophisticated technology, one can find the religiosity of the Japanese. One can see a number of Buddhist and Shinto shrines all over Japan, both in rural and urban areas. Even though, average Japanese may not be concerned about his or her religion, yet they are very particular in carrying some religious obligations, which they believe may bring them good fortune. It is common to see most of the Japanese visiting Buddhist Shrines on New Year's Eve praying for good fortune in the New Year and the following day, on the New Year's Day, they visit the

---

496 "Address to the Bishops of Japan on their 'Ad Limina' Visit, September 2, 1985," *Insegnamenti di Giovanni Paolo II*, 8.2 (1985): 559.

497 Henry Van Straelen, *Donde Va El Japon?* (Madrid: Editorial Catòlica, 1961), 319-320.

498 See Noriyuki Miyake, "A Challenge to Pentecostal Mission in Japan," *AJPS* 9:1 (2006): 83-97.

Shinto Shrine to please the *kamigami* (gods). The Japanese also have many superstitious beliefs.[499]

Japanese language is very complex. There are many ambiguous terms. The Japanese word for ambiguity is *aimai*. "Ambiguity or *aimai*, is defined as a state in which there is more than one intended meaning, resulting in obscurity, indistinctness, and uncertainty."[500] Japanese society expects that people must express their opinions in ambiguous terms. Japanese never refuse anyone outright; they convey their refusal in a roundabout way. Japanese do express their opinions but first they listen to others' opinions. They reply in a tone, which seems that they have almost accepted the other person's opinion. However, it is only towards the end of the conversation one can understand whether the opinion is accepted or not. The Japanese language has various terms, which express ambiguity. *Chotto* (but), *demo* (but), *maemotte kangaeteokimasu* (I will think about it) are some of the examples. If there are any differences of opinion, Japanese will surely resort to one of the above terms to express his or her differences indirectly.[501]

Group mentality works very strongly in the Japanese soceity. In the past when agriculture was the only means of survival, Japanese had to depend on each other for agricultural activities. This dependence on each other taught them to have good relations with their neighbors. Therefore, Japanese have group mentality working in them. They feel secure to belong to a group and would do anything to remain loyal to that group. This group mentality has also brought along with it the sense of *uchi* ('in group') and *soto* ('out group'). Japanese make a clear demarcation in their personal relationships. One's family members, colleagues at office or school are 'in group' people. Strangers and foreigners are 'out group' people.[502]

Right from childhood, parents/guardians teach their wards, to behave themselves when they are before outsiders. *Tatemae* means

499 See Noriyuki Miyake, "A Challenge to Pentecostal Mission in Japan," *AJPS* 9:1 (2006): 69-70.

500 Roger Davies and Osamu Ikeno, eds. *The Japanese Mind: Understanding Contemporary Culture* (Tokyo: Tuttle Publishing, 2002), 9.

501 Ibid., 11.

502 Ibid., 11.

the way to behave in public. One can express opinions freely (*honne*) between the 'in group' people. *Honne* means real feelings.[503] Japanese would never express their real feelings when they are among strangers or foreigners. It is an unwritten rule, which all follow.[504]

Striking contrasts in the behavior of the Japanese people and the ambiguity of the terms makes the mission work a Herculean task. Japanese consider foreign missionaries as 'out group' people. Hence, it is obvious that Japanese would not let them know their real feelings. It takes a long time and patience to build a relationship of trust with them.

4.3.2 Love for Nature

Japanese feel close to nature. Shinto, the traditional religion of Japan focuses on living in harmony with nature. It considers as offensive to destroy nature. It considers nature as a friend and benefactor. Unlike the occidental mentality of 'conquest of nature', the Japanese like to live with the nature.[505] Nature is a sign of beauty and spontaneity. The construction of Japanese temples and houses is in harmony with the nature. One can find a small garden around the temples and houses, which immediately gives a sense of vicinity to nature.

The closeness to nature also indicates that Japanese prefer practical things to Divine. Keeping this in mind the missionaries will have to convey the message of Christ first through instances of daily life. Just as Jesus explained the truth about the Kingdom of God in simple parables from daily life, the missionaries too will have to take into account the existential circumstances of the Japanese, to give the message of Christ in a form, which is both simple and appealing. If the missionaries try to impose theological doctrines right from the beginning, it is very probable that the message may neither be accepted nor understood.

503 Joy Hendry, *Understanding Japanese Society*, 3rd ed. (Abingdon: Routledge Curzon, 2003), 49.

504 Roger Davies and Osamu Ikeno, eds. The Japanese Mind: Understanding Contemporary Culture, 115-116.

505 Daisetz T. Suzuki, *Zen and Japanese Culture* (New York: Princeton University, 1959), 334.

4.3.3 Respect, Manners and Love for Beauty

Japanese language has nouns and verbs to express politeness (*Keigo* honorific expression). Among these honorific expressions, there are two categories; one is Sonkeigo, which the Japanese use when addressing elders, one's seniors at the place of work or a person who belongs to a higher status in the society. The other is *Kenjougo*, which the Japanese use when addressing oneself or a person of lower status. They expect that when one speaks about oneself in public, one must use *Kenjougo* expressions. Japanese consider it rude or proud to brag about one's achievements in public. No matter how well a person does, the Japanese expect the person to use expressions, which do not praise one.

Japanese use gestures like *ojigii* (to bow) to greet people. Instead of shaking hands with others, Japanese consider bowing as good manners and a sign of respect.[506] Aesthetics is very important in Japan. "Beauty is everywhere in Japan. It is everywhere in Japan, and where there are Japanese."[507] Aesthetics is a part of their life. Beauty is very important for Japanese. It is an expression of Japanese spirituality. Forms of art like *Sadou* (tea ceremony), *Ikebana* (flower arrangement), *Shodou* (calligraphy) and *Hanga* (woodblock print) express the love for beauty. The external form is very important for the Japanese. It is common to pack a gift beautifully. At times, the package may be more expensive than the gift itself. Japanese 'eat with their eyes'. It means that the along with the taste of the food itself, Japanese are concerned how it appears.[508]

Thus, the missionaries must take into account the sense of beauty, respect and manners when they are engaged in mission work. A missionary must be very sensitive to the local customs and manners. In no way can the missionary give any impression of impoliteness or imprudence otherwise, the Japanese would discard both, the message and the messenger.

506 Association for Japanese Language Teaching, *Japanese for Busy People: Teacher's Manual*, 3rd ed. (Tokyo: Kodansha International, 2006), 24.

507 Pearl Sydenstricker Buck, *The People of Japan* (New York: Simon and Schuster, 1966), 63.

508 See Charles A. Moore, ed. *The Japanese Mind: Essentials of Japanese Philosophy and Culture* (Minneapolis: East-West Press, 1967), 296.

4.3.4 Intuitive and Contemplative

Japanese are intuitive and contemplative. Traditional Japanese religions emphasize the meditative and contemplative side of the spirituality. Silence is an important aspect of their worship. The Japanese sense of religion is quite different. The characteristics of Japanese religiosity are "eclecticism, flexibility, and lack of intellectual concern, lack of universality, and the down-to-earth realism and practicality."[509] Japanese do not have clear-cut concepts of transcendentalism or universalism. The purpose of their practicing religion is to live in peace and get maximum benefits. *Wa* (harmony, peace, tranquility) is very important for the Japanese. Japan has blended major religions like Shinto and Buddhism, though they have completely different philosophies. The Japanese have also modified the Buddhist philosophy and ethics to suit their concept of harmony and life style.[510]

It would not be an easy task for the missionaries to make Christ's message appealing to Japanese, who have flexible concepts about the divine. In spite of the all the difficulties, a missionary will have to take into account these facts, which are a part of life for the Japanese.

4.3.5 The Search for Right Approach to Spread the Charismatic Renewal Movement

The CCRM must consider all the above-mentioned characteristic features in order to attract people to its spirituality. It is a difficult but not an impossible task. The CCRM prayer meetings have clapping, praising and singing in a loud voice. Japanese may not readily welcome these features. They prefer silence.[511] Therefore, it is very important that out of over-enthusiasm one must not force anyone to join in praising loudly or clapping. A person participating in the prayer meeting must have complete liberty to pray as he or she wills. However, in spite of this difficulty the CCRM has many

509 See Charles A. Moore, ed. *The Japanese Mind: Essentials of Japanese Philosophy and Culture* (Minneapolis: East-West Press, 1967), 297.

510 Ibid.

511 Okumura, *Tabunka ni Ikiru Shukyou* [Religions Living in Cultural Pluralism], 197-198.

features, which can be useful in attracting the Japanese. One of the features is strong fellowship among the people involved in CCRM. The Japanese have a strong sense of belonging to a particular group. If the Japanese who participate in the CCRM prayer groups find a community of people strongly knitted together in love and hope, there is a chance that they can be easily attracted to such a group.

The economic recession, unhealthy cutthroat competition and decline of familial values, has brought a lot of distress in the Japanese society. Suicides, mental illness, *Karoshi* (when a person dies because of being forced to work for long hours and days together without proper rest), and depression are common social problems found in Japanese society. The strong and the rich in the society alienate the weak and the poor. In such a situation, people are seeking for a place where they can find some support and love. If the CCRM community can provide them such a space, then they can attract them to their prayer meetings. If the Japanese see love and fellowship existing among the group members then they would believe in the message of Christianity.

Japanese have a great love for nature. They have a great admiration for the nature because of its splendor and grandeur. However, they are still seeking to know the power behind this magnificent nature. Christianity can offer them the answer to this question. It is God, who is the creator of all things.

Pope Benedict XVI in his message of June 3, 2006 to the participants of the Second World Congress of Ecclesial Movements and New Communities noted the role of the Holy Spirit in the creation of the world. He urged all to protect nature from abuses.

> The Bible says first of all that the Spirit of God was moving over the chaos, over the waters of the abyss. The world in which we live is the work of the Creator Spirit. Pentecost is not only the origin of the Church and thus in a special way her feast; Pentecost is also a feast of creation. The world does not exist by itself; it is brought into being by the creative Spirit of God, by the creative Sacred Scriptures. For this reason Pentecost also mirrors God's wisdom. In its breadth and in the omni-

> comprehensive logic of its laws, God's wisdom permits us to glimpse something of his Creator Spirit. It elicits reverential awe. Those very people who, as Christians, believe in the Creator Spirit become aware of the fact that we cannot use and abuse the world and matter merely as material for our actions and desires; that we must consider creation a gift that has not been given to us to be destroyed, but to become God's garden, hence, a garden for men and women. In the face of the many forms of abuse of the earth that we see today, let us listen, as it were, to the groaning of creation of which St. Paul speaks (Rom 8: 22); let us begin by understanding the Apostle's words, that creation waits with impatience for the revelation that we are children of God, to be set free from bondage and obtain his splendour.[512]

New Religious Movements are on an increase in Japan. Even though, Japan is a fully literate and people have knowledge of science and technology they easily fall prey to cults, which promise healing, a quick solution to all the problems and prosperity. One of the instances of such dangerous cults is the notorious *Aum Shinrikyo* (*Aum* is a Sanskrit word with a wide meaning of "all," "divine." *Shinrikyo* is a Japanese word and it means Religion of Truth). The whole world was shocked to know about the lethal nerve gas sarin tragedy, which happened on March 20, 1995. Five gas containers of the extremely lethal nerve gas sarin were spewing deadly fumes at five different subway stations of Tokyo. This incident left 12 people dead and more than 5,500 people who needed medical attention.[513] The police investigations revealed that the followers of *Aum Shinrikyo* planted these gas containers. The police raided the headquarters of *Aum Shinrikyo*, which was at Kamikuishiki, 70 miles southwest of Tokyo and found secret laboratories where the followers produced this gas; besides it, they found $7.9 million in cash and 22 pounds of

512 "Message to the Second World Congress of Ecclesial Movements and New Communities, June 3, 2006," *Insegnamenti di Benedetto XVI*, 2.1 (2006): 757-765.

513 Robert Snow, *Deadly Cults: The Crimes of True Believers* (Westport: Praeger Publishers, 2003), 15.

gold. Apart from these things, the police found 50 people who were wandering around the headquarters who were mentally unsound and 7 people who were kept as prisoners. The police also found that the cult had murdered a dozen people and had charred their bodies in industrial micro oven. The police arrested the founder of this cult, Shoko Asahara and many of his disciples who were involved in the sarin gas incident. Shoko Asahara had founded this cult in 1989. He claimed to have received enlightenment during his visit to India. Some cult magazines published pictures showing Asahara floating in air. This made him famous within no time. Within a short span of 6 years, (i.e. from 1989 to 1995) *Aum Shinrikyo* claimed a membership of 50,000 people belonging to all occupations. Youth became easy prey of the cult. Apart from the youth, there were renowned scientists, industrialists, politicians, doctors, top level Self-Defense forces' personnel and lawyers.[514] One of the reasons cited for such a large number of people joining *Aum Shinrikyo* is the sense of belongingness to the group that the members experienced. People who had hardly received any love or attention from their families or anyone in society found the cult as a warm welcoming place. Even though, Asahara subjected them to strict asceticism, they accepted it as a means to salvation. Magical powers of Shoko Asahara (though later the police proved these as fake) also attracted them.

Such a tragic incident cannot pass away without having any serious repercussions on society. The Japanese began to be more suspicious of all religious movements including Christianity. This incident has still left deep scars on some people's minds. There is an aversion for religions. The Japanese government too tried to reform the Religious Corporation Laws, to tighten its hold on all religious organizations.[515] In spite of such tragic incidents, the Japanese people still become easy prey of cults, which promise quick relief from all problems, healings and material prosperity. In such a situation on one

514 Robert Snow, *Deadly Cults: The Crimes of True Believers* (Westport: Praeger Publishers, 2003), 16-18.

515 Mark R. Mullins, "The Legal and Political Fallout of the 'Aum Affair'," in *Religion and Social Crisis in Japan: Understanding Japanese Society Through the Aum Affair*, eds. Robert J. Kisala and Mark R. Mullins (New York: Palgrave, 2001), 77-78.

hand, the Japanese can mistake the CCRM, which also emphasizes the use of the charisms of healing and prophecy, as a cult movement. On the other hand, these very features of the CCRM can attract the disenchanted youth and others to Christ.[516] The CCRM must be very conscious of the prevailing situation in Japan and must not give space for misunderstanding. The teachings about the use of charisms like prophecy, healing and tongues should be in line with the official teachings of the Church. The CCRM must not over emphasize these charisms and yet at the same time, should encourage people to know about the reality of these charisms. The Life in the Spirit seminars, conventions, retreats and workshops are good platforms to impart the right teaching to all those who have no background of Christianity or the CCRM. Leaders must make it clear that the healings and prophecies happening during the CCRM meetings are not magic. No one can claim any healing or miracle. It is the sovereign power of God. The CCRM must convey the message that Christianity is not a religion, which promises a bed of roses but a deep loving relationship with the person of the Jesus Christ. Jesus never taught that His disciples would have an easy life, quick material success and benefits. Rather He said, "If any want to become my followers, let them deny themselves and take up their cross and follow me" (Mt 16:24). Most of the promises of healing and other material benefits of the cults come with a heavy price tag. The cults make a brisk business by exploiting the ignorance of the people. However, Jesus loves and heals unconditionally. He offers salvation free. One must receive it humbly and wholeheartedly. If these fundamental truths of Christianity reach the hearts of the Japanese, they will be greatly attracted to the person of Christ.

The traditional religions of Shinto and Buddhism, especially Zen forms the base of Japanese spirituality. Unlike Western spirituality, the Japanese believe truth or enlightenment does not belong to the realm of reason but intuition. The heart is the seat of the prayer. In other words, the heart is the place where God dwells. The CCRM can greatly attract people because it also focuses on the prayer of the

516 Fischbeck, "Kami no Miwaza wo Hada de Taikenshita" [Personal Experience of God's Wonders], in *Shu no Ibuki: Bassui Ban* [Breath of the Lord: Excerpts], Vol. 4, 63-64. Original In Japanese. [Translation mine].

heart, where God's Spirit dwells.[517] It is remarkable to know that the CCRM prayer meetings, which are full of loud praises, also give time for deep praise and worship in silence. It is in this silence where one encounters God.

Japanese are very good observers. They observe things with meticulous precision. When they are with Catholics, especially Charismatics, they will keenly observe whether the message, which they proclaim, matches their lives. Following is one of the texts from Acts of the Apostles that can give us a key insight about a model Christian community.

> They devoted themselves to the apostles' teaching and fellowship, to the breaking of bread and the prayers. Awe came upon everyone, because many wonders and signs were being done by the apostles. All who believed were together and had all things in common; they would sell their possessions and goods and distribute the proceeds to all, as any had need. Day by day, as they spent much time together in the temple, they broke bread at home and ate their food with glad and generous hearts, praising God and having the goodwill of all the people. And day by day the Lord added to their number those who were being saved. (Acts 2:42-47)

The model community of the Acts of Apostles is a dream in this modern age. However, the CCRM emphasizes renewal of spiritual life. Pope Benedict XVI in his message of May 22, 2006 to the participants of the Second World Congress of Ecclesial Movements and New Communities noted the importance of true witnesses of Christ.

> Christ still continues today to make resound in the hearts of so many that 'come, follow me' which can decide their destiny. This normally happens through the witness of those who have had a personal experience of Christ´s

517 Paul Green, "*Yami no Naka de Shu no Mikao wo Miru*" [To Behold Lord's Face in the Darkness], in *Shu no Ibuki: Bassui Ban* [Breath of the Lord: Excerpts], Vol. 4, 39-40. Original in Japanese. [Translation mine].

> presence. On the faces and in the words of these 'new creatures', his light becomes visible and his invitation audible.[518]

To live a life based on the Gospel values of Christ is not an easy endeavor. It cannot be lived by good will or human reasoning alone. It needs much more than that; it needs God's power, the power of the Holy Spirit. The early Christian community had a great influence because of their witness of mutual love for one another. If Christians, especially Charismatics, want to carry out the work of evangelization, they too must be communities, which witness the love of Christ through their lives. A person who encounters Christ is transformed and transfigured. The effects can been felt not only in the internal spiritual realm but also in the very life of the person. Bishop Albert Marie DeMonléon in his address during the First World Congress of Ecclesial Movements and New Communities held from May 27-29, 1998 at Rome noted that,

> That the meeting with the Lord leaves its mark on the face and on the outward conduct of those who have experienced it, should be no cause for surprise. The communion with the living Christ is not only a purely interior spiritual reality: it is reflected in the whole person; it is something that can be remarked from outside, that others can see.[519]

Thus, the CCRM has to consider the various issues of the Japanese culture and language to spread its spirituality in Japan.

518 "Message to the Participants of the Second World Congress of Ecclesial Movements and New Communities, May 22, 2006," *Insegnamenti di Benedetto XVI*, 2.1 (2006): 662-665.

519 Albert Marie DeMonléon, "The Movements as Places of a Transfigured Humanity," in *Movements in the Church,* 152.

Conclusion

The CCRM spread to Japan in 1972. It grew steadily even though Catholics are a minority in Japan. The aim of the CCRM is the spiritual renewal of the Catholics. It has contributed in the renewal of the Church in Japan. The many testimonies published in *Ikeru Mizu*, the official newsletter of the CCRJ demonstrate that the CCRM has influenced the spiritual lives of the people. The conversion in the lives of the Catholics can galvanize the work of evangelization. Pope John Paul II noted in his Encyclical *Redemptoris Missio* that, "We cannot preach conversion unless we ourselves are converted anew every day."[520]

The CCRM organizes various programs to educate people about the importance of the interior renewal in the Holy Spirit. The CCRM encourages people to use the charisms of the Holy Spirit during the prayer meetings and in their daily lives for the growth of the Church. Many Catholics have rediscovered the beauty of their Christian vocation. They read the Bible meditatively and celebrate the sacraments with a great joy.

The CCRM has also helped in integrating the migrants with the Japanese Church. The commonalties of the characteristic features of the CCRM worldwide, helps the migrants to come closer to the

520 "Encyclical *Redemptoris Missio*," *AAS* 83.1 (1991): 293-294.

Charismatics in Japan. This indirectly helps them to build a rapport with the Japanese Catholics.

The CCRM helps the Church in evangelization and ecumenism. It also helps in promoting inter-religious dialogue, even though it has not organized any formal program for it.

Renewal is a process. The CCRM has significantly contributed in this process of renewal. The future of the Catholic Church largely depends on Catholics, who have a strong spiritual life. Their lives will bear testimonies. Thus, the Church needs the support of the CCRM to be relevant and vibrant in Japan. The CCRM has the potential to turn the flame of the Spirit into a mighty fire in Japan.

Appendix 1

ICCRS Statues

Preamble[521]

The Catholic Charismatic Renewal (CCR) is a grace of renewal in the Holy Spirit with a worldwide character and many expressions in the Catholic Church, but it is neither uniform nor unified. It does not have a single founder nor a group of founders, and has no membership lists. Rather it is a flow of grace that allows individuals and groups to express themselves in different ways and forms of organization and activities, often quite independent of one another, in different stages and modes of development, with differing emphases. Nevertheless, they share the same fundamental experience and espouse the same general goals. This pattern of loose-knit relationships is found at the diocesan and national levels as well as at the international level. These relationships are very often characterized by free association, dialogue and collaboration rather than by integration into an ordered structure. Leadership is characterized more by offering service to those who want

521 See ICCRS, *Then Peter Stood* Up., 105-114. ICCRS website has the statues as well as the copies of pontifical decrees. See http://www.iccrs.org/Dettaglio.php?id_liv3=231 [accessed on September 4, 2014.]

it rather that by governance. In several realities the CCRM organizes itself like an Ecclesial Movement, but there are also structures such as Communities, Networks, Schools of Evangelization, Television Stations, Associations, Religious Institutes and Seminaries, as well as Publishing Houses, Musicians, Missionaries, and Preachers. All of these, though not formally associated in a specific structure have a "charismatic" profile.

The central goals of CCRM, or Catholic Pentecostal Renewal as it is also called, include:

1. To foster mature and continuous personal conversion to Jesus Christ, our Lord and Saviour.
2. To foster a decisive personal receptivity to the person, presence and the power of the Holy Spirit. These two spiritual graces are often experienced together in what is called in different parts of the world a baptism in the Holy Spirit, or a release of the Holy Spirit, or a renewal of the Holy Spirit. They are most often understood as a personal acceptance of the graces of Christian initiation and as an empowering for personal Christian service in the Church and in the world.
3. To foster the reception and use of the spiritual gifts (charismata) not only in the CCRM but also in the broader Church. These gifts, ordinary and extraordinary are abundantly found among laity, religious and clergy. Their proper understanding and use in harmony with other elements of the Church life is a source of strength for Christians on their journey towards holiness and in the carrying out of their mission.
4. To foster the work of evangelization in the power of the Holy Spirit, including the evangelization of the unchurched, the re-evangelization of nominal Christians, the evangelization of culture and social structures. CCRM especially promotes sharing in the Church's mission by proclaiming the Gospel in word and deed, and by bearing witness to Jesus Christ through personal testimony and through those works of faith and justice to which each one is called.

5. To foster the ongoing growth in holiness through the proper integration of these charismatic emphases with the full life of the Church. This is accomplished through participation in a rich Sacramental and liturgical life, and appreciation of the tradition of Catholic prayer and spirituality, and ongoing formation in Catholic doctrine. This is guided by the Church's Magisterium, and participation in the pastoral plan of the Church.

ICCRS In order to serve needs for communication, co-operation and co-ordination, a Council and an international Office were set up in 1978 under the auspices of Leon Joseph Cardinal Suenens, named by Pope Paul VI as his Episcopal Adviser to the Charismatic Renewal on the international level. The Council was formed of leaders from around the world and the Office was established first in Brussels and later in Rome. On May 23rd, 1984, Pope John Paul II named Bishop Paul J. Cordes to succeed Cardinal Suenens as his representative to the Council. Since 1978 the Council has developed an international organisation which, on one hand, promotes communication and co operation among Renewal organisations on the national level, and on the other hand provides a channel of communication and co operation for the international CCRM with the Holy See. This organisation is known as ICCRS, International Catholic Charismatic Renewal Services. ICCRS is an institution which works in communion with the Holy See, and is open to welcome and represent all the Charismatic expressions in the world that have the same spiritual inheritance, and share the same doctrine in communion with the Magisterium of the Church. ICCRS consists of an international Council which shares and establishes the central goals, objectives and projects, having an office located in Vatican City, responsible for carrying out the decisions of the Council. In pursuing its goals and objectives ICCRS seeks to offer helpful service to the CCRM. It seeks also to gather wisdom, insight and experience, and to make it available world-wide. When ICCRS presents teaching or pastoral advice, issues guidelines, or offers on-site training, it does so as a servant offering help, not as an authority expecting compliance. In relating to national and local expressions of CCRM, ICCRS desires to stress its commitment to this servant role. It has therefore a moral authority and an authority of service. ICCRS does not, however, seek to impose its authority but only to offer its services. The relationship between ICCRS and national and local expressions of CCRM in no way limits the relationships between these groups and their local and national bishops. Nor does the relationship with ICCRS in any way limit the freedom of any individual or group in the CCRM to relate to the Holy See.

A. Nature

Art. 1. International Catholic Charismatic Renewal Services, known as ICCRS, is at the world level the principal coordinating organization of the Catholic Charismatic Renewal (CCR). Its mission is service and promotion of the CCRM all over the world, under the Holy Spirit's action, in close contact with the Holy See. Under Pope John Paul II, ICCRS has been directed to relate to the Holy See through the Pontifical Council for the Laity.

Art. 2. ICCRS is a juridical personality "ad instar", i.e. corresponding to a private association of the faithful (cf. CC 321-329, 116, §2).

Art. 3. ICCRS has a special concern for the faithfulness to the Catholic Church of Charismatic Renewal participants and for their obedience to the Pope as well as to the other Bishops, according to the Church's teachings.

Art. 4. In accordance with the ecclesiology and the "spirituality of communion" (Novo Millennio Ineunte 43), ICCRS strives to maintain cordial relationships of respect and friendship with spiritual movements that exist within the Catholic Church, avoiding in its policies special privileges in accordance with the Apostle's teachings in Phil. 2:1-11 and Eph. 4:2-7.

Art. 5. While preserving its Catholic identity, ICCRS maintains fraternal bonds with other Christian communities believing in the shared possession of the Holy Spirit. But ICCRS does not initiate any international ecumenical activity without obeying the Church's norms on this issue, first having consultation, where required, with the Holy See or the diocesan Bishop.

Art. 6. In order to be of service to all the participants within the CCRM, ICCRS makes a special effort to welcome Renewal participants who call upon it and seek to meet their needs.

Art. 7. In giving these services ICCRS does not have any jurisdictional authority over the CCRM, since this is directly under the diocesan Bishop. However, ICCRS acknowledges a moral influence in the CCR world wide by reason of the services it provides described in these statutes. All these services are offered in strict collaboration with the Pontifical Council for the Laity. To improve these services, ICCRS may appoint Episcopal counsellors and other advisors for specific purposes.

B. Objectives of ICCRS

Art. 8. ICCRS serves the CCRM world wide as a centre of unity, communication and co-operation in order to fulfil Christ's desire: "That they may all be one" (Jn. 17:21) and to keep Christ's body without divisions (1 Co. 12:4-31). This unity has to be understood within the context of diversity, since inside the CCRM different forms and manifestations can be, and in fact, are present. ICCRS' service embraces the following:

Helping all CCRM leaders of the world through constant communication. This is accomplished by:

preparing different material about CCRM and placing it at their disposition;

participating, through its members, in conferences, congresses, assemblies, etc., in order to encourage security, communion, peace and joy as well as solid doctrine;

helping with financial aid, visits and exchanges among the different centres of mutual enrichment; and

helping to promote those approaches or decisions which would be more prudent and in conformity with the Church's intentions in that which concerns evangelization, pastoral work, etc.

In all this, and, in general, in all matters ICCRS resolves to act with a great respect for the principle of subsidiarity.

Assisting CCRM and the Bishops in the encouragement and in the discernment of charisms, following the doctrine of Vatican II (*LG* 12,2).

Working for mutual understanding between the CCRM and the Church, following the Popes' orientations, and encouraging at an international level the collaboration among the CCRM, Bishops and theologians.

Stimulating CCRM participants to work for the evangelization of the world "We are ruled by Christ's love for us" (2 Cor 5:14) in the third millennium after Christ's birth. This is a challenge given by the Roman Pontiff. ICCRS accepts it, trusting in the Holy Spirit's special assistance, working to focus CCRM's energies from the most developed areas towards those which are less developed or poor.

Serving as an information centre for the CCRM and for all those who wish to know about it.

In its spirit of service and in accordance with the direct request of the Pontifical Council of the Laity, ICCRS will maintain a relationship of dialogue and collaboration with the "Catholic Fraternity of Covenant Communities", established as a Private Association of the Faithful by the Holy See. The President of ICCRS may from time to time invite the President of the Catholic Fraternity to attend part of a Council meeting.

Art. 9. ICCRS, to better obtain the above-mentioned aims or objectives, commits itself to fulfil the following services:

Visiting by the President or other members, in so far as possible, CCRM national co-ordinators and CCRM centres around the world. Their visits are to coincide, if possible, with some important event which will gather a considerable number of CCRM participants. They are also to exchange with the leaders their impressions on their programs and projects and offer services in so far as possible to these leaders.

Communicating regularly with CCRM leaders throughout the world through letters, the ICCRS Newsletter for leaders, and other writings.

Organising world-wide conferences and congresses for CCRM leaders as well as supporting other initiatives and proposals for other kinds of conferences of meetings on national and international levels.

Preparing theological and pastoral studies about the CCRM, known as ICCRS Documents, and gradually developing them in such a way that the subjects for an adequate catechesis for CCR participants will be covered.

Promoting other writings and publications on CCRM in different parts of the world and facilitation of their translation into other languages.

Maintaining frequent contact with the Holy See through the Pontifical Council for the Laity.

Visiting the different dicastries or offices of the Holy See to keep them informed of the CCRM world wide progress and to dialogue with them on CCRM theological and pastoral aspects.

Equitably distributing financial aid for the development and promotion of CCRM in the poorest regions of the world in accordance with ICCRS' means, following the advice of the ICCRS Project Fund Committee.

C. Structures of ICCRS

Art. 10. The goals, objectives and projects of ICCRS will be promoted by its Council. In the services offered to the regions and countries of the world, ICCRS has no juridical authority over the CCRM.

1. ICCRS Council Composition

Art. 11. The members of ICCRS comprise the ICCRS Council. ICCRS' Council consists of a President and 13 councillors, one of whom is the Vice-President, chosen in the following way: 5 from The Americas-ss2 from North America (possibly one English-speaking and one French-speaking), 1 Portuguese-speaking from Latin America, 1 Spanish-speaking from South America, and 1 Spanish-speaking from Central or North America, 3 from Europe - one from Northern Europe, one from Southern Europe, and one from Eastern Europe, 2 from Africa - one from the English-speaking nations and one from the French-speaking ones, and 3 from Asia-Oceania - one from Eastern Asia, one from Middle and South-East Asia, and one from Oceania.

Art. 12.The Council may admit new members from particular ministries and from any areas not adequately represented, provided a majority of 2/3rds of the Council are in favour.

Art. 13.ICCRS has its official Office in Rome. Any change of location must be approved by a majority of 2/3rds and in accordance with the Pontifical Council for the Laity. Mission of each member.

Art. 14. It is the duty of the President to:
keep in contact with and consult other members;
implement the decisions of ICCRS;
convoke and preside over ICCRS' meetings and to prepare an agenda after consultation with other members;
represent ICCRS to the Holy See and all other entities;
appoint the Director in consultation with Council members and assign his/her duties;
authorise major expenditures by councillors.

Art. 15. The Vice-President helps, assists, and advises the President, and when necessary represents the President.

Art. 16. The Councillors:
are obliged to attend ICCRS' meetings;
must keep frequent contact with the President and the ICCRS Office and provide information asked of them;
must serve on the ICCRS committees and sub-committees to which they are appointed;
must send an annual detailed report to ICCRS on the situation of CCRM in their geographic area or particular area of concern, giving a real assessment of the Renewal;
must strive to live up to CCRM standards and to be authentic examples to their geographic group or particular area;
must seek to represent ICCRS in their own geographic or particular area of concern and within that context will generate financial support to enable ICCRS to carry on its mission;
may jointly on the basis of common language, geographical

proximity or other common interest gather CCRM participants to study the possibilities for mutual assistance, exchange of services, personnel and publications, or the holding of joint assemblies, congresses, etc. In order to encourage this co-operation, ICCRS will wherever possible set up regional sub-committees, consisting of the ICCRS Director and the ICCRS Councillors from that region, together with 3 or 4 members elected by the National Service Committees of the region. The sub-committee would be chaired by one of the ICCRS Councillors. The ICCRS Council members will decide how such elections are to be conducted. The President of ICCRS may by right attend any meetings of a regional sub-committee as a full member.

Art. 17. The Pontifical Council for the Laity:
The President of the Pontifical Council or his representative is invited to attend ICCRS' meetings and committees.
assists the ICCRS Council and its Office in a theological and spiritual basis;
ensures that the central goals of the Catholic Charismatic Movement and of ICCRS corresponds to the Magisterium of the Catholic Church and especially to the teachings and orientation of the Holy Father with regard to Charismatic Renewal;
promotes unity within the plurality of the Catholic Charismatic Movement at the international level;
he is consulted especially with regard to important decisions and programs (such as, for example, the choice of a President, changes in the Statutes and headquarters).
Elections.

Art. 18. The duration of the mandate. ICCRS' members are elected for a three year period. They can be re-elected for one or two further consecutive 3 year terms (six more years). In special circumstances, ICCRS can extend the mandate for one further period of three years.

Art. 19. Procedures for the nomination New members of ICCRS are elected by the electing members having regard for the following criteria:
leadership in the CCRM requires belonging to the Catholic

Church;

leadership in the CCRM and full commitment to the CCRM (not merely a representative, an information gatherer, a counsellor or an Episcopal delegate and without a commitment to the CCRM);

representative of a qualified section of the CCRM (for example, the Covenant Communities) or of a particular linguistic or cultural reality committed to social and pastoral activities of the CCRM;

understanding well the progress and evolution of CCRM;

persons specially prepared, capable of working with others, of good judgement and with imagination and creativity for the particular services of ICCRS;

persons well known for their good reputation and committed to Christ and to the Church.

For the selection of candidates the following procedure is to be followed:

The out-going ICCRS member is entitled to nominate two or more candidates from the region.

ICCRS will write to all National Service Committees in the region, inviting each NSC to nominate a suitable candidate.

Other CCRM leaders and realities may also be invited to submit names in accordance with the same provisions.

Nominations received in the Office must include a full Curriculum Vitae (CV) of the candidate, with a recommendation from the NSC and/or other regional entities regarding the suitability of that person to be a candidate.

Each nomination received must include a letter from the local Bishop or relevant Church authority, attesting to the suitability of the candidate for the position of an ICCRS Councillor.

When proposing a new representative to a geographical region, the person proposed should be based in that region.

Art. 20. Procedures for the election.

Each and every one of ICCRS members has a voice and vote in the election.

Discussion and dialogue takes place between existing members of ICCRS, followed by a time of prayer and discernment.

For the election of a new member a majority of 2/3rds of the ICCRS members is required. For re-election a simple majority is required.

A member does not participate in the discussion or vote on his/her own re-election.
When an ICCRS member relinquishes a position on the Council, the successor does not necessarily have to come from the same country, even though a geographic area must be taken into consideration.
Any change in a member's responsibility or area of ministry which is approved by ICCRS, does not imply that member's resignation from ICCRS unless the Council feels that the individual no longer fulfils the criteria listed in Art. 19.
Voting is conducted by secret ballot.

Art. 21. The President is elected by the ICCRS members from nominations approved by the Pontifical Council for the Laity.

Art. 22. If it be the judgement of the majority of the Council members that the President is not fulfilling the presidential duties, then, after fraternal dialogue with the President and after proper consultation with the Pontifical Council for the Laity, the members, having presented it to the Lord, may, in charity, request the incumbent to resign.
If the President refuses, the Vice-President takes the office of Presidency and convokes an extraordinary ICCRS meeting to study the matter and to act consequently. The President will not attend the meeting, but may submit in writing the reasons for not resigning and must be given an opportunity to respond to any new allegations made during the extraordinary meeting. If, after full discussion at the meeting and any necessary dialogue with the President, a vote has to be taken, the procedure will follow Canon 119 §2, and the decision will be communicated to the Pontifical Council for the Laity.
If a new President is to be elected, the procedure will follow the norm established in Art. 21. After the election of the new President, a further vote will be taken to decide if the deposed President will remain a member of the Council.
ICCRS meetings and committees.

Art. 23. The ICCRS Council meets at least once a year for four or five days. The meeting consists of prayer, personal sharing, reports on the various regions and business matters.

Art. 24. Various committees function within ICCRS, of which two are essential:
The Executive Committee comprising the President and two or three members as chosen by ICCRS, one of whom should be the Vice-President. The Director would normally be invited to attend, but without a vote. Minutes are taken by a person authorised by the President. The mission of the executive committee is to make decisions on urgent matters presented between two ICCRS sessions, whenever it is not possible to wait until the next meeting. Afterwards the measures that were taken must be examined by ICCRS in its regular meeting to confirm or modify them.
The Financial Committee comprising of the President and two members as chosen by ICCRS. The Director would normally be invited to attend, but without a vote. Its purpose is to evaluate the financial situation of ICCRS and to resolve urgent financial problems of the Council and of ICCRS and of the projects decided by it.
All the committees will present annually a complete report of their activities to the ICCRS Council.

2. ICCRS Office

Art. 25. The ICCRS Office serves the ICCRS' Council, providing the necessary administration to implement the Council's decisions. It is equipped with sufficient equipment in order to accomplish the work entrusted to it and to preserve the archives. It has the necessary personnel, according to ICCRS' criteria, chosen from different parts of the world, with the special representation of the languages most spoken within the CCRM.

Art. 26. The Executive Director is chosen by the ICCRS Council members, and may but need not be a member of the Council. Among his many tasks, the Director will when requested represent ICCRS on behalf of the President.

Art. 27. ICCRS' Office is managed by the Executive Director under the supervision of the President and on the basis of the Council's guidelines. The tasks of the office consist of co-ordination and administration in many different ways. For example:

Co-ordination and Administration: Keeping in order and up-to-date ICCRS' lists of leaders area by area, undertaking correspondence, informing members of important news received from their areas, managing the Newsletter, the International Library and the Web pages, arranging and attending Council meetings and taking minutes of the proceedings, being available to the President and Council members for correspondence, translation etc., publishing ICCRS' books, supervising ICCRS' conferences and other meetings, producing special reports on the CCRM situation in different parts of the world etc.

Accounting and Financial matters: Keeping the accounting books according to modern means and practices so they can be examined by the ecclesiastical authority according to Canon 325, producing an annual balance sheet with a profit and loss statement, preparing an annual budget for ICCRS' members, raising financial resources to enable ICCRS to carry on its mission, dealing with the payment of salaries and wages, the reimbursement of expenses, and the payment of accounts etc., all according to the guidelines given by ICCRS and its President.

The task of receiving visitors is an important concern for the Office.

D. Interpretations and amendments to statutes

Art. 28.

On the right interpretation and application of the above statutes the ICCRS Council has exclusive authority (see the appendix).

For everything which is not regulated by the above statutes, the rules of Canon Law are to be applied.

Art. 29. Changes to the above statutes require consent by a 2/3rds majority of the ICCRS Council members before submitting proposed amendments to the Pontifical Council for the Laity for approval.

Appendix 2

The Statues of the Catholic Charismatic Renewal Services of Japan

Preamble[522]

The CCRM, which started after the Second Vatican Council in 1967 in USA at Duquesne University, reached Japan in 1972. It began at a prayer meeting organized at Hatsudai Catholic Church in Tokyo. In 1973, the CCRJ organized the first "Life in Spirit Seminar" in Tokyo and the next year it organized a seminar in Kansai region too. Gradually CCRJ organized prayer meetings in different regions of Japan. After the first National CCRM convention in 1975, CCRM spread rapidly to different regions on Japan. As regional prayer meetings were getting stronger and having deeper fellowship, the CCRJ decided to organize regions on district basis and to conduct CCRM conventions in every district.

522 Catholic Charismatic Renewal of Japan, National Service Committee, "Statues of the Catholic Charismatic Renewal Services of Japan," (Tokyo: Catholic Charismatic Renewal of Japan, 2000). Original draft is in Japanese. [Translation mine.]

CCRJ started in 1981, in order to represent Japan at International Leaders' Conference at Rome. CCRJ is a forum to discuss the common policies of the CCRM activities in Japan. Again in 1983 all the CCR Service Team members from various districts came together to attend the National Service Team Conference and decided the rules and regulations of the CCRJ. Leaders decided to rename the CCRM in Japan. Initially they called it "Charismatic Renewal" but later changed to "Renewal brought by the Holy Spirit."

In 1980s, Kanto region took the lead to direct the various activities of CCRJ, but in the 1990s, each district started its independent functioning. With this development, the services of the National Service Team and National CCRJ became indispensable to coordinate the activities of various district level CCRM prayer meetings. Again, in the international arena, CCRJ established relationship with ICCRS and Catholic Charismatic Council for Asia-Pacific (CCCAP).[523]

On the occasion of the Holy Year 2000, the following Statutes are decided after having deliberations and the consent of all those involved with the activities of CCRJ.

(Statute regarding the name of the CCRM in Japan)
Article 1: The gathering of the CCRM in Japan shall be called *Nihon Katorikku Seirei Ni Yoru Sasshin* (Renewal in the Japanese Catholic

---

523 Bart Pastor from Philippines along with some leaders of CCRM in Asia and Oceania formed a regional group known as Catholic Charismatic Council for Asia-Pacific (CCCAP). For a number of reasons CCCAP did not continue to function beyond the nineties, and for a time, there was no regional link between the countries of Asia and the Pacific region. To fill this prevailing vacuum the President of ICCRS and some other leaders decided to form a sub-committee of ICCRS in the region of Asia-Oceania similar to the committees in Europe and in Africa. The leaders formed the ICCRS Sub-Committee for Asia-Oceania (ISAO) at an inaugural meeting held in Singapore from December 8-10, 2006. The aims and objectives of ISAO are to serve the Renewal through coordination, promotion, sharing of experiences, reflections and resources in the various regions of the world. These aims are in accordance with the Statutes of ICCRS. This was reported by, Allan Panozza, "ICCRS Sub Committee Asia-Oceania: ISAO," *Leadership Formation,* 13, No. 3 (May-July 2007): 3.

Church brought by the Holy Spirit). In English it shall be called, The Catholic Charismatic Renewal in Japan (CCRJ).

(Statute regarding the Office of CCRJ)
Article 2: The Office of CCRJ will be established at, Shimomeguro 2-23-29, Meguro Ku, Tokyo, Japan.

(Statute regarding the aim of CCRJ)
Article 3: The aims of this renewal are to make a baptized person conscious of the Holy Spirit received at the reception of the Sacraments of initiation, encourage a Catholic to make prayer the center of his or her life, to live a life of great faith and to lead him or her towards the work of evangelization.

(Statute regarding the Prayer Meeting)
Article 4: The smallest unit of CCRJ is the Prayer Group. Each group shall independently organize praise and worship meetings.

(Statute regarding the district)
Article 5.1: A district consists of all the prayer groups in a definite geographical area and its work is to deliberate upon the matters common to all the groups.
5.2: The geographical demarcation of each district is determined according to the clauses included in Article 6 and after the deliberations of the National Service Team.
5.3: The management of each district is carried out by all the prayer groups in a particular district. However, it is necessary that the Leader of the district must be a Catholic.

(Statute regarding National Service Conference)
Article 6.1: A National Service Conference is to be established to deliberate upon all the common matters pertaining to the CCRJ in the spirit of prayer.
6.2: National Service Conference shall consist of members elected by each district for National Service Team and all the members of the National Service Committee as mentioned in Article 7.
6.3: Each district must elect more than 1 and less than 3 people to serve as permanently responsible member(s) of the National Service Conference.

6.4: The election method as well as the term of each member of the National Service Conference is to be determined by the deliberations done by each district. However, it is necessary that the members of National Service Conference must be Catholic.
6.5: The member of National Service Conference has the obligation to represent the district from which he or she is elected and to deliberate upon matters pertaining to the CCRJ at national level.
6.6: National Service Conference must hold a meeting at least once in a year.
6.6.1: The Chairperson of the National Service Conference must be elected among the members of this Conference.
6.6.2: Chairperson shall steer the meetings, prepare minutes, and with the approval of the attendants of the meeting preserve them.
6.7: The Financial Year of the National Service Conference shall begin every year on the First of January and shall end on the Last day of December.

(Statute regarding the National Service Committee)
Article 7.1: A National Service Committee is to be established to determine the policies of the National Service Conference and the various services of CCRJ.
7.2: The National Service Committee shall consist of members elected by the members of the National Service Conference. The number of members of National Service Committee and all other details are to be determined by the consultation of the members of the National Service Conference.
7.2.1: The National Service Committee must deliberate to choose a member who would have the responsibility to represent the National Service Committee.
7.2.2: The term of the members of the National Service Committee will be for 2 years. However, it is possible for a member to seek re-election.
7.2.3: A member of the National Service Committee must be Catholic.
7.3: The members of the National Service Committee, as per the directives of each district must represent the CCRJ in Japan as well as abroad.

7.4: The National Service Committee has the right to divide the work and decide the person responsible for each work after deliberations. The person responsible for each service is obliged to represent the CCRJ when he or she carries out the work assigned to him or her.
7.5: The National Service Committee must plan, suggest and enforce the various activities and projects of CCRJ.
7.5.1: The purpose of the National Service Committee is to organize appropriate prayer meetings, retreats, workshops, etc..
7.5.2: To establish rapport, support and give suggestions to each district from the point of view of National CCRJ.
7.5.3: To publish the newsletter *Ikeru Mizu* (The Living Waters) of CCRJ and also to introduce literature, books about the CCRM in general.
7.5.4: To represent CCRJ, to establish rapport and attend meetings at international level.
7.5.5: To prepare and manage the budget of the National Service Committee.
7.5.6: To do all other activities which are appropriate for the growth of CCRM.
7.6: The National Service Committee must meet at least twice in a year. The quorum is half of the total members of the National Service Committee.
7.6.1: The Chairperson is to be elected among the members of the National Service Committee. Chairperson can decide the rules by the general consent of all the members present.
7.6.2: The Chairperson must prepare the minutes of the meetings within a month, and preserve a copy in the office of National Service Committee. He must also send a copy of the minutes to each member of the National Service Committee and National Service Team.
7.7: The Financial Year of the National Service Committee shall begin every year on the First of January and shall end on the Last day of December.

(Statute regarding supplementary provisions)
Article 8.1: The details of the Statues of the CCRJ are to be worked out by the deliberations of the National Service Conference.

8.2: All members of National Service Conference and National Service Committee shall not receive remuneration. However, one can claim the expenses involved in the work of CCRJ.
8.3: National Service Committee can establish an office with the consent of the National Service Conference for facilitating the work of CCRJ.

(Statute regarding the day of enforcement of the Statutes)
Article 9.1: These Statutes shall be implemented from July 24, 2000.
9.2: The Statutes of CCRJ, 1983 are abolished.
Detailed Regulation:
(The demarcation of districts)
Article1: According to the provisions of Article 5.2 of the Statutes, the five districts of CCRJ will be Hokkaido district, Northeast district, Kanto district, Kansai and Japan West.
(The numerical strength of the National Service Committee)
Article 2: According to the provisions of Article 7.2 of the Statutes, the numerical strength of the National Service Committee must be above four but less than seven.
(Regarding the day of enforcement of the Detailed Regulations)
Article 3: These Detailed Regulations shall be implemented from July 24, 2000.

Appendix 3

Statues of Japan Ecumenical Association

On May 24, 1968, the Japan Ecumenical Association had its inaugural session at Oriens Institute for Religious Research. The following is the prospectus and statutes published on the occasion of the opening session.

The Japan Ecumenical Association[524]

The Church, aware that she must witness to the Gospel of Christ in our times of rapid change, feels the need for self-renewal.

We Christians who believe in God, our Father, and in His Son whom He sent into this world for our salvation, are conscious of the issues which divide us. We hope, however, with the help of God, to overcome our divisions and reach that unity for which the Lord prayed.

As Christians of Japan we realize that we are but few in the midst of a vast number of compatriots who do not yet know Christ. We pray that the Holy Spirit may unite us so that we may give better

524 Kishi Chitose, "The State of the Ecumenical Movement in Japan," in *The Japan Christian Yearbook 1969-1970*, 180-184.

witness to God s Kingdom and proclaim the Good Tidings to many brethren.

To that effect we wish to examine what divides us that it may be eliminated, and to investigate what unites us that it may be strengthened.

As Christians particularly interested in the solution of these problems and basing ourselves upon the common heritage of faith, we acutely felt the need to discuss them with one another and to search for their solution in fraternal collaboration. It seems to us that the task ahead can be expressed in the following points:

1. To promote whatever might foster in this country the unity of the Church through contact, dialogue and cooperation;
2. To study from the ecumenical point of view all problems which we face in our proclamation of Christ's Gospel to this nation;
3. To promote contact, dialogue and cooperation with the other religions in Japan and with the leaders of Japanese society;
4. To establish contact and friendly relations with similar organizations here and abroad.

These goals call for a permanent organization, such as does not yet exist within the Church of Japan. Hence a group of interested people met and decided to establish The Japan Ecumenical Association.

These persons intend to participate in the work of the Association, not in the name of the Church to which they be long nor as representatives of that Church, but in a personal and private capacity, on their own initiative and borne by their sense of faith and by their desire to engage in dialogue and cooperation with one another.

It is their fervent wish and prayer that this initiative may bring increased vigor to the Church and signal the advent of a new era of missionary proclamation in Japan.

Tokyo, May 24, 1969
The Promoters, Japan Ecumenical Association

Statutes of the Japan Ecumenical Association

Name:
Article 1: The Association is called "The Japan Ecumenical Association" (JEA).

Offices :
Article 2: At present, JEA has two offices. One is located in the Nihon-Seisho-Shingakko, 492, 1-chome, Shimoochiai, Shinjuku-ku, Tokyo. The other is at Oriens Institute for Religious Research, 2-28-5, Matsubara, Setagaya-ku, Tokyo.

Purpose :
Article 3: JEA consists of group of Christians who, on the basis of their common faith and aware of their present divisions, intend to overcome them mainly through the study of whatever could lead to that unity for which Christ has prayed. Hence they wish:

1. To foster all contact, dialogue and cooperation contributing to Church unity;
2. To study, from the ecumenical point of view, a missionary approach to Japanese society ;
3. To promote contact, dialogue and cooperation with non-Christians in Japan and with the leading circles of Japanese society ;
4. To maintain liaison with similar organs here and abroad.

Activities :
Article 4 :
Toward the achievement of these goals, the Association intends to undertake the following
activities :
1. Studies and inquiries related to ecumenism;
2. Conferences and meetings for research and mutual consultation, retreats, and contact with branch organizations;
3. Publication of ecumenical news and other material relevant to ecumenism;
4. Liaison with similar organizations here and abroad ;
5. Other activities congenial to the purpose of the Association.

Membership:
Article 5:
JEA has two kinds of members:

1. Regular members: Those who share the purpose and activities of the Association;
2. Associate members: Those who, upon request of the directorate, give assistance to the Association.

Organization :
Article 6: JEA organizes a general meeting every year. At this meeting, reports are read on activities,
plans and finances; officers are elected and business is conducted as called for by the purpose of the Association.
Article 7: JEA has the following officers:

1. Several directors.
2. Several executive secretaries.

Tenure is for a period of two years; officers can be re-elected.
Article 8: The directors constitute the directorate. They govern the Association according to the decisions of the general meeting. The president of the board of directors unifies and represents the Association. The executive secretaries carry out their duties according to the instructions of the directorate.
Article 9: If need be, JEA may set up branches as well as sectional committees.

Finances:
Article 10: 1. JEA expenditures are defrayed by membership fees, revenue and donations.
2. Membership fees are as follows: regular members: 1000 per annum; associate members: amount determinated by the member himself.

Supplementary rules:
Article 11: The statutes of the Association may be changed by a two-thirds majority vote at the general meeting.
Article 12: The above statutes take effect on May 24, 1969.

Bibliography

A. Ecclesial Documents

1. General

Vatican Council II. http://www.vatican.va/archive/hist_councils/ii_vatican_council/index.htm

Catechism of the Catholic Church. http://www.vatican.va/archive/ENG0015/_INDEX.HTM

Catholic Bishops' Conference of Japan. *Dai Ikkai Fukuin Senkyo Suishin Zenkoku Kaigi (NICE I) Kadai* [First National Incentive for Catholic Evangelization Conference (NICE I)]. Tokyo: Catholic Bishops' Conference of Japan, 1986.

_____. *Statistics of the Catholic Church in Japan 2014.* Tokyo: Catholic Bishops'Conference of Japan, 2014.

_____. *An Overview of the History of the Catholic Church in Japan.* http://www.cbcj.catholic.jp/eng/ehistory/table02.htm.

Catholic Commission of Japan for Migrants, Refugees and People on the Move, *Survey of the Number of Faith* (Tokyo: Catholic Commission of Japan for Migrants, Refugees and People on the Move, 2005), 1-2. http://www.jcarm.com/eng/survey/survey05.pdf

Pontifical Council for Interreligious Dialogue and the Congregation for the Evangelization of the Peoples. *Dialogue and Proclamation, May 19, 1991. AAS* 84.1 (1992): 414-468.

Pontifical Council for Promoting Christian Unity. *Directory for the Application of Principles and Norms for Ecumenism, March 25, 1993, AAS* 85 (1993): 1039-1119.

Pontificum Consilium Pro Laicis. *Movements in the Church.* Vatican: Pontifical Council for Laity, 1999.

_____. *Pastors and the Ecclesial Movements: A Seminar for Bishops.* Vatican: Libreria Editrice, 2009.

Francis, "Address to the Participants in the Plenary Assembly of the Pontifical Council for Inter-religious Dialogue, November 28, 2013." http://w2.vatican.va/content/francesco/en/speeches/2013/november/do cuments/papa-francesco_20131128_pc-dialogo-interreligioso.html.

Benedict XVI. "Homily on the Occasion of the Imposition of the Pallium and Conferral of the Fisherman's Ring for the Beginning of the Petrine Ministry of the Bishop of Rome, April 24, 2005." *Insegnamenti di Benedetto XVI*, 1.1 (2005): 25.

_____. "Message to the Participants of the Second World Congress of Ecclesial Movements and New Communities, May 22, 2006." *Insegnamenti di Benedetto XVI*, 2.1 (2006): 662-665.

_____."Message to the Second World Congress of Ecclesial Movements and New Communities, June 3, 2006." *Insegnamenti di Benedetto XVI*, 2.1 (2006): 757-765.

_____. "Homily on the Occasion of Solemnity of Pentecost, June 4, 2006." *Insegnamenti di Benedetto XVI*, 2.1 (2006): 766-768.

_____. "Address to His Excellency Mr. Kagefumi Ueno, Ambassador of Japan to the Holy See, November 13, 2006." *Insegnamenti di Benedetto XVI*. 2.2 (2006): 615-617.

_____. "Letter to Venerable Kahjun Handa on the occasion of the 20th Anniversary of the Religious Summit Meeting on Mount Hiei, June 23, 2007." *Insegnamenti di Benedetto XVI*, 3.1 (2007): 1176-1177.

_____. "Address to Bishops of Japan on their 'Ad Limina' Visit, December 15, 2007." *Insegnamenti di Benedetto XVI*, 3.2 (2007): 854-857.

_____. "Homily on the Solemnity of Pentecost, May 11, 2008." *Insegnamenti di Benedetto XVI*, 4.1 (2008):763-767.

_____. "Address to Participants in a Meeting Organized by the Catholic Fraternity of Charismatic Covenant Communities and Fellowships, October 31, 2008." *Insegnamenti di Benedetto XVI*, 4.2 (2008): 597- 599.

_____. "Homily on the Solemnity of Pentecost May 11, 2008." *Insegnamenti di Benedetto XVI*, 4.1 (2008): 763-767.

_____. "Address to Participants in a Meeting Organized by the Catholic Fraternity of Charismatic Covenant Communities and Fellowships, October 31, 2008." *Insegnamenti di Benedetto XVI*, 4.2 (2008): 597-599.

John Paul II. "Address to Representatives of the Shinto Religion, February 28, 1979." *Insegnamenti di Giovanni Paolo II*, 2.1(1979): 478-479.

_____. "Address to Some Representatives of Buddhism and Shinto in Japan, February 20, 1980." *Insegnamenti di Giovanni Paolo II*, 3.1 (1980): 438-439.

_____."Address to the Bishops of Japan on their '*Ad Limina*' Visit on May 20, 1980." *AAS* 72.1 (1980): 400.

_____. "Address to Representatives of Non Christian Religions of Japan, February 24, 1981." *Insegnamenti di Giovanni Paolo II*, 4.1 (1981): 506-509.

_____. "Apostolic Exhortation *Christifideles Laici.*" *AAS* 81.1 (1989): 443-448.

_____. "Audience with the Bishops of Southern France, December 16, 1982." *Insegnamenti di Giovanni Paolo II*, 5.3 (1982): 1611-1617.

_____. "Address to the Bishops of Japan on their 'Ad Limina' Visit, September 2, 1985," *Insegnamenti di Giovanni Paolo II*, 8.2 (1985): 555-559.

_____. "Encyclical *Redemptoris Missio*," *AAS* 83.1 (1991): 249-340.

_____."General Audience of December 5," *Insegnamenti di Giovanni Paolo II*, 13.2 (1990): 1381.

_____. "General Audience of April 17, 1991." *Insegnamenti di Giovanni Paolo II*, 14.1(1991): 785-789.

_____. "Address to a Group of Religious Representatives from Japan Participating in the 5th International Meeting of Peace, October 7, 1991." *Insegnamenti di Giovanni Paolo II*, 14.2 (1991): 770-771.

_____. "General Audience of October 5, 1994." *Insegnamenti di Giovanni Paolo II*, 17.2 (1994): 441-442.

_____. "Address to the Members of the Catholic Fraternity of Charismatic Covenant Communities, November 14, 1994." *Insegnamenti di Giovanni Paolo II*, 17.2 (1994): 775-777.

_____. "Apostolic Letter *Tertio Millennio Adveniente*." *AAS* 87 (1995): 26.

_____. "Encyclical *Ut Unum Sint*." *AAS* 87 (1995): 934-981.

_____. "Address to Bishops of Japan on their '*Ad Limina*' Visit, February 25, 1995." *AAS* 88 (1996): 1025-1030.

_____. "Message of the Holy Father on Occasion of the XIII World Youth Day, November 30, 1997." *Insegnamenti di Giovanni Paolo II*, 20.2 (1997): 886.

_____. "Address to the National Service Committee of the Italian "Renewal in the Spirit", April 4, 1998." *Insegnamenti di Giovanni Paolo II*, 21.1 (1998): 701-703.

_____. "Address to the World Congress of Ecclesial Movements and New Communities, May 27, 1998." *Insegnamenti di Giovanni Paolo II*, 21.1 (1998): 1062.

_____."Address to Ecclesial Movements and New Communities, May 30, 1998." *Insegnamenti di Giovanni Paolo II*, 21.1 (1998): 1119-1125.

_____. "Address to the Eight Meeting of the Catholic Fraternity of Charismatic Covenant Communities and Fellowships, June 1, 1998." *Insegnamenti di Giovanni Paolo II*, 21.1 (1998): 1262-1265.

_____. "General Audience of September 16, 1998." *Insegnamenti di Giovanni Paolo*, 21.2 (1998): 470.

_____. "Address to the Participants in the International Conference for Catholic Charismatic Leaders, October 30, 1998." *Insegnamenti di Giovanni Paolo II*, 21.2 (1998): 886-887.

_____. "Address to the Bishops of Japan on their '*Ad Limina*' Visit on March 31, 2001." *AAS* 93.2 (2001): 531.

_____. "Address to the National Congress of the Italian "Renewal in the Holy Spirit, March 14, 2002." *Insegnamenti di Giovanni Paolo II*, 25.1 (2002): 359-361.

_____. "Celebration of the First Vespers of Pentecost on May 29, 2004." *Insegnamenti di Giovanni Paolo II*, 27.1 (2004): 713.

Paul VI. "Encyclical *Ecclesiam Suam.*" *AAS* 56 (1964): 609-659.

_____. "Apostolic Exhortation *Signum Magnum.*" *AAS* 59.1 (1967): 465-475.

_____. "Address of Pope Paul VI to the Members of the Secretariat for Christian Unity, April 28, 1967." *Insegnamenti di Paolo VI*, 5(1967): 193.

_____. "*Lo Spirito Santo Animatore e Santificatore,* November 29, 1972." *Insegnamenti di Paolo VI*, 10 (1972): 1210-1213.

. "The Announcement of the Holy Year 1973, May 23, 1973." *Insegnamenti di Paolo VI*, 11(1973): 470-472.

_____. "Address on Occasion of the First International Leaders' Conference, October 10, 1973." *Insegnamenti di Paolo VI*, 11(1973): 971-972.

_____. "Apostolic Exhortation *Marialis Cultus.*" *AAS* 66 (1974): 113-168.

_____. "Address to a Group of Japanese, September 5, 1974." *Insegnamenti di Paolo VI*, 12 (1974): 789-790.

_____. "General Audience of October 16, 1974." *Insegnamenti di Paolo VI,* 12(1974): 937-940.

_____. "Address of Pope Paul VI to the Participants of the Third International Catholic Charismatic Renewal Congress, May 19, 1975." *AAS* 67 (1975): 364-368.

_____. "Address to the Representatives of Shinto, February 26, 1975." *Insegnamenti di Paolo VI,* 13 (1975): 184-185.

_____. "Apostolic Exhortation, *Evangelii Nuntiandi.*" *AAS* 68 (1976): 5-76.

John XXIII."Prayer to the Holy Spirit for the Success of the Ecumenical Council." *AAS* 51 (1959): 832.

B. Pentecostalism, Charismatic Renewal Movement

Alva, Reginald. *Mary and the Catholic Charismatic Renewal Movement.* Delhi: ISPCK, 2012.

_____. "The Ecumenical Calling of the Catholic Charismatic Renewal Movement." *Academia*, 5 (January 2013): 268-273.

_____." Marian Devotion After the Second Vatican Council." *Academia*, 6 (June 3103): 149.

_____. "The Dangers of Overstressing on Healing in Japan." in *Church + Society in Asia Today*, 16, No. 3 (December 2013): 175-185.

_____. *The Spirituality of the Catholic Charismatic Renewal Movement.* New Delhi: Christian World Imprints, 2014.

Anderson, Allan. *An Introduction to Pentecostalism.* Cambridge: Cambridge University Press, 2004.

_____. *Spreading Fires: The Missionary Nature of Early Pentecostalism.* New York: Orbis Books, 2007.

Akimoto, Shinsuke. "*Ikuno Katorikku Kyoukai no Shijiunsetsu: Mokusokukai wo Testudatte.*" [Lent at Ikuno Catholic Church: Helping to Conduct the Retreat]. *Ikeru Mizu*, No. 56 (Spring 2000): 7-8.

Asanuma, Yonago. "*Watashi no Hiza ga Iyasareru to ha.*" [My Knee was Healed]. in *Jesus 2000: Shu no Eiko he no Maneki* [Jesus 2000: Invited to Partake in the Glory of the Lord]. Tokyo: Catholic Charismatic Renewal of Japan, National Service Committee, 2000.

Ashio, Riko. "*Inori no Tsudoi ha Ikiteiru.*" [The Prayer Meetings are Alive]. *Ikeru Mizu*, No. 70 (Fall Edition 2003): 10.

Cassidy, Jeremiah. "*Yurushu no Saiten.*" [Festival of forgiveness]. *Ikeru Mizu,* No. 47 (Special Edition 2003): 3.

Catholic Charismatic Renewal of Japan. *Inori no Tsudoi he no Tebiki.* [A Manual for Prayer Meetings]. Tokyo: Catholic Charismatic Renewal of Japan, 1994.

_____. *Iesus 2000: Shu no Eiko he no Maneki. [Jesus 2000: Invited to Partake in the Glory of the Lord*]. Tokyo: Catholic Charismatic Renewal of Japan, National Service Committee, 2000.

_____. *2001 Seirei ni Yoru Sasshin Kanto Taikai: Dai Rokkai Hokokusho, Oki ni kogidase.* [Sixth Catholic Charismatic Renewal Convention, 2001: Put Out Into the Deep]. Tokyo: Catholic Charismatic Renewal of Japan, Kanto Region, 2001.

Cavnar, Jim. *Participating in Prayer Meetings.* Ann Arbor: Word of Life, 1974.

Csordas, Thomas. *Language, Charisma, & Creativity: Ritual Life in the Catholic Charismatic Renewal.* New York: Palgrave, 2001.

De Monléon, Albert Marie "The Movements as Places of a Transfigured Humanity." in *Movements in the Church.* Vatican: Pontificum Consilium Pro Laicis, 1999.

DeMontigny, Armand. "*Inore Taezu Inore*, 1." [Pray Unceasingly Pray, 1]. in *Shu no Ibuki: Bassui Ban.* [Breath of the Lord: Excerpts]. Vol. 1. Tokyo:Catholic Charismatic Renewal of Japan, 1992.

_____. "*Inore Taezu Inore*, 2." [Pray Unceasingly Pray, 2]. in *Shu no Ibuki: Bassui Ban.* [Breath of the Lord: Excerpts]. Vol. 2. Tokyo: Catholic Charismatic Renewal of Japan, 1992.

_____. "*Mottomo Sugureta Inori Ha Sanbi Desu.*" [The Best Prayer is Praise], in *Shu no Ibuki: Bassui Ban.* [Breath of the Lord: Excerpts]. Vol. 2. Tokyo: Catholic Charismatic Renewal of Japan, 1992.

_____. "*Shoukyoku to Karisuma Sasshin.*" [Parishes and CCRM]. in *Shu no Ibuki: Bassui Ban.* [Breath of the Lord: Excerpts]. Vol. 4. Tokyo: Catholic Charismatic Renewal of Japan, 1992.

_____. "*Are Kara Mou Juu Nen.*" [Already Ten Years After It]. in *Shu no Ibuki: Bassui Ban.* [Breath of the Lord: Excerpts]. Vol. 6. Tokyo: Catholic Charismatic Renewal of Japan, 1993.

De Paoli, Ambrose . "Message to National CCRM Convention." in *Jesus 2000: Shu no Eiko he no Maneki. [Jesus 2000: Invited to Partake in the Glory of the Lord].* Tokyo: Catholic Charismatic Renewal of Japan, National Service Committee, 2000.

Editorial Board of *Ikeru Mizu*. "*Sei Coronban Kai Senkyo Gojuu Shunen wo Iwatte.*" [Celebrating 50 Years of Mission of the Society of St. Columban Mission]. *Ikeru Mizu*, No. 52 (Spring Edition 1999): 11.

_____. "*Seirei Sasshin wo Meguru Q & A.*" [Questions and Answers Regarding Catholic Charismatic Renewal]. *Ikeru Mizu*, No. 72 (Spring Edition 2004): 9.

_____. "*Nagoya de Seirei Korin no Tsudoi Hirakareru.*" [Pentecost Meet at Nagoya]. *Ikeru Mizu,* No. 68 (Summer Edition 2003): 5-6.

_____. "*Yamaura Moto Sama no Shinko no Akashi.*" [The Testimony of Faith of Mr. Moto Yamaura]. *Ikeru Mizu*, No. 73 (Summer Edition 2004): 3- 4.

_____. "*Seirei ni Yoru Sasshin Semina wo Ukete.*" [Participating in Life in the Spirit Seminar]. *Ikeru Mizu*, No. 86 (Fall Edition 2007): 9-10.

_____. "*Dai 23 Kai Seirei ni Yoru Sasshin Hokkaido Tai Kai no Hokoku: Anatagata ha Yo no Hikari Desu.*" [Report of the 23rd Hokkaido Regional CCRM Convention: You are the Light of the World]. *Ikeru Mizu,* No. 90 (Fall Edition 2008): 5.

_____. "*Dai Nijuusan Kai Seirei ni Yoru Sasshin Hokkaido Taikai no Hokoku.*" [Report of the 23rd Hokkaido Regional CCRM Convention]. *Ikeru Mizu,* No. 90 (Fall Edition 2008): 5.

_____. "*Dai 24 Kai Seirei ni Yoru Sasshin Hokkaido Tai Kai no Hokoku.*" [Report of the 24th Hokkaido Regional CCRM Convention]. *Ikeru Mizu,* No. 93 (Fall Edition 2008): 7.

Fischbeck, George. "*Kami no Miwaza wo Hada de Taikenshita.*" [Personal Experience of God's Wonders]. in *Shu no Ibuki: Bassui Ban.* [Breath of the Lord: Excerpts]. Vol. 4. Tokyo: Catholic Charismatic Renewal of Japan, 1992.

_____. "*Baransu no Aru Inori no Seikatsu wo.*" [Balanced Prayer Life]. in *Shu no Ibuki: Bassui Ban.* [Breath of the Lord: Excerpts]. Vol. 5. Tokyo: Catholic Charismatic Renewal of Japan, 1993.

_____. "*Kirisuto no Onrei ni Okeru Iyashi.*" [Healing Through the Spirit of Jesus]. in *Shu no Ibuki: Bassui Ban.* [Breath of the Lord: Excerpts] Vol. 5. Tokyo: Catholic Charismatic Renewal of Japan, 1993.

Fujisaki, Naoe. "*Shounan Chiku no Seirei ni Yoru Seikatsu Sasshin Semina.*" [Life in the Spirit Seminar at Shounan Regional]. *Ikeru Mizu,* No. 83 (Fall Edition 2005): 7.

Fukuhara, Keiko "*Hitori no Shingakusei ni Yotte.*" [Through One Seminarian]. *Ikeru Mizu,* No. 46 (Special Edition 1997): 5.

Girard, Jean Raymond. "*Yurushi no Hiseki ha Kijun Desu.*" [Sacrament of Reconciliation is the Base]. *Ikeru Mizu,* No. 47 (Special Edition 2003): 4.

Govorounova, Alena "Pentecostalism and Shamanism in Asia and Beyond: An Inter- disciplinary Analysis," in *Pentecostalism and Shamanism in Asia.* Edited by Paul Swanson. Nagoya: Nanzan Institute for Religion and Culture, 2013.

Green, Paul. "*Yami no Naka de Shu no Mikao wo Miru.*" [To Behold Lord's Face in the Darkness]. in *Shu no Ibuki: Bassui Ban* [Breath of the Lord: Excerpts]. Vol. 4. Tokyo: Catholic Charismatic Renewal of Japan, 1992.

Hamao, Stefen Fumio. Address to the Participants of the Fourth World Meeting of Families: Renewal Movements and the Evangelization of the Families in Diaspora. http://www.vatican.va/roman_curia/pontifical_councils/migrants/documents/rc_pc_migrants_doc_2003037_renewal_hamao_en.html#_ftnref28.

Hashimoto, Chikara. "*Kita no Chi ni Seirei no Hi ga.*" [The Fire of the Holy Spirit in the North]. *Ikeru Mizu*, No. 46 (Special Edition 1997): 3-4.

_____. "*Kyouko no Nihon No Kyokai he no Messegi.*" [Holy Father's Message to the Church of Japan]. *Ikeru Mizu*, No. 61 (Summer Edition 2001): 1-2.

Hata, Motoyuki. "*Atarashi Uta wo Utaou.*" [Let Us Sing a New Song]. *Ikeru Mizu,* No. 50 (Fall Edition 1998): 4-5.

_____. "*Shu no Fukkatsu Omedetou Gozaimasu.*" [Happy Easter]. *Ikeru Mizu* No. 64 (Spring Edition 2002): 1-2.

_____. "*Okinawa de Shinko Sasshin no Tameni no Mokusokai Hirakareru*" [Convention for Renewal of Faith at Okinawa], *Ikeru Mizu*, No. 65 (Summer Edition 2002): 3.

Hattori, Aiko. "*Seirei no Hi ha.*" [The Fire of the Holy Spirit], *Ikeru Mizu*, No.46 (Special Edition 1998): 5-6.

Hayashi, Mikiko "*Osaka ni Seirei no Hi ga.*" [The Fire of the Holy Spirit in Osaka]. *Ikeru Mizu*, No. 46 (Special Edition 1997): 7.

Hocken, Peter. "Alpha Course." in *The New International Dictionary of Pentecostal and Charismatic Movements.* Edited by Stanley M. Burgess and Eduard M. Van Der Maas. Grand Rapids: Zondervan, 2003.

_____. "Charismatic Movement." in *The New International Dictionary of Pentecostal and Charismatic Movements.* Edited by Stanley M. Burgess and Eduard M. Van Der Maas. Grand Rapids: Zondervan, 2003.

_____. "Clark, Stephen." in *The New International Dictionary of Pentecostal and Charismatic Movement.* Edited by Stanley M. Burgess and Eduard M. Van Der Maas. Grand Rapids: Zondervan, 2003.

_____. "Martin, R. Francis." in *The New International Dictionary of Pentecostal and Charismatic Movements.* Edited by Stanley M. Burgess and Eduard M. Van Der Maas. Grand Rapids: Zondervan, 2003.

_____. "Martin, Ralph." in *The New International Dictionary of Pentecostal and Charismatic Movements.* Edited by Stanley M. Burgess and Eduard M. Van Der Maas. Grand Rapids: Zondervan, 2003.

_____. "Montague, George T." in *The New International Dictionary of Pentecostal and Charismatic Movements.* Edited by Stanley M. Burgess and Eduard M. Van Der Maas. Grand Rapids: Zondervan, 2003.

_____. "O'Connor, Edward Dennis." in *The New International Dictionary of Pentecostal and Charismatic Movements.* Edited by Stanley M. Burgess and Eduard M. Van Der Maas. Grand Rapids: Zondervan, 2003.

_____. "Ranaghan, Kevin Mathers and Dorothy." in *The New International Dictionary of Pentecostal and Charismatic Movements.* Edited by Stanley M. Burgess and Eduard M. Van Der Maas. Grand Rapids: Zondervan, 2003.

_____. "The Impact of the Charismatic Movement on the Roman Catholic Church." in *Journal of Beliefs & Values.* Vol. 25, No. 2 (August 2004): 205-216.

Heron, Benedict. *Praying for Healing: The Challenge*. Mumbai: St. Paul's Press, 1989.

Hinata, Tsuneko. "*Kumamoto no Seirei ni Yoru Sasshin no Okori.*" [The Beginning of the CCRM in Kumamoto]. *Ikeru Mizu*, No. 46 (Special Edition 1997): 10-11.

Hocken, Peter. "The Impact of the Charismatic Movement on the Roman Catholic Church." in *Journal of Beliefs & Values*. Vol. 25, No. 2 (August 2004): 205-216.

Hollenweger, Walter. *Pentecostalism: Origins and Developments Worldwide*. Peabody: Hendrickson Publishers, 1997.

Hosoi, Soshi. "*Dai Juu Kai Kansai Taikai ni Sankashite.*" [Participating in 10th Kansai Regional CCRM Convention]. *Ikeru Mizu,* No. 73 (Winter Edition 2003): 6.

Hymes, David. "Japan." in *The New International Dictionary of Pentecostal and Charismatic Movements.* Edited by Stanley M. Burgess and Eduard M. Van Der Maas. Grand Rapids: Zondervan, 2003.

Iizuka, Midori "*Seirei ni Yoru Seikatsu Sasshin Semina wo Ukete.*" [Participating in Life in the Spirit Seminars]. *Ikeru Mizu,* No. 83 (Winter Edition 2003): 6.

Imashiro, Toshiko. "*Inochi wo Kaetekudasaru Seirei.*" [The Holy Spirit Who Changes Lives]. *Ikeru Mizu,* No. 50 (Fall Edition 1998): 3.

International Catholic Charismatic Renewal Office. *Life in the Spirit Seminars.* Rome: International Catholic Charismatic Renewal Office, 1993.

International Catholic Charismatic Renewal Services. *Then Peter Stood Up.* Rome: ICCRS, 2000.

_____. Doctrinal Commission. *Baptism in the Holy Spirit.* Vatican: ICCRS, 2012.

Irei, Shoko. "*Okinawa Taikai ni Sankashite.*" [Participating in Okinawa Regional CCRM Convention]. *Ikeru Mizu,* No. 55 (Winter Edition 1998): 6.

Ishibashi, Kashi. "*Tsuchisaki Kyokai de no Semina ni Sankashite: Junbisareteita Michi.*" [Participating in the Seminar at Tsuchisaki Church: The Way Prepared]. *Ikeru Mizu,* No. 75 (Winter Edition 2005): 7.

Ishida, Kaneko. "*Taikai Jimukyoku ni Yoserareta Akashi no Naka Kara.*" [Testimonies Sent to Convention Office]. *Ikeru Mizu,* No. 82 (Fall Edition 2006): 3-4.

Ishii, Machiko. "*Dai Juugo Kai Seirei Ni Yoru Sasshin Hokkaido Taikai wo Oete.*" [Finishing 15th Hokkaido Regional CCRM Convention]. *Ikeru Mizu,* No. 57 (Summer Edition 1998): 11.

Ishii, Shirou. "*Dai JuuYon Kai Seirei ni Yoru Sasshin Hokkaido Taikai Hirakareru.*" [14th Hokkaido Regional CCRM Convention Opens]. *Ikeru Mizu*, No. 53 (Summer Edition 1999): 2-4.

Ishikawa, Yukiko. "*Sono Hi Iyasareta HaiShuyou.*" [Lung Tumor was Healed That Day] in *Jesus 2000: Shu no Eiko he no Maneki.* [Jesus 2000: Invited to Partake in the Glory of the Lord]. Tokyo: Catholic Charismatic Renewal of Japan, National Service Committee, 2000.

Ishizaki, Takaki. "*Touhoku Taikai ni Sankashite.*" [Participating in the Northeast Regional CCRM Convention]. *Ikeru Mizu*, No. 55 (Winter Edition 2000): 3.

Ito, Mariko. "*Seirei no Hi ga Tomosareta.*" [The Fire of the Holy Spirit], *Ikeru Mizu*, No. 46 (Special Edition 1997): 6.

Itou, Mikiko. "*Sankasha no Koe Kara.*" [Participants Testimonies]. *Ikeru Mizu,* No. 71 (Winter Edition 2003): 6.

Joshua. "*Hajimete no Sankasha no Koe.*" [From First Time Participants]. *Ikeru Mizu*, No. 93 (Summer Edition): 7.

Kanna, Francisca Riko. "*Okinawa ni Seirei no Hi wo Hakonde.*" [Carrying the Fire of the Holy Spirit in Okinawa]. *Ikeru Mizu*, No. 46 (Special Edition 1997): 13.

Kaseman, Wakako. "*Doitsu no Seirei Sasshin Kara: Shisuta Marugarita no Hataraki.*" [CCRMin Germany: Activities of Sister Margarita]. *Ikeru Mizu,* No. 89 (Summer Edition 2008): 6-7.

Katayama, Hiroko. "*Konan Regional no Seirei no Kaze.*" [The Holy Spirit's Breeze in Konan Regional], *Ikeru Mizu*, No. 46 (Special Edition 1997): 3-4.

Kato, Reiko. "*Shu no Heian.*" [Peace of the Lord]. *Ikeru Mizu,* No. 70 (Fall Edition 2003): 10-11.

Kawaoka,Testuko. "*Shu ha Ima Ikiteorareru.*" [The Lord is Living]. *Ikeru Mizu*, No. 94 (Fall Edition 2009): 5.

Kimura, Ichigen. "*Watashitachi ha Heiwa to Yurushi wo Tsutaeru Messenja.*" [We are the Messengers of Peace and Forgiveness]. *Ikeru Mizu*, No. 65 (Summer Edition 2002): 2.

Kitamura, Kuniko. "*Dai* JuuYon *Kai Seirei ni Yoru Sasshin Hokkaido Taikai Hirakareru*" [14th Hokkaido Regional CCRM Convention Opens], *Ikeru Mizu*, No. 53 (Summer Edition 1999): 3. Original in Japanese. [Translation mine].

Kobayashi, Arikata. *Shinsei he no kadode* [Entrance to New Life] (Tokyo: Catholic Charismatic Renewal of Japan HSRO, 2006), 11-16.

Kobayashi, Atsu. "*Korinzu Shinpu ni Yoru Dai Seinen wo Mukaeru Mokusokai.*" [Retreat by Fr. Collins: To Prepare for the Great Holy Year]. *Ikeru Mizu,* No. 55 (Winter Edition 2000): 9-10.

_____. "*Zainichi Burajirujin ni Yori Seirei Sasshin Taikai ni Sankashite.*" [Participating in the CCRM Convention Organized by Brazilians Living in Japan]. *Ikeru Mizu,* No. 61 (Summer Edition 2001): 1-2.

Kurozawa, Momoko. "*Torinashi no Houshi ni Manekarete.*" [Called to the Ministry of Intercessory Prayers]. *Ikeru Mizu,* No. 50 (Fall Edition 1998): 12-13.

Kyono, Keiko. "*Shu no Ibuki ga Fuku.*" [The Breath of the Lord], *Ikeru Mizu*, No. 47 (Special Edition 1998): 6.

_____. "*Shu Yo, Inochi no Pan wo Kudasai.*" [Lord Give Us the Bread of Eternal Life]. *Ikeru* Mizu, No. 79 (Winter Edition 2006): 11.

_____."*Koinonia Tsukuri no Reshipi.*" [Recipie for Kononia]. *Ikeru Mizu,* No. 106 (Fall Edition 2012): 6.

Lachapelle, Andre. "*Hokuto Chiku ni Seirei no Atarashii Ibuki ga.*" [New Breath of the Holy Spirit in Northeast Region]. *Ikeru Mizu,* No. 46 (Special Edition 1997): 2.

Lafont, Martin. "*Inori de Kami no Koe wo Kiku.*" [To Listen to God's Voice Through Prayer]. in *Shu no Ibuki: Bassui Ban [Breath of the Lord: Excerpts]*. Vol. 2. Tokyo: Catholic Charismatic Renewal of Japan, 1992.

_____. "*Yogen ni Tsuite.*" [About Prophecy]. in *Shu no Ibuki: Bassui Ban* [Breath of the Lord: Excerpts]. Vol. 2. Tokyo: Catholic Charismatic Renewal of Japan, 1992.

Lessard, Noel. "*Futsu no Shisai.*" [Ordinary Priest]. *Ikeru Mizu,* No. 47 (Special Edition 1998): 10-11.

Macnutt, Francis. *Healing.* Notre Dame: Ave Maria Press, 1974.

Masuda, Noriko. "*Inori no Tsudoi wa Ikiteiru.*" [The Prayer Meeting is Living]. *Ikeru Mizu,* No. 52 (Spring Edition 1999): 3.

Mathy, Francis. "*Seirei No Mitashi Ha….*" [Baptism in the Holy Spirit is…]. in *Shu no Ibuki: Bassui Ban.* [Breath of the Lord: Excerpts]. Vol. 1. Tokyo: Catholic Charismatic Renewal of Japan, 1992.

_____. "Kirisuto ni Yoru Kyoudoutai." [Community in Christ]. in *Shu no Ibuki: Bassui Ban.* [Breath of the Lord: Excerpts]. Vol. 2. Tokyo: Catholic Charismatic Renewal of Japan, 1992.

_____. "*Rei no Shikibetsu no Sho Mondai.*" [Problems in Discernment of the Spirits]. in *Shu no Ibuki: Bassui Ban.* [Breath of the Lord: Excerpts]. Vol. 2. Tokyo: Catholic Charismatic Renewal of Japan, 1992.

_____. "*Rei ni Okeru Deai: Jibun to Hito to Kami.*" [Encounter in the Spirit: Self, Others and God]. in *Shu no Ibuki: Bassui Ban.* [Breath of the Lord: Excerpts]. Vol. 3. Tokyo: Catholic Charismatic Renewal of Japan, 1992.

_____. "*Utage no Ato ni.*" [After the Wedding Banquet]. *Ikeru Mizu,* No. 47 (Special Edition 1998): 1-2.

_____. "What in the World is going on?- Japan." *Pentecost Today.* 26, No.4 (October- December 2001): 4, 15.

Matsumura, Kiyoko. "*14 Nen Buri ni Iyasarete.*" [14 Years Old Sickness Healed]. in *Jesus 2000: Shu no Eiko he no Maneki.* [Jesus 2000: Invited to Partake in the Glory of the Lord]. Tokyo: Catholic Charismatic Renewal of Japan, National Service Committee, 2000.

McDonnell, Kilian and others. *Theological and Pastoral Orientations on the Catholic Charismatic Renewal.* Notre Dame: Word of Life, 1974.

_____. "Holy Spirit and Christian Initiation." in *The Holy Spirit and Power: The Catholic Charismatic Renewal.* Edited by Kilian McDonnell. New York: Doubleday & Company Inc., 1975.

_____. *Presence, Power, Praise: Documents on the Charismatic Renewal.* Vol.1. Collegeville: Liturgical Press, 1980.

_____. ed. *Open the Windows: The Popes and Charismatic Renewal.* South Bend: Greenlawn Press, 1989.

_____ and George T. Montague. *Christian Initiation and Baptism in the Holy Spirit: Evidence from the First Eight Centuries*. Collegeville: The Liturgical Press, 1991.

_____ and George T. Montague, eds. *Fanning the Flame: What Does Baptism in the Holy Spirit Have to Do with Christian Initiation?* Collegeville: The Liturgical Press, 1991.

Miyake, Noriyuki. "A Challenge to Pentecostal Mission in Japan." *AJPS* 9:1 (2006): 83-97.

Mizoguchi, Akira. "*Kami no Mikotoba to Inori no Sekatsu.*" [Word of God and Prayer Life]. in *Shu no Ibuki: Bassui Ban.* [Breath of the Lord: Excerpts]. Vol. 2. Tokyo: Catholic Charismatic Renewal of Japan, 1992.

_____. "*Karisuma to Hiseki.*" [Charisms and Sacraments]. in *Shu no Ibuki: Bassui Ban.* [Breath of the Lord: Excerpts]. Vol. 2. Tokyo: Catholic Charismatic Renewal of Japan, 1992.

Muroi, Kunio. "*Kami Chushin de Ikiteikitai.*" [I Want to Live A God-Centered Life]. in *Jesus 2000: Shu no Eiko he no Maneki.* [Jesus 2000: Invited to Partake in the Glory of the Lord]. Tokyo: Catholic Charismatic Renewal of Japan, National Service Committee, 2000.

Nakadai, Yuuko. "*Inori no Tsudoi ha Ikiteiru.*" [Prayer Meetings are Alive]. *Ikeru Mizu,* No. 59 (Winter Edition 1998): 6.

Nakamoto, Kiyoko. "*Fukuoka de no Seirei Sasshin ha Kono Yoni Hajimatte.*" [CCRM Began in Fukuoka This Way]. *Ikeru Mizu,* No. 46 (Special Edition 1997): 9-10.

Nakamura, Kazuko. "*Boukou Shuyou Gan ga Iyasareta.*" [Bladder Cancer Healed]. *Ikeru Mizu,* No. 70 (Fall Edition 1998): 7.

Nakamura, Tomotaro. *"Nihon ni Okeru Katorikku Seirei ni Yoru Sasshin no Ayumi."[The History of the Catholic Charismatic Renewal of Japan].* Tokyo: Catholic Charismatic Renewal Center, 2008.

O'Connor, Edward Dennis. "The Hidden Roots of the Charismatic Renewal in the Catholic Church." in *Aspects of Pentecostal – Charismatic Origins.* Edited by Vinson Synan. Plainfield: Logos International, 1975.

_____. *The Pentecostal Movement in the Catholic Church.* Notre Dame: Ave Maria Press, 1979.

Okada, Peter Takeo. "*2001 Nen Seirei Ni Yoru Sasshin Kanto Taikai ni Yosete.*" [On the Occasion of Kanto Regional CCRM Convention 2001] in *2001 Seirei ni Yoru Sasshin Kanto Taikai: Dai Rokkai Hokokusho, Oki ni Kogidase. [Sixth Catholic Charismatic Renewal Convention, 2001: Put Out Into the Deep].* Tokyo: Catholic Charismatic Renewal of Japan, Kanto Region, 2001.

_____. "*Dai Nana Kai Seirei ni Yori Sasshin Kanto Taikai Sankasha no Minasama he.*" 7th Kanto Regional CCRM Convention: To All the Participants]. *Ikeru Mizu,* No. 71(Winter 2004): 3.

_____, Jun Ikenaga and Mitsuaki Takami. "*NICE I Kara 20 Shunen: Pauro Toshi to Reppukushiki wo Mukaete.*" [Twenty Years After NICE I: Approaching the Pauline Year and Beatification Ceremony]. Tokyo: Catholic Bishops' Conference of Japan, 2008.

Okuyama, Aiko. "Seito no Majiwari no Naka de." [Among the Communion of Saints]. *Ikeru Mizu,* No. 49 (Summer Edition 1998): 6-8.

Oouchi, Nobuko. "*Taikai Jimukyoku ni Yoserareta Akashi no Naka Kara.*" [Testimonies Sent to Convention Office]. *Ikeru Mizu,* No. 82 (Fall Edition 2006): 5.

Painter, Clement. "*Seirei no Hi ha Firipin Ni.*" [The fire of the Holy Spirit in Philippines]. *Ikeru Mizu,* No. 46 (Special Edition 1997): 14-15.

Raly, Caspian. "*Dai Juu Gokai Seirei ni Yoru Sasshin Zenkoku Taikai wo Kaerimite.*" [Evaluation of 15th National Catholic Charismatic

Renewal Convention]. *Ikeru Mizu*, No.56 (Spring Edition 2000): 3.

Ranaghan, Kevin and Dorothy Ranaghan. *Catholic Pentecostals.* New York: Paulist Press, 1969.

_____. "Charismatic Movement and Charismatic Renewal." *New Covenant* 12, No. 11. (June 1983): 20-21.

Ri, Sadami. "*Michibikareru Mama Ni.*" [To Be Led]. *Ikeru Mizu*, No. 50 (Fall Edition 1998): 3.

Sakai, Keiko. "*Dai Juuni Kai Seirei ni Yoru Sasshin Kansai Taikai.*" [12th Kansai Regional CCRM Convention]. *Ikeru Mizu,* No. 77 (Summer Edition 2005): 6-7.

Sakakura, Keizi. "*Seirei Sasshin Madoguchi Shisai Toshite: Herumenein.*" [As a Liaison Priest of the CCRM: Hermeneutics]. *Ikeru Mizu,* No. 68 (Spring Edition 2003): 1- 2.

Sasaki, Haku. "*Seirei ni Ikasareta Atarashii Seikatsu.*" [A New Life in the Holy Spirit]. in *Shu no Ibuki: Bassui Ban.* [Breath of the Lord: Excerpts]. Vol. 1. Tokyo: Catholic Charismatic Renewal of Japan, 1992.

_____. "*Seirei ni Yoru Kore Kara no Michi.*" [The Way Ahead in the Spirit]. in *Shu no Ibuki: Bassui Ban.* [Breath of the Lord: Excerpts]. Vol. 3. Tokyo: Catholic Charismatic Renewal of Japan, 1992.

_____. "*Dai Seinen ni Ibuki wo Ukete.*" [Receive the Breath During Great Holy Year]. *Ikeru Mizu,* No. 56 (Spring Edition 1999): 1-2.

Sasaki, Shinichi. "*Seirei Sasshin to Watashi.*" [CCRM and Me]. *Ikeru Mizu,* No. 50 (Fall Edition 1998): 7-8.

Sato, Francis Keiichi "*Niigata Kyouku: Sato Keiichi Shikyou no Kotoba.*" [Niigata Diocese: Words from Bishop Keiichi Sato]. in *Jesus 2000: Shu no Eiko he no Maneki. [Jesus 2000: Invited to Partake in the Glory of the Lord].* Tokyo: Catholic Charismatic Renewal of Japan, National Service Committee, 2000.

Schneider, Bernadine. "*Sanbi ni Inori ni Tsuite: Seisho to Tomoni Inori.*" [About Prayer of Praise: To Pray with the Scriptures]. in

Shu no Ibuki: Bassui Ban. [Breath of the Lord: Excerpts]. Vol. 3. Tokyo: Catholic Charismatic Renewal of Japan, 1992.

_____. "*Seirei Kitekudasai.*" [Come Holy Spirit]. *Ikeru Mizu,* No. 50 (Fall Edition 1998): 11.

Shimamoto, Francis Xavier Kaname. "Message to National CCRM Convention." in *Jesus 2000: Shu no Eiko he no Maneki. [Jesus 2000: Invited to Partake in the Glory of the Lord].* Tokyo: Catholic Charismatic Renewal of Japan, National Service Committee, 2000.

Shirayanagi, Peter Seiichi. "*Aa, Kami no Tomi to Chie to Chishiki no Fukasa. Kami no Sadame ha Satorigataku, Sono Michi ha Kiwamegata: Roma 11:33.*" [O the Depth of the Riches and Wisdom and Knowledge of God. How Unsearchable are His Judgments and how Inscrutable his Ways: Rom 11:33]. *Ikeru Mizu,* No.46 (Special Edition 1998): 1.

_____. "*Shirayanagi Sukikyo no Kowa.*" [Cardinal Shirayanagi's Lecture]. in *Jesus 2000: Shu no Eiko he no Maneki. [Jesus 2000: Invited to Partake in the Glory of the Lord].* Tokyo: Catholic Charismatic Renewal of Japan, National Service Committee, 2000.

_____. "*2001 Nen Seirei Ni Yoru Sasshin Kanto Taikai ni Yosete.*" [On the Occasion of Kanto Regional CCRM Convention 2001]. *in 2001 Seirei ni Yoru Sasshin Kanto Taikai: Dai Rokkai Hokokusho, Oki ni Kogidase. [Sixth Catholic Charismatic Renewal Convention, 2001: Put Out Into the Deep].* Tokyo: Catholic Charismatic Renewal of Japan, Kanto Region, 2001.

_____. "*Kanto Taikai ni Goshusseki no Kyodai, Shimai no Minasama.*" [To All the Participants, Brothers and Sisters, of Kanto Regional CCRM Convention], *Ikeru Mizu,* No. 71 (Winter 2004): 3-4.

Shlemon, Barbara Leahy *Healing the Hidden Self.* Mumbai: Asian Trading Corporation, 1987.

Souma, Nobuo. "*Shinri no Rei ha Hito wo Jiyu ni Suru.*" [The Spirit of Truth Will Set You Free]. in *Shu no Ibuki: Bassui Ban. [Breath of the Lord: Excerpts].* Vol. 2. Tokyo: Catholic Charismatic Renewal of Japan, 1992.

Stewart, John Marie. *Laying the Foundation: A History of the Disciples of the Lord Jesus Christ.*Channing: Disciples of the Lord Jesus Christ, 2005.

Suenens, Léon Joseph. *Co responsibility in the Church.* Translated by Francis Martin. New York: Herder and Herder, 1968.

_____. *A New Pentecost?* New York: The Seabury Press, 1975.

_____. *Ecumenism and Charismatic Renewal: Theological and Pastoral Orientations.* Ann Arbor: Servant Books, 1978.

_____. *Open the Frontiers: A Spiritual Testimony from Cardinal Suenens in Conversation with Karl-Heinz Fleckenstein.* London: Darton, Longman and Todd, 1980.

Sugiura, Yuko. "*Kakuchi no Inori no Tsudoi no Hataraki Kara.*" [The Happenings in Each Region]. *Ikeru Mizu,* No. 78 (Fall Edition): 12.

Suzuki, Masakazu. "A New Look at the Pre-War History of the Japan Assemblies of God." *Asian Journal of Pentecostal Studies* Vol. 4, No.2 (2001): 242-243.

Tamasaki, Abiko. "*Seirei ni Yoru Seikatsu Sasshin Semina ni Sankashite.*" [Participating in the CCRM Life in the Spirit Seminar]. *Ikeru Mizu,* No. 46 (Special Edition 1997): 15.

Terada, Masaaki. "*Shu ga Hataraiteorareru Koto wo Chokkan.*" [I Perceived that the Lord is Indeed Working]. *Ikeru Mizu,* No. 74 (Fall Edition 2004): 5-6.

_____. "*Yokohama, Shounan Chiku no Hataraki.*" [The Happenings at Yokohama and Shounan Region]. *Ikeru Mizu,* No. 79 (Fall Edition 2006): 9.

Thigpen, Paul. "Catholic Charismatic Movement." in *The New International Dictionary of Pentecostal and Charismatic Movements.* Edited by Stanley M. Burgess and Eduard M. Van Der Maas. Grand Rapids: Zondervan, 2003.

Tominaga, Mayumi. "*Reiteki Iyashi ni Kansh.a*" [Thanks for the Spiritual Healing]. *Ikeru Mizu,* No. 94 (Fall Edition 2009): 2.

Tsuboi, Aiko. "*Houshasenn de Yowatteita Watashi wo.*" [I was Getting Weak Because Of Radiation]. in *Jesus 2000: Shu no Eiko he no*

Maneki. [Jesus 2000: Invited to Partake in the Glory of the Lord]. Tokyo: Catholic Charismatic Renewal of Japan, National Service Committee, 2000.

Tsuchida, Masatoshi. "*Anata wo Shounin ni Suru.*" [I Will Make You My Witness]. *Ikeru Mizu*, No. 49 (Summer Edition 1998): 4.

Tsuchido, Paul Shew. "A Forgotten History: Correcting The Historical Record of the Roots of Pentecostalism in Japan." *Asian Journal of Pentecostal Studies* Vol.5, No.1 (2002): 29-30.

_____. "Pentecostals in Japan." in *Asia and Pentecostal: The Charismatic Face of Christianity in Asia*. Edited by Allan Anderson and Edmond Tang. Carlisle: Regnum Books International, 2005.

Walsh, Vincent. *Key to Charismatic Renewal in the Catholic Church.* St. Meinrad: Abbey Press, 1977.

Watanabe, Tsue. "*Dai JuuYon Kai Seirei ni Yoru Sasshin Hokkaido Taikai Hirakareru*" [14th Hokkaido Regional CCRM Convention Opens], *Ikeru Mizu*, No. 53 (Summer Edition 1999): 3.

Word of God. *The Life in the Spirit Seminars Team Manual.* Ann Arbor: Servant Books, 1979.

Yamada, Hiromi. "*Tokyo de no Zenkoku Taikai ni Sankashite.*" [Participating in National CCRM Convention at Tokyo]. *Ikeru Mizu,* No. 47 (Special Edition 1998): 7.

Yamaguchi, Kayoko. "*Seirei Sasshin Okinawa Taikai ni Sankashite.*" [Participating in the Okinawa Regional CCRM Convention]. *Ikeru Mizu*, No. 55 (Winter Edition 2000): 5.

Yamaoka, Shuko. "*Kansai Taikai de no Iyashi no Akashi Kara.*" [Healing Testimonies at Kansai Regional CCRM Convention]. *Ikeru Mizu*, No. 75 (Winter Edition 2005): 5-6.

Yano, Machiko. "*Funago ni mo Seirei no Kaza ga.*" [The Wind of the Holy Spirit in Funago Too]. *Ikeru Mizu*, No. 46 (Special Edition 1997): 8-9.

Yasuda, Toyoo. "*Okinawa de Shinko Sasshin no Tameni no Mokusokai Hirakareru.*" [Convention for Renewal of Faith at Okinawa]. *Ikeru Mizu*, No. 65 (Summer Edition 2002): 3.

Yuriko, Nigo. "*Seirei ni Yoru Sasshin Semina ni Sankasareta Katagata no Kansobun kara.*" [Reflections from the Participants of the Life in the Spirit Seminar]. *Ikeru Mizu,* No. 98 (Fall Edition 2010): 9-10.

Yoshioka, Chiyoko. "*Taikai Jimukyoku ni Yoserareta Akashi no Naka Kara.*" [Testimonies Sent to Convention Office]. *Ikeru Mizu,* No. 82 (Fall Edition 2006): 4.

C. Other Works Consulted

Association for Japanese Language Teaching. *Japanese for Busy People: Teacher's Manual.* 3rd ed. Tokyo: Kodansha International, 2006.

Barrett, David and Todd Johnson, "The Catholic Charismatic Renewal, 1959-2025," in *Then Peter Stood Up*. Rome: ICCRS, 2000.

_____. *World Christian Encyclopedia: A Comparative Survey of Churches and Religions in the Modern World.* New York: Oxford University Press, 1982.

_____, George Kurian and Todd Johnson. *World Christian Encyclopedia: A Comparative Survey of Churches and Religions in the Modern World.* 2 Vols. 2nd ed. New York: Oxford University Press, 2001.

Boxer, Charles. *The Christian Century in Japan, 1549-1650.* London: Cambridge University Press, 1951.

Buck, Pearl Sydenstricker. *The People of Japan.* New York: Simon and Schuster, 1966.

Cary, Otis. *History of Christianity in Japan.* Vol. 1& 2. New York: Fleming H. Revell, 1909.

Chitose, Kishi. "The State of the Ecumenical Movement in Japan." in *The Japan Christian Yearbook 1969-1970.* Edited by Ryokzo Hara, James Colligan, Lan Macleod. Tokyo: Kyo Bun Kwan, 1970.

Davies, Roger and Osamu Ikeno, eds. *The Japanese Mind: Understanding Contemporary Culture.* Tokyo: Tuttle Publishing, 2002.

ammond, Richard. *A History of Christianity in Japan*. Grand Rapids: William B. Eerdmans, 1971.

Ellwood, Robert. "New Religions in Japan." in *The Encyclopedia of Religion*. Vol. 10. Edited by Mircea Eliade. New York: Macmillan Publishing Company, 1987.

England, John. et al., eds. *Asian Christian Theologies: A Research Guide to Authors, Movements, Sources*. Vol. 3. Delhi: ISPCK, 2004.

Ford, James Ishmael. *Zen Master Who?:A Guide to the People and Stories of Zen*. Somerville: Wiston Publications, 2006.

Hendry, Joy. *Understanding Japanese Society*. 3rd ed. Abingdon: Routledge Curzon, 2003.

Hori, Ichiro. *Folk Religion in Japan: Continuity and Change*. Edited by Joseph Kitagawa and Alan L. Miller. Chicago: University of Chicago Press, 1968.

Jansen, Marius. The Making of Modern Japan. Cambridge: Harvard University Press, 2000.

Japan Assemblies of God. *Mikotoba ni Tachi, Mitama ni Michibikarete: Nihon Assemburizu ob Goddo Kyodan Soritsu Goju Nenshi. [Standing on the Word of God, Guided by the Holy Spirit: The Fifty Years History of the Founding of Japan Assemblies of God]*. Tokyo: Japan Assemblies of God, 1999.

Jennes, Joseph. *A History of the Catholic Church in Japan, from Its Beginnings to the Early Meiji Era (1549-1873)*. Tokyo: Oriens Institute for Religious Research, 1973.

Karan, Pradyumna. *Japan in the Twenty-First Century: Environment, Economy and Society*. Lexington: University Press of Kentucky, 2005.

Latourette, Kenneth Scott. *A History of the Expansion of Christianity: The Great Century in Northern Africa and Asia, A.D.1800-A.D.1914*. Vol. 6. London: Eyre and Spottiswoode Limited, 1944.

Laures, Johannes. *Kirishitan Bunko: A Manual of Books and Documents on the Early Christian Missions in Japan*. 3rd ed. Tokyo: Sophia University, 1957.

Ministry of Education, Culture, Sport, Science and Technolog Japan, "*Zenkoku Jinja Kyokai Nado Shukyo Dantai, Kyoshi, Shinjasu*" [National Statistics of Shrines, Churches etc, Religious Organizations, Adherents]. http://www.e- stat.go.jp/SG1/estat/List.do?bid=000001052797&cycode=0

Moffett, Samuel Hugh. *A History of Christianity in Asia*. Vol. 2. New York: Orbis Books, 2005.

Moore, Charles. ed. *The Japanese Mind: Essentials of Japanese Philosophy and Culture*. Minneapolis: East-West Press, 1967.

Mudroch, James and Isoh Yamagata. *A History of Japan during the Century of Early Foreign Intercourse (1542-1651)*. Vol. 2. Kobe: The Chronicle, 1903.

Mueller, George. *The Catechetical Problem in Japan: 1549-1965*. Tokyo: Oriens Institute for Religious Research, 1967.

Mullins, Mark. *Christianity Made in Japan: A Study of Indigenous Movements*. Honolulu: University of Hawaii Press, 1998.

_____. "The Legal and Political Fallout of the 'Aum Affair'." in *Religion and Social Crisis in Japan: Understanding Japanese Society Through the Aum Affair.* Edited by Robert J. Kisala and Mark R. Mullins. New York: Palgrave, 2001.

Naofusa, Hirai. "Shinto." in *The Encyclopedia of Religion*. Vol. 13. Edited by Mircea Eliade. New York: Macmillan Publishing Company, 1987.

Noriyoshi, Tamaru. "Buddhism in Japan." in *The Encyclopedia of Religion*. Vol. 2. Edited by Mircea Eliade. New York: Macmillan Publishing Company, 1987.

Kessler, Diane and Michael Kinnamon, *Councils of Churches and the Ecumenical Vision*. Geneva: WCC Publications, 2000.

Koschorke, Klaus Frieder, Ludwig and Mariano Delgado, eds. *A History of Christianity in Asia, Africa and Latin America, 1450-1990: A Documentary Source Book*. Grand Rapids: William B. Eerdmans Publishing Company, 2007.

Gerald O'Connell, *Vatican Cardinal Applauds Japan for Interreligious Dialogue*. August 14, 2009. This article is

Dr... about the interview of Cardinal Jean-Louis Pierre Tauran to Radio Vatican on August 12, 2009 following his return from a trip to Japan. UCAN (Union of Catholic Asian News) published excerpts of this interview in their website. http://www.ucanews.com/story-archive/?post_name=/2009/08/14/cardinal- applauds-japan-church-for-interreligious-dialogue&post _id=50794

Okumura, Ichiro. "*Kirisutokyo to Bukkyo to no Taiwa no Ayumi.*" [The History of Dialogue Between Christianity and Buddhism]. in *Shoshukyo Taiwa.* [Interreligious Dialogue]. Edited by Catholic Bishops' Conference of Japan, Department of Interreligious Dialogue. Tokyo: Catholic Bishops' Conference of Japan, 2006.

_____. *Tabunka ni Ikiru Shukyou.* [Religions Living in Cultural Pluralism]. Vol. 2. Tokyo: Oriens Institute for Religious Research, 2009.

Oxley, Simon. *Creative Ecumenical Education: Learning From One Another*. Geneva: WCC Publications, 2002.

Rogers, Minor. "Kami." in *Abingdon Dictionary of Living Religions.* Edited by Keith Crim, Roger A. Bullard, Larry D. Shinn. Nashville: Abingdon, 1981.

Samson, George Bailey. *A History of Japan*, Vol. 2. Stanford: Stanford University Press, 1963.

Schütte, Josef. 'Japan, Martyrs of.' in *New Catholic Encyclopaedia.* Vol. 7. New York: McGraw-Hill Book Company, 1967.

Schwade, Arcadio. 'Japan.' in *New Catholic Encyclopaedia.* Vol. 7. New York: McGraw-Hill Book Company, 1967.

Smith, Howard. "Kami." in *A Dictionary of Comparative Religion.* Edited by S.G.F. Brandon. New York: Charles Scribners's Sons, 1970.

Snow, Robert. *Deadly Cults: The Crimes of True Believers.* Westport: Praeger Publishers, 2003.

Spae, Joseph. *Christianity Encounters Japan.* Tokyo: Oriens Institute for Religious Research, 1968.

______. *Shinto Man.* Tokyo: Oriens Institute for Religious Research, 1972.

Straelen, Henry Van. *¿Donde Va El Japon?* Madrid: Editorial Catòlica, 1961.

Suzuki, Daisetz. *Zen and Japanese Culture.* New York: Princeton University, 1959.

Turnbull, Stephen. *The Kakure Kirishitan of Japan: A Study of Their [The hidden Christians]Development, Beliefs and Rituals to the Present Day*. Surrey: Japan Library, 1998.

World Health Organization, *Statistics of Suicide Rates in Japan* posted on their web page. http://www.who.int/mental_health/media/japa.pdf.

Index